THE LORD
OF HISTORY

By the same author

HOLY PAGANS OF THE OLD TESTAMENT
Translated by Felix Faber

JEAN DANIÉLOU, S.J.

THE LORD
OF HISTORY

Reflections on the
Inner Meaning of History

Translated by Nigel Abercrombie

Meridian Books
THE WORLD PUBLISHING COMPANY
Cleveland and New York

A MERIDIAN BOOK

Published by The World Publishing Company
2231 West 110th Street, Cleveland, Ohio 44102
First Meridian Printing September 1968
© Longmans, Green and Co., Ltd., 1958
Reprinted by arrangement with Henry Regnery Company
114 West Illinois Street, Chicago, Illinois 60610
Library of Congress Catalog Card Number: 58-59636
Printed in the United States of America   220.95

First published in France by Editions du Seuil, Paris
under the title "Essai sur le Mystère de l' Histoire"

IMPRIMI POTEST J. D. BOYLE, S.J., VICE-PRAEP. PROV.
ANGL. SOC. JESU. DATUM LONDINI DIE 28 MAII 1958.
NIHIL OBSTAT JOHANNES M. T. BARTON, S.T.D., L.S.S., CENSOR
DEPUTATUS. IMPRIMATUR ✠ GEORGIUS L. CRAVEN, EPUS
SEBASTOPOLIS, VIC. GEN. WESTMONASTERII, DIE 2A JUNII 1958.

CONTENTS

Contents

ACKNOWLEDGEMENTS

We are indebted to his Grace the Archbishop of Westminster, and Messrs. Burns Oates & Washbourne Ltd. for extracts from Mgr. Ronald Knox's version of the Bible.

PREFACE TO THE ENGLISH EDITION

ISTORY, like morals, may be considered on either of two distinct levels of intelligibility. The chronicle of past events may be more or less comprehensive and accurate, more or less penetrating and persuasive; at this scientific and critical level, the discipline of history corresponds to the practical discipline of the good life—it is essentially empirical, as the other is essentially pragmatic. This is the context in which Lord Acton's ideal of a chaste impartiality in historical writing is permanently valid, and Aristotle's dictum (that history is less philosophical than poetry) commands assent. Exactly so in morals—courage, chastity, kindness are autonomous values; though, at another level of understanding, the eternal worth of these virtues may be seen to depend entirely upon godliness: and the intellectual worth of history proves likewise to depend upon revelation.

It is with history in this latter sense, alone, that Father Daniélou has concerned himself in this book.

In the Introduction, he shows how the bare possibility of history (as distinct from chronicle) arises from the revealed knowledge of God's creative work, and why this particular dimension of thought was discovered late in time.

The next ten chapters investigate a variety of contemporary topics from the point of view of history as a *succedaneum* of the Christian revelation.

Part II of the book elucidates some of the principles and techniques of history itself, so understood, exhibiting the kind of continuity and the kind of progress to be found in it.

In the last six chapters, the author looks at the present

and future course of history, to see in what sense the Christian 'makes' history.

In the preface to the original French edition, Father Daniélou explained that parts of the work had been composed in lecture form: the present translation follows the printed French text closely enough for this remark to have some application still—it seemed that more would have been lost than gained by any attempt to disguise the book as a treatise.

Quotations of Scripture are taken from the Knox version (or, occasionally, from its footnotes), with two exceptions: biblical material in patristic passages, which is commonly not in verbal agreement with the Vulgate, is given in the form which the context seems to require; and Father Mackey's version of St François de Sales (p. 296), including a quotation from St Paul, stands unaltered.

NIGEL ABERCROMBIE

Lewes.
Easter 1958.

INTRODUCTION

I

THE Bible is a record of the evidence for certain events, certain historical works of God: as, the covenant with Abraham, the birth and resurrection of Jesus Christ, and Pentecost. Consequently the Christian outlook is primarily determined by a series of divine operations, tracing a distinct line of development: each of these events marks a new stage in the actualization of God's design, and a mutation of human life. Two aspects of the whole process are of especial importance: first the nature of the event itself, and of the divine decision transforming reality; and secondly the succession of events, exhibiting at once a certain continuity and a certain discontinuity, i.e. by definition, progress.

If we now examine the forms of thought and philosophical systems current at the time when Christianity first made its appearance in the world, it is clear that they were by no means ready to assimilate this Christian conception: on the contrary, they were wholly antagonistic thereto.

In the first place, there was the influence of Greek thought: here, that which is divine consists in the unmoved eternal order of Ideas. Immutable law, whether of nature or of society, represents to the senses the changeless eternity of the intelligible world. The phenomenon of movement itself is an imitation of immobility, being conceived as cyclical, both in the regular motions of the heavenly bodies and in the eternal recurrence which governs the course of history, so that the same events will be everlastingly repeated. By going round in a circle, even change thus conforms to the stable eternity of the ideal world, and no longer implies innovation. No such thing as an event can ever infringe the eternal order.

The opposition is fundamental between this conception and the Christian belief in a unique, irrevocable value belonging to the historical Incarnation. In the Epistle to the Hebrews, Christ is said to have entered 'once' (ἅπαξ) into the holy place, that is, when he ascended into God's heaven: something was then irrevocably gained. Nothing can ever again divide human nature from the Divinity; there is no possibility of a relapse; mankind is essentially saved. All that remains is the business of extending to the individual members of the species that which has been secured for all humanity. The event, then, has finally effected a qualitative change at a given moment in time, so that things can never be the same again. The words 'past' and 'present' have here their full meaning. It is this belief in the irreversibility of salvation that gives rise to the Christian virtue of hope, in contrast to the characteristic melancholy which flows from the Greek acceptance of an endless repetition.

Curiously enough, the earliest Christian theologians were slow to realize the originality of their own position, and in fact began by trying to eliminate it. Thus Origen held that the spiritual creation existed in a state of perfection from the first, and is presumably co-eternal with the Word:[1] but it fell: consequently the purpose of the Incarnation was to restore a pre-existing condition of affairs. There is nothing new in history. It would have been better if nothing happened at all, and everything had remained in its primordial stability. Similarly Eusebius[2] teaches that Christ brought about no innovation of truth, but came simply to re-establish the pure religion of primitive man, for which Judaism had been a temporary substitute. In both these instances, we find the same Greek idea of perfection as something which has always been the same.

[1] *de Princ.* I: 2, 10.   [2] *Dem. Ev.* I: 6.

In St Augustine's *City of God*, there is a vivid awareness of the Christian conception of history, in all its paradoxical originality. Sacred history is here seen to consist of positive beginnings which subsequently last for ever. The notion is refractory to the normal processes of human understanding, which is accustomed to conceive reality under a two-fold classification: there are things that have neither beginning nor end, which Philo called θεῖα, the things of God, and there are things that have a beginning and an end, namely corruptible material things. The possibility of things that have a beginning but no end is offensive to reason: it seems to derive directly from Christian thought. In the *City of God*, all the great creative decisions of God which have determined the course of history are seen to be of this kind: the creation of the world (XI: 4), and of mankind (XII: 13), the Covenant with Abraham, which St Augustine called *articulus temporis* (XVI: 12), and the resurrection of Christ and life eternal, determining the everlasting destiny of man (XII: 21). St Gregory of Nyssa gave expression to the same conception of history when he wrote that 'it proceeds from beginnings to beginnings, by successive beginnings that have no end'.[1]

This example is enough to indicate the method which characterizes the theology of history: it consists precisely in the use of scriptural principles for the resolution of questions to which these principles were not, in scripture, explicitly applied. In the case mentioned in the foregoing paragraph, the particular principle to be applied belongs properly to the Covenant: it is this, that God's promises are irrevocable because of his faithfulness; men may be unfaithful, and thus withdraw themselves from the beneficial enjoyment of the promises, but they cannot have the promises withdrawn. So the union of the divine and human natures in Christ, which took place at a given moment in time, is thenceforward permanent, irrespective of all the

[1]*Hom. Cant.* P.G. 44: 981C.

possible sinfulness of mankind. St Augustine takes over this principle as applicable also to such matters as the creation, or the eternal destiny of man, for these have the same quality of occurring in time (or with time, in the case of the creation of the world), but once for all thereafter.

*   *   *

II

In conflict with the trend of Greek thought, which may fairly be taken as representative of pure reason, the aspect of the Christian outlook on history that came into prominence was the absolute significance of individual events. In controversy with the representatives of Judaism, a second aspect of the same outlook had to be more precisely formulated: this was the interrelation between those events. There is no such thing as history unless events, besides having some importance, can be shown to be in some way continuous. It is just this latter point which distinguishes the idea of 'historicity', as understood by existentialists, meaning no more than the present decision of an individual free will, from the idea of sacred history, wherein the individual fits into the pattern of a larger and objectively planned arrangement of reality.

Jews and Christians agree in believing that the religious institutions of Jewry, such as the circumcision, the sabbath, and the temple, are of divine origin; but Christians simultaneously hold that Christ abolished these institutions. How is this apparent contradiction to be explained? Can a good thing ever be no good? The problem was insoluble with the intellectual equipment of the ancient thinkers. Consequently we find that the earliest Christian writers such as the pseudo-Barnabas, and Justin, were actually driven to declare that the Jewish forms never were good, on the hypothesis that their only valid significance was always the spiritual sense enshrined in them, while the literal practice of the rites themselves was always wrong. This desperate attempt to dispose of the difficulty plainly undervalued the Old Testament, in the same sort of way as the gnostics who repudiated it altogether.

St Irenaeus was the first to discover and propound without ambiguity the basis of a definitive solution. Here again it was highly offensive to pure reason, for it introduced the notion of time, καιρός, as a necessary element in the formation of value-judgements concerning reality. Thus it must be confessed, on the one hand, that the Old Testament is good, and that it is the work of the same God who made the New Testament. On the other hand the values of the Old Testament were provisional; they are no longer to be prized when once their due season, their καιρός, has elapsed. The error of the Jews is strictly an anachronism, because they would arrest the development of God's plan, and perpetuate an obsolete pattern of reality. Origen, following Melito of Sardis, described the Old Testament as a preliminary sketch —something indispensable at one stage, but of no further use once the work is finished;[1] or as a lamp, which it is absurd to keep alight after sunrise.[2] The Christian attitude towards the Old Testament is simply the gratitude that a grown man should feel for the education he had as a child.[3]

This, then, is the second distinctive feature of the Christian view of history; the historical process is seen as an economy of progress. The Old and the New Testaments belong to one scheme of things, but mark two successive stages in its development. St Irenaeus explains this design of succession as a system of pedagogy. Everything that belongs to the temporal order must be imperfect at first.[4] God himself consented to this law of original imperfection. Before granting the plenitude of revelation to his people, he began by familiarizing them gradually with his ways, that is, by educating them.[5] 'Thus he called them from what was secondary to what was essential, from types to realities, from

[1] *Hom. Lev.* X: 1.   [2] *Com. Matt.* X: 9.   [3] ibid.
[4] *Adv. Haer.* IV: 11, 2.   [5] ibid. IV: 9, 1.

temporal things to eternal, from fleshly to spiritual, from earthly to heavenly.'[1]

The mention of 'types', or 'figures', here is of cardinal importance, for the typological method of exegesis defines the relationship of the Old Testament to the New, explaining both the similarities and the differences between them. So the Flood, the resurrection of Christ, and holy baptism all conform to one basic structural type: in all three, there is a judgement of God, importing the destruction of the sinful world, the old man; in each case, the righteous is spared, to be the origin of a new manhood. So again, the crossing of the Red Sea prefigured both the Resurrection, and Baptism, being an exercise of divine power to save the people from the bondage of the powers of evil. In this way, typology gives expression to the specific intelligibility that belongs to history as such. Without it, the events recorded would convey no assimilable meaning to our bewildered comprehension; the key is in the possibility of reference back to earlier manifestations of the same ways. Thus the Annunciation of the Blessed Virgin Mary belongs to a series of annunciations, to Sarah, to Hannah, to Zacharias, while at the same time surpassing them all.

*   *   *

III

Enough has been said to illustrate the essentially historical character of the Christian notion of reality; but there remains a further point: the two categories of event, and progress, do not exhaust the topic. If they did, we should be faced with a theory of indefinite progress, on the model of contemporary theories of evolution. Any such view would leave out of account the further, essential truth, that Christianity is not only progress, but itself the goal of progress. This third and final characteristic of the Christian

[1] *Adv. Haer.* IV: 14, 3.

outlook on history is its eschatological quality; the idea of an end, ἔσχατον, is of capital importance in the system, from three distinct points of view. First, history is not conceived as an indefinite progress, but as finite in scope; it is a determinate, circumscribed design, called by the Fathers of the Church the cosmic week, which is to be followed by the eighth day, representing the life of the world to come. Secondly, Christianity is itself the term of development: Christ professedly comes 'late in time', and inaugurates the stage that will not pass away. So there is nothing beyond Christianity. It is indeed ἔσχατος, *novissimus*, the last thing. And it is the everlasting juvenescence of the world, which makes everything else obsolete. Thirdly, the end of history has already taken place, because the incarnation and the ascension of Christ fulfil its purpose.

It is the great merit of O. Cullmann's book, *Christ and Time*, that it gives powerful emphasis to this truth: Christ's resurrection being the decisive event in all history, nothing that can ever happen will equal it in importance. This disposes at once of all the errors of evolutionism. No progress now can ever bring about for us what we have already got in Christ; that which is beyond all progress is here and now in him; the last state exists already in the Christian mysteries. Consequently no identification is permissible between the Christian hope and a belief in progress: they are radically different things. We have said that Christianity gives a metaphysical value to the idea of innovation: but as it now appears that Christ is the ultimate event, he is, in a sense, the culminating and final innovation. It is a further peculiarity of the Christian outlook on history that the centre of interest is neither at the beginning, as it was for the Greeks, nor at the end, as it is in evolutionary theories, but in the middle. It follows that history differs in kind between B.C. and A.D. History before Christ was a preparation and an awaiting. Once he is come, the essential business is to hand on (παράδοσις) the sacred and now immutable trust delivered once and for all. The idea of tradition thus acquires a real meaning, because the world to come is there already.

Granted that the last days have come with Christ's gift of eternal life, a new problem of another sort arises, not now from the impact of Christianity upon other systems of thought, but from the actual historical situation of Christianity itself. If it be said that the coming of Christ has altered the state of mankind, the objection has to be met that, in the world about us, no change is in fact apparent. It is as old as Origen: 'It is obvious in the fall of Jericho (which prefigured the defeat of the Powers by the cross of Christ) that the devil and his army was destroyed. How then is it that these have still so much power against the servants of God? . . . Again, the apostle Paul says that Christ has raised us up in his resurrection, and seated us with himself in heaven—yet we believers do not seem to be resurrected, or in heaven.'[1] Origen supplies the answer, in the same passage: 'The coming was indeed fulfilled in Christ's abasement, but we hope for another coming in glory. The first was called "shadow" in a mystical text of holy scripture: "Under his shadow we shall live among the heathen." Hence we know that many things are but a shadow in the time of the first coming.'[2] The Church stands in relation to the Second Coming much as the Law stood in relation to the first: 'The Apostle says that the Law is a shadow of good things to come. . . . But we no longer live in their shadow, because we are no longer subject to the Law, . . . we are under a better shadow, for we live under Christ's shadow among the heathen.'[3]

The whole life of the Church is characterized by this constant eschatological reference. Present knowledge 'through a glass, in a dark manner' points towards vision 'face to face'. The visible organization of the Church prefigures the heavenly hierarchy. The sacraments are types and pledges of eternal

[1]*Hom. Jos.* VIII: 4. [2]ibid.
[3]*Comm. in Cant.* III (P.G. 13: 153).

rewards. Origen says of Baptism that 'in the regeneration through fire and the spirit, we shall be conformed to the body of Christ's glory as he sits on the throne of his majesty'.[1] The holy Eucharist is specifically both the nourishment of wayfarers and an anticipation of the eschatological banquet. The whole Christian position is determined by the expectation of the Second Coming: but there is no knowing just when it will be.

This last question notoriously exercised men's minds a great deal in the earliest Christian times. Their preoccupation with Christ's coming again provoked a variety of speculative suggestions, some based on the 'weeks of years' in Daniel, others on the idea of seven millennia. Hippolytus supposed that Christ was born in the middle of the sixth millennium, so that the Second Coming would be in A.D. 500.[2] St Augustine, in his earlier writings, put the Incarnation at the beginning of the same millennium, giving A.D. 1000 as the date of the Second Coming. But Christ had already warned his first disciples against all such computations; and the demonstrated error of the conclusions shows their absurdity. God keeps the secret of that day and hour of the Second Coming. Nevertheless it is always imminent, and the Christian attitude of mind intrinsically depends upon the expectation of it, just as the Christian outlook on history is defined in terms of it.

* * *

IV

Consideration of the lapse of time before the Second Coming leads us to examine the current history of the Christian Church. St Augustine says that sacred history continues *usque ad praesentia tempora*. This is a point of importance. Sacred history is not restricted to the contents of

[1]*Com. Matt.* 15: 23.   [2]*Comm. Dan.* 4.

the Bible, but is still going on: we are living in sacred history. God still accomplishes his mighty works, in the conversion and sanctification of souls.[1] The particular significance of this point is missed in the usual Protestant presentations of the theology of history, where sacred history tends to be identified with what is recorded in the Scriptures, and no reference is made to the Church as continuing God's work through the infallible *magisterium* and the unfailing efficacy of the sacraments. On this understanding the age of the New Israel is less happily circumstanced than the age of the Old: the Incarnation would thus appear to have arrested the course of history. Such is the position associated with the name of Barth: it can be called a sort of post-Christian gnosticism. From this point of view, the only important event is the resurrection of Christ. The final salvation of men flows from this event, solely in proportion to their belief in it: but there is no working out of salvation in the course of historical time. History brings no increment of real value, and consequently no progress: there is really no point in it. The Barthian preoccupation is therefore with the past event of the Resurrection, more than with the present life of the Church.

Cullmann does indeed repudiate this extreme position, and the fact is worth noting. He acknowledges 'an existing kingdom of Christ and the life of the Holy Spirit in the Church'. But he objects to the Catholic presentation that it over-emphasizes the importance of the growing Church and the living tradition. Our reply must be that the Catholics' appreciation of the development of the Church does not in any way diminish their faith in the unique importance of the fact of the Resurrection; but it does imply recognition of the positive worth of current history, consisting in the growth of the mystical body through the work of the Spirit.

[1]"All these things that we read of as having been foretold and fulfilled in the past, are still being done under our eyes in the present'—*de cat. rud.* 45.

What has been already accomplished once for all time is the union of manhood and godhead in Jesus Christ. What is awaited at the end of all time is the manifestation of Christ's victory, in the transfiguration of the universe and the general resurrection of bodies. But what is now in progress is something invisible, yet supremely real, the building up in charity of that mystical body of Christ that shall be revealed in the last day.

This, then, is the purport and import of current history: the Christian mission. Christ delays his second coming because his Gospel must first 'be preached all over the world, so that all nations may hear the truth; only after that will the end come'.[1] This, be it noted, was already the answer that St Augustine gave to those men of his time who thought that the fall of Rome meant the end of the world: that could not be so, because the Gospel had not yet been preached to the barbarians. Nor is the Christian mission simply to teach the word to individuals of all countries: it is to evangelize the civilizations represented by the real leaders of every people, so that Christianity may find its appropriate and authentic expression in the idiom of every racial community, and the Church be like a bride *circumdata varietate*,[2] as the Psalmist says. It is a work of ages.

The need to wait until the rest of the world has been evangelized is the explanation and justification, for those who belong to the earliest group of Christian peoples, of the delay of the Second Coming. It is thus really their missionary charity that alone can help them to put up with it. Their distinct vocation is to further the spread of Christianity, whereby they actually hasten the coming of the Lord. But in the meanwhile they have their distinct temptation and risk, like other ripe fruit, which is to fall into decay. The threat of interior decay is the characteristic problem of Christendom: there was a crisis in the sixteenth century, when the Churches were divided; there is another

[1] Matt. 24: 14.　　[2] Ps. 44:10 (Vulgate).

in the twentieth, with the growth of communism. Thus the question of Christian unity has to be seen in historical perspective, just as much as the conversion of the heathen, or of the Jews.

The Christian mission is what gives substance and consistency to the history of our era. It is the intrinsic reality underlying the phenomena of secular history. It means the progressive building-up in love of the incorruptible body of Christ which shall go through the fire of judgement. Being the work of the Holy Ghost, the mission continues the mighty works, the *mirabilia Dei*, recorded in the two Testaments: the chosen people were brought out of Egypt, Christ was brought back from the dead, in the power of the self-same Spirit through whom the souls of men are saved in baptism. The work of the Spirit is accomplished through the preaching of the word and through the sacraments, which are themselves, as Cullmann clearly recognized, the continuation in the Church of the *Wunder* in the Bible.

The mere geographical extension of the mission is not, however, the whole meaning of current history. As we have already seen, the Christian outlook implies a notion of progress; there is an element of progress in Church history, and notably in the history of dogma. Of course the object and content of revelation is unchanging; there can be no question here of what is called evolution in the modernist sense: but there is a development of dogma, because the Holy Ghost enables the living Church in its teaching office to define certain aspects of revealed truth which are not explicitly spelt out in the Scriptures. Karl Thieme has clearly brought out the strictly historical quality of these definitions: they are not just the result of theological analysis, nor even of the inner mind of the Church; they correspond to particular historical situations, indicating the main turning-points in the Church's life. Mohler and Newman recognized in this development one of the distinguishing characteristics of current sacred history.

Continuing thus the series of the wonderful works of God in the world, the life of the Church is traversed by the fact of sin. The powers of evil which were destroyed by the cross of Christ retain the appearance of effective hostility until the Second Coming. Christ's Church is thus at odds with sin as the people of Israel were in former times. In this context, St Augustine distinguished between two different kinds of trial. There is first the opposition of the outside world, where the limiting case is martyrdom: 'The more copiously the Church is watered with the blood of martyrs, the more it grows.'[1] This is the point of insertion of the whole theology of martyrdom, which belongs to the theology of history inasmuch as it embodies and typifies the conflict between sacred and secular history. Martyrdom is thus seen as the archetypal form of conflict with evil, as the summit of Christian sanctity through conformation to Christ, and as the official proclamation of the Gospel to the accredited representatives of the earthly city.

Secondly, however, the enmity of the devil is evinced by divisions within the Church, as well as by persecutions from without: as St Augustine said, 'this vine, as the Lord had foretold, had to be purged, and the unfruitful branches taken away, whence came schisms and heresies, the work of men who sought not the Lord's glory, but their own'.[2] And here should follow the theology of the separation of the Churches and of the return to unity, as Fr Congar has written it: the history of heresy thus acquires a valid theological significance.

*   *   *

V

So far we have been concerned with the nucleus of sacred history, which is coterminous with the history of the

[1] *de cat. rud.* 44.   [2] ibid.

Church; but this is not the whole of history. We have to consider the relationship of history commonly so-called, the history of civilizations and empires, with the history of salvation: as to which, opinions vary widely. In St Augustine's view, the history of the city of God, which coincides with the history of the Church, is altogether distinct from and antagonistic to the history of the city of Satan, which corresponds to political history. At the opposite extreme, certain evolutionist theories of modern times tend to merge the history of the Church into the universal march of progress: and some Christian thinkers, who would not go so far as that, would prefer to confine the strictly historical facts of progress within the realm of secular history, leaving to the Church indeed the function of impregnating history with the Christian spirit, but not that of making history at all.

On this subject, three observations may conveniently be made here.

First, the interaction of sacred and secular history is an established fact. The Christian outlook embraces the whole field of historical reality. St Irenaeus, in primitive times, saw that universal history was all part of the Divine dispensation; and in this respect he was only expounding the doctrine of Genesis. The Creator and the Redeemer are one and the same God. Civilization is not devils' work: society and culture belong to creation, they are part of the work of God's hands. They represent the organization of a world that has fallen from grace, but is not essentially evil. E. C. Rust rendered valuable service by his clear demonstration of the way in which the totality of world history fits into the pattern of the Christian synthesis.[1] It is a two-way relationship. On one hand, extrinsically, the history of the Church is affected on the surface by the fate of cultures. The Church may be regarded not only as transcendent, but also as incarnate; and from the latter point of view, the history

[1] *The Christian Understanding of History* (1947).

of the Church is a record of the various and successive
Christian civilizations—Palestinian, Byzantine, Medieval,
Baroque, Romantic and modern. (For there is nothing
wrong, despite certain suggestions to the contrary, in such
multiple incarnations of the Church in the different forms
of social order: the harm lies in attempts to identify the
Church exclusively with any one of these forms.) It is also
true that the Church exercises a reciprocal influence on the
cultures into which it is adopted. Thus on these extrinsic
considerations, the history of Christianity falls within
general history, being one of its most important consti-
tuents. But from another point of view the history of
civilizations falls within the history of salvation. This is not
because of any strictly religious value to be attributed to
human progress, whether technical or social: by Christian
standards this is something indifferent in itself, being capable of evil as well as of good. Whenever a community or a
culture assumes the attributes of absolutism, becoming an
end in itself, it is in conflict with the city of God. Thus in
practice St Augustine's view often proves to be accurate,
because it often happens that political organisms are really
the city of Satan. The fallen angels of the nations, Mammon, Wotan, Apollo . . . are still there to be aroused;
even since Christ's victory on the cross they have still a
semblance of power until the judgement day. But on the
other hand it is equally possible for any civilization to be
subject to God's law. In this case, while human progress
itself can never be of any avail to salvation, it is at least 'that
which is saved', as St Augustine said of free will; and so the
operations of mankind are not in vain. Each one of us shall
be in eternity whatever we make of ourselves in this world.
The new heavens and the new earth shall be our own universe, just as the labours of men have contrived to shape it,
only transfigured: so true it is that the history of civilizations, no less than the history of the natural creation, belongs within sacred history in the largest sense.

Nevertheless, this interaction of sacred and secular history, which constitutes an integral part of the history of salvation, is not the whole of it, or even its most important aspect; the second of our observations at this stage must be to insist that the primary and specific element in history is sacred history itself, that is, the succession of the wonderful works of God through the efficacy of the word and the sacraments: for herein alone consists the real inwardness and hidden substance of the historical process. All the rest, such as the series of Christendoms in which *Ecclesia una* is embodied, is but the outward vesture of reality. The progress of the Church is not just the record of its influence on technical and social developments: the activity of the Church is not to be measured primarily in terms of its success in humanizing social conditions, or inculcating a right use of leisure, or improving the workers' standard of living. Important as they are, these things are secondary; the essential work of the Church is the liberation of the souls of men from spiritual bondage, though the Church also works for their economic enfranchisement.

The fact of the matter is that the world of human social organization is already obsolete. In this third observation we find another application of strictly historical criteria. The coming of Christ has brought the kingdom of God into being. The only real society now is that of God's people, the Church. Christ's universal and exclusive kingship is an accomplished fact. Earthly civilization survives under a sort of stay of execution until the end of the world. In this particular situation we may see the antinomy which is the tragic drama of Christianity, for the Christian belongs at once to a world that has ceased to be, and to a world that is not yet; as plainly appears, for instance, in the case of war, which arises from the obsolete condition of society, altogether contrary to the Gospel, yet Christians are in it. Hence the Church and temporal society can never enjoy the harmonious relationship of two parallel organizations, where one might be the other's complement and crown. They are two successive periods of history, in dramatic conflict

*   *   *

VI

Seeing Christianity and culture face to face, we have been led to consider how they stand in relation to each other in regard to the whole history of salvation. There is another species of confrontation which is of capital importance for the Church today, though it was already one of the pre-occupations of such an early writer as Clement of Alexandria: namely, the position of Christianity in relation to the heathen religions.[1] Once again, there are various schools of thought, diametrically opposed to each other. The evolutionary theory of Comparative Religions regards Christianity as a stage in the development of the religious attitude, evolving naturally from earlier forms. At the other extreme, some theologians tend to dismiss all pagan systems as one mass of errors and superstitions, totally lacking any trace of goodness and truth, fit only to be demolished to make room for the Gospel.

As before, it is possible to find in the theology of history a resolution of these difficulties, which preserves what is valid in both theories, and enables us to see how the heathen religions fit into the broad picture of the history of salvation.

In the first place, there is an element of truth in the nature-cults. They belong to the earliest of all the covenants, that made with Noah, wherein God is revealed through the regularity of natural processes, but not yet, as in the covenant with Abraham, through the singularity of historical events. In the rhythms of bodily life, and the movements of the stars, and the succession of the seasons, we can learn something of God and his ways: they are

---

[1]The special case of Islam falls rather to be considered under the same heading as Judaism, for while the latter is an anachronistic survival, the former is a regression.

L.H.–C

hierophanies, affording us the knowledge of a personal Providence whose faithfulness is attested by their unvarying recurrence. That is the gist of the scriptural account of the promise made to Noah, where the subject-matter was the order of nature, and a rainbow was the attestation. The same doctrine is implicit in the Epistle to the Romans: 'from the foundations of the world men have caught sight of his invisible nature, his eternal power and his divineness, as they are known through his creatures'.[1] It is defined in the Acts: 'the living God . . . allowed Gentile folk everywhere to follow their own devices; yet even so he has not left us without some proof of what he is; it is his bounty that grants us rain from heaven, and the seasons which give birth to our crops, so that we have nourishment and comfort to our heart's desire.'[2]

The fact remains that this primitive revelation is nowhere to be found free of corruption. That is not to deny the soundness of its foundation; but things have since gone awry. So Emil Brunner was justified in saying that 'no religion in the world is without some elements of truth. No religion is without its profound error.'[3] The same thought appears in the Epistle to the Romans, just after the verse from which the previous quotation was taken: mankind 'exchanged the glory of the imperishable God for representations of perishable man, of bird and beast and reptile'.[4] Idolatry consists in taking the things of nature, wherein God is revealed, as objects of worship. Thus paganism is ambivalent, and incurs condemnation on one hand while exciting compassion on the other. It is truly both a kind of 'toothing-work', from which the building of Christianity may be securely developed, and also the chief obstacle to its progress.

The heathen religions obstruct the march of Christianity because of their obsolescence as much as by their corrup-

[1]Rom. 1: 20.   [2]Acts 14: 14–17.
[3]*The Mediator* (trs. Wyon, 1934), p. 33.   [4]Rom. 1: 23.

tion. It is once again a question of historical development. The covenant with Noah was the true religion of mankind until the covenant with Abraham was made; but from that moment it was superseded. From the time of the Gospel it has been doubly obsolete; it is anachronistic twice over. What is wrong with the heathen religions is that they have not made room for revelation. They have not succeeded in playing their difficult part in what Guardini calls the drama of the forerunners: their function was to make way for that which should succeed them, as John the Baptist did for Jesus, and Melchizedek for Abraham at the meeting-point of the covenants.[1] But the forerunner is always tempted not to give way, tempted to withstand history, by trying to stop the unfolding of God's design and fix the pattern at the moment of his own contribution: if he does that, the forerunner becomes an antagonist. Guardini gives the example of Buddha as a great forerunner of the Gospel, who may well turn out to be its last opponent.

The supersession of the primitive revelation of nature by the historic covenant does not involve its annihilation, but rather its fulfilment, just as the Old Testament is fulfilled in the New. In both cases, all the real values of the former are taken over into the latter and raised to a higher plane. So, in Genesis, the narrative of Creation and the Fall of Man embodies mythical material, enriched with new meaning. So, too, the Jewish Passover is a celebration of the historical Exodus within the framework of a vegetation-ritual of spring, and itself came afterwards to serve as the liturgical framework for the festival of the Resurrection. Seen in the full context of the history of salvation, the sequence of religious systems is not a mere succession, or a natural evolution, but a series of advances under the creative impulsion of the Holy Ghost.

*   *   *

[1]See J. Daniélou, *Advent* (trs. Sheed; 1950), p. 58.

The Christian conception of history was plainly not the result of any systematic process of reasoning. As questions arose out of the circumstances of the Church's continued existence in time, so the Church was induced to work out its own idea of the history of salvation. The theology of history became possible only when Christianity had become aware of the fact of its own duration, and enucleated the inner significance of that fact.

PART I

PART I

CHAPTER ONE

SACRED AND PROFANE HISTORY

IT was a just observation of Father Thornton's that
although Christianity is itself independent of any particular type of culture—and therefore independent of
modern society—yet, as every organism must, it 'lives by
virtue of its "response" to the environment in which it has
been placed by the Creator'.

There is a real problem, though this is not always recognized, about the situation of Christianity in the modern,
technocratic world. A worker, a scientist, an economist of
the present day may well, and in fact often does, find the
outward forms of Christian life bafflingly strange, simply
because these derive, as a matter of history, from patterns
of social existence that are quite obsolete. Thus he gains an
impression that Christianity itself belongs to the past,
and corresponds to a state of affairs that no longer exists.

Such views are characteristic of a whole field of contemporary thought. Christianity, regarded as a social phenomenon, is felt to be essentially transient. Its intrinsic worth
may not be challenged, but its permanent relevance is
denied. It represents a stage, perhaps an essential stage, in
human development; but this stage will be left behind.
Evidence is produced to show the actual decadence of the
system, presaging its early dissolution.[1] On the other hand,
in direct contradiction to these opinions, there is a school of

[1]Notably in the Marxist view, according to which the phenomenon of
religion itself (not merely Christianity) is due to vanish in the new social
order. Other less radical writers hold that Christianity represents a
particular phase in the religious history of mankind; and is at the present
time giving way before the advent of new religions.

23

thought so anxiously committed to safeguard the transcendence of Christianity as to divorce it altogether from the
historical process; but this is escapism, a flight from reality,
a withdrawal from the human struggle. It is a return to the
gnostic denial of natural values, a condemnation of creaturely existence. We have seen how this pessimistic conception of history is incompatible with the Christian position.

If we are to have an effective grasp of the whole problem,
we must recognize a two-fold relationship between Christianity and history. On the one hand, Christianity falls
within history. It emerged at a given point in the sequence
of historical eventuation. It provides a constituent part of
the fabric of recorded facts. To this extent, it belongs to the
historian's province to describe its appearance in the chronicle of documented reality. But on the other hand, history
falls within Christianity: all secular history is included in
sacred history, as a part, a prolegomenon, a preparatory
introduction. Profane history covers the whole period of this
world's existence, but Christianity is essentially the next
world itself, present here and now in a mystery. The fundamental reality of Christianity is 'to come', not just in relation to a particular moment of time, but in relation to all
historical time, past, present and future. It is indeed
novissimus, the last thing: with Christianity, the end is
already achieved. But in the mystery of the being and
working of the Christian Church, this thing which is
beyond history exists now in historical fact.

Both aspects of this two-fold relationship are equally
essential. Take first the inclusion of Christianity in history:
this is a real incarnation. As Christ himself belonged to one
nation, one culture, one period of time, so the Church is
embodied in successive cultural forms—which are themselves no less transitory than the very civilizations they
represent. Karl Marx may show how the economic conditions of first-century Galilee were reflected in the primitive
Christianity; or how the Byzantine orthodoxy conformed to

the theocratic theory of the Eastern emperors; or how the Reformation followed the economic expansion of the Renaissance, disrupting the medieval forms of social organization: he is discussing what we may call successive Christendoms. In Marxist terminology, these unstable, more or less ephemeral phenomena belong to the superstructure, not to the unchanging, permanently valid infrastructure, which is represented by the Church itself.

The distinction is clearly applicable to the circumstances of the present day. There has been, over the last four centuries, a perfectly normal materialization of Christianity in terms of western civilization. This Christianity of the *bourgeois* has borne fruit in miracles of charity and holiness. But our world is now in the throes of such a cultural crisis as previous history hardly records: the old world of the *bourgeois* is in collapse, with all its categories of civilized life and behaviour. This is something quite independent of individual preferences, neither to be applauded nor deplored: but we are witnessing the last convulsions of a dying world, a dying culture; and everything about the Church that intrinsically belongs to this particular culture dies with it. The Christianity of the *bourgeois* has had its day, and Christian people are well aware of the fact: only, what is passing is not Christianity itself, but the particular embodiment of Christianity in a given social organization.

This is critical for the purposes of our analysis. Christianity ineluctably requires, always, both an incarnation and a detachment. Incarnation, solidarity, is a matter of simple duty. Any attempt to withdraw the Christian religion from its historical settings, into some timeless ideality, is a plain case of mistaken identity. There are critics of our present-day movement towards a workers' Christianity, who complain that this movement is a dangerous error, comparable with Constantine's, when he incorporated fourth-century Christianity into the forms of Byzantine civilization, or with the error of the seventeenth-century Jesuits who imbued

Christianity with the culture of the new triumphant *bour-
geoisie*. On the contrary, these earlier incarnations were not
mistakes, either; they are only obsolete, or obsolescent. As
we have seen, this all-important issue is a question of
chronology. The emergence of new social patterns does not
mean that the old patterns were not right in their day, but
only that they are no longer right.

For detachment is just as much a matter of duty as integration. Christianity is not finally identified with any of the
types of culture in which it is successively embodied. Just
as the distinctive error of Judaism has been a refusal to die
and rise again, or a failure to grow up, so it is, in a measure,
with those who would petrify Christianity in its former
shapes, preserving the incrustations of social custom that
belong to past ages. Each one of us is under the obligation
to 'die daily' and to be born again 'a new man': St Paul
meant what he said, and his language has an application to
Christianity itself, which must necessarily adopt the forms
of human societies, becoming incarnate as the appropriate
Christendom of its time—but each successive Christendom
will be only provisional, and transitory; garments to be put
away when they are worn out. The stripping off of these
familiar coverings is always a painful business. That is the
nature of the crisis through which we are passing at the
present time. It would be wrong to underestimate the scale
and the difficulty of the process, or to be impatient (as sometimes people are) with the slow and gradual responses of
the Church in such a deeply tragic situation, where every
decision is loaded with immeasurable consequence.

This is the crux of the business. A middle way must be
found between two opposite and equally dangerous errors.
On one hand there is what Cardinal Suhard called *inté-
grisme*, a conservative attachment to inadequate categories
and conceptions wrongly identified with imperishable truth.
This archaizing tendency takes various forms, according to
the particular stage of history chosen to represent the ideal

of Christianity—it may be a nostalgic hankering after the Primitive Church of the first centuries, or a more or less romantic medievalism, or a desperate attachment to the vanishing outline of *bourgeois* Christendom. On the opposite side there is the danger of modernism, whereby the necessary process of adaptation is allowed to endanger the essential structure of the *depositum fidei*, discarding the substance along with its ephemeral accidents.

Of course, any exaggerated concern with the outward forms of religious activity would be symptomatic of a certain superficiality in spiritual understanding. If we have insisted upon the contemporary need for a renewal of these patterns, we are at least entitled to emphasize also our conviction that this does not affect the heart of the matter. What is required of the Church is primarily that it should bestow the gift of Christ's life upon men: what is required of priests is primarily that they should be holy. It is not so important that they should be up to date. Many Christian institutions show their age without loss of vital energy. The roots of Benedictine monachism obviously lie deep in an irrecoverably archaic economic system; the *Summa* of St Thomas is inextricably bound up with the Aristoteleanism of the thirteenth century; the Ignatian spiritual method is conceived in terms of chivalry: but all the same, St Benedict is still the father of all monks, St Thomas the doctor of all schools, and St Ignatius the master of the *Spiritual Exercises*. We are not such iconoclasts as to pull down our cathedrals to make room for reinforced concrete churches; there is in fact room for both.

With these qualifications, then, it is clear how and to what extent the Church is a part of history, and subject to the laws that govern the rise and fall of civilizations. The complementary assertion, and much the more important, is that secular history is entirely comprised within sacred history. The latter is strictly the whole of history; the former, a distinct and limited subdivision. As Cullmann has well shown,[1] this has been the Christian philosophers' point of view from primitive times: for though it is true that Christians as such were then chiefly concerned with those historical events upon which our salvation depends, yet they also passed judgement on secular history itself. The Bible insists that God the Lord of creation is one and the same as God the Redeemer of his people: St Irenaeus makes the same point against the gnostics. The history of salvation embraces not only the history of mankind, but the whole of cosmic history.[2] It is not to be conceived as an intrusive enclave within the round of nature and natural history, but as embracing this physical development, for which indeed it provides the meaningful structure: the person of the Redeemer is himself the Creative Word.

In the Christian tradition, the history of salvation begins, not with the choosing of Abraham, but with the creation of the world. St Augustine constantly makes his point. The *narratio plena* starts with 'in the beginning God made heaven and earth'. So the shape of catechetical instruction follows the order of holy scripture, which itself constitutes the authentic and authoritative chronicle. St Irenaeus held the same position, and emphasized this line of thought with particular reference to the gnostics' doctrine of two demiurges, one creating, the other redeeming. Thus the creation of the universe is the first step in God's plan, which is to culminate only in the creation of new heavens and a new earth. Creation is a wonderful work of God. In it appears the absolute immediate dependence of all that is upon the divine will. But it remains an historical event, itself the inauguration of the time-process, and as such belongs to the general history of salvation.

[1] *Christ and Time* (trs. Filson; 1951), pp. 20–21.

[2] St Cyril of Jerusalem expresses this point finely: 'By the spirit of prophecy [that is, a religious intuition of history], man, for all his littleness, sees the beginning and the end of the universe, and the middle term of time, and knows the succession of empires' (*Cat.* XVI: 16. P.G. 33: 941 B).

Then, as we have just observed, the final consummation of this history is to consist in another cosmic event—the resurrection of the body, or, to use what is really a more appropriate terminology, the creation of the new cosmos, for this event, properly understood, is not simply a physical transformation of mankind, but of the whole creation. So the history of salvation extends from one cosmic event to another, each involving the totality of existence. St Augustine explicitly traces the parallelism of these two creations, in reply to the heathen who find the Christian hope of resurrection a principal stumbling-block: 'Why should you not believe you will exist again after this existence, seeing you exist now after non-existence? . . . Is it harder for God . . . who made your body when it was not, to make it anew when it has been?'[1]

It is not only the beginning and the end of our history that consist in actions on a cosmic scale. The central point is also a creative act, the resurrection of Christ, himself the Word of God, by whom all things were made, who is to come in the fullness of time to make all things new.

As he is the almighty Word of God, whose invisible presence is among us and in all the world, so the effects of his power extend throughout the world in height and depth and length and breadth: for all things are under the rule of salvation through the Word of God, and the Son was crucified for all things, marking creation with the sign of his cross. For it was necessary and fitting that he who took visible form should bring all visible things into a share of his crucifixion: thus his personal influence is sensibly effective in the whole world of visible things. For it is he that lightens in the heights, that is, the heavens, and he that plumbs the deeps, that is, the underworld: he, that spans the length from East to West, and bridges the immeasurable breadth from North to South, bringing the whole race of men in every quarter to the knowledge of his Father.[2]

[1] *de cat. rud.* 46.
[2] Irenaeus, *Dem. Apost.* 34: Patrol. Orient. XII: p. 773.

The point has lost none of its significance in our own time. Modern man is accustomed to think of the universe in evolutionary terms. If we cannot show that the cosmic order itself is subject to the sovereign influence of Christ's redemption, then the history of salvation is liable to be merged in the world-process: the person of Christ fades into a universal *Werden*, the impersonal evolutionary trend. Traces of such a conception can be detected in some modern Christian theories of evolution:[1] but it is essential for us to establish that the creative action of the Word is not the blind working of an immanent force. Envisaged from the point of view of the history of salvation, the entire universe is the field of activity of the creative Word who made it, and maintains it in being, and came when it had fallen under the sway of alien Powers, not to destroy, but to set it free and transform it.

Within this frame of reference, how shall the relationship of the Church to political and economic society be expressed? In this question also there are two contrary extremes. On one view, the progress of science and material civilization appears to be directly related to the kingdom of God, so that the former may almost be represented as a means—even the means *par excellence*—of advancing the latter. This is clearly a dangerous position, involving a devaluation of the Church's currency, a disregard of the spiritual law of the Church's life and growth, in favour of scientific or political action conceived as intrinsically religious. At the opposite pole, social and technological advances are sometimes regarded as wholly indifferent, or even diabolically hostile to the kingdom of God. Science is presented as an attempt of the human reason to usurp the Creator's prerogative: political activity, as an aggressive symptom of the human lust for power, seeking world domination.

[1]Lampert points out this danger in his *Apocalypse of History* (Faber & Faber, 1948).

Neither thesis is admissible. Organized society derives
from the plan of creation, and cannot be radically evil. For
this reason, when political organization is made an end in
itself, whether as nationalism, democracy, progress or what
not, it represents the city of Satan over against the city of
God.

This was formerly an essential element of Christian
teaching, as may be seen in St Augustine's *De catechizandis
rudibus*:

> Two cities, one of sinners and one of saints, are to be found
> throughout history from the creation of mankind until the end
> of the world: at the present day they are mingled together in
> body, but separate and distinct in will; in the day of judgement,
> they will be separated bodily. All men who take pleasure in the
> lust of power and the spirit of domination, in the pomps and
> vanities of the world, and all spiritual substances who approve
> these things and take pride in subjecting men to themselves,
> all these are united in one city: even when they fight among
> themselves over such advantages, they are none the less borne
> down together in the same direction by one and the same
> burden of cupidity, and bound together by common behaviour
> and deserts. On the other hand, all such as humbly seek the
> glory of God . . . belong together in one city.[1]

St Augustine's presentation of this theme reveals the
dramatic quality of the history of salvation. There are, as he
says, angels as well as men in both cities. The drama of
mankind is unfolded in the context of a wider conflict, between the spiritual Powers that hold men captive, and the
angels of God under the kingship of Christ. The human
tragedy is a visible representation of this spiritual warfare.
St Augustine follows the general patristic tradition in recognizing a connexion between fallen angels and human
idolatry. The opposition of the two cities divides the worshippers of the true God from the worshippers of idols; and
the worship of idols consists in treating human productions

[1]*de cat rud.* 31.

as absolute realities. The wicked spirits of the gentile nations are still at work, and resume their power whenever a people or a class or a social group of any kind becomes an end in itself: or in the limiting case when mankind as a whole makes an idol of humanity.

Alternatively, the earthly city can be assimilated and taken up into the history of salvation; the principalities and powers of this world can become part of the city of God, when 'earthly rulers themselves forsaking those idols in whose name they were wont to persecute Christians, acknowledge and worship the one true God and Christ our Lord', and when they 'afford peace to the Church—albeit a temporal peace—and quiet opportunity to build up her spiritual edifice'.[1] But there is no middle way between these alternatives of war and peace. No autonomous secular order can exist as part of God's ordinance 'without integration in the order of Christ and His Church. Outside this pattern, apart from the sovereign jurisdiction of God, everything belongs to the city of Satan, the world and the flesh. It remains true, however, as St Augustine reminds us, that the line of demarcation is not visibly drawn—a man may be a member of the visible Church and yet belong to the city of Satan; and *vice versa*.

These are then the basic principles for a religious interpretation of the history of mankind in society. The history of civilization does not conform to a law of continuous evolutionary progress; nor does it consist in a Spenglerian succession of discontinuous and independent cultures; it is to be regarded as a series of καίροι, moments of decision, crises, each representing at once the break-up and the condemnation of a society that has committed the sin of ὔβρις in the pride of life—each consisting also in a parallel renewal of the Church through purgation. These decisive moments, times and seasons, each reflect the supreme καίρος of the passion and resurrection of Jesus, as they also antici-

[1] *de cat. rud.* 37.

pate the ultimate καίρος of the Last Judgement. Bultmann's conception of the Judgement as an abiding reality
is thus reconcilable with faith in the judgement to come;
for each individual, judgement is always with us in a continuous present, but for the whole world of created existence there must be a confrontation of crises, a verdict of
damnation and salvation. The Judgement is in truth always
upon us, yet still withheld; history consists in a perpetual
judgement of the world, whereof the Second Coming will
be simply the final pronouncement.

L.H.—D

CHAPTER TWO

CHRISTIANITY AND CULTURES

AMONG the most important developments of our age is the formation of modern nation-states by peoples hitherto subject to the Western hegemony. In the Far East, Japan was the first to be emancipated. China is for the time being under the Communist yoke, but has at any rate broken away from the economic control formerly exercised by Great Britain and the United States. India, now independent, aims at the quality and status of a great power. Something of the same kind is happening in the Near East, where the Arab world is notoriously in a state of ferment. Egypt has followed Turkey on the road to national autonomy; and last but not least, the state of Israel has been refounded after a break of two millennia. None of these revolutions is exclusively political; in each case there has been a cultural awakening as well. India and Israel may look to the West for industrial or scientific methods and skills, but they are also determined to foster and revive their own religious, literary and social traditions. The political upheavals of the Arab peoples are accompanied by manifestations of intense religious activity. The Oriental races exploit the resources of modern technology for the benefit of their own distinct philosophies of life.

This development brings the Church up against a serious problem. Hitherto we have been content to think of civilization as meaning Western civilization—which, during the ages, we have moulded into Christian patterns. We now have to recognize the existence and vitality of other civilizations, which are not Christian. It is of no use in this

context to insist that Chritianity is universal; any such pretension is liable to involve a most dangerous fallacy. As long
ago as the third century Tertullian believed that the whole
world was Christian. True, there were Christians at that
time in all the known world, that is throughout the Mediterranean basin; but they were mostly Roman settlers.
Christianity had not made much impression on the native
populations. When the Roman civilization collapsed, the
true state of affairs was discovered plainly enough: the
Romans retreated from Africa and the shores of the Black
Sea—and Christianity vanished along with them. Since
then, Christianity has penetrated to every quarter of the
globe; but once again, the spread of the gospel has not gone
much beyond the Portuguese, Spanish, or French trading-
posts, or outside the zone of immediate Western influence.
The same consequence appears today. As the range of European rule is restricted in the former colonial territories, so
Christianity is in retreat. Our religion is still regarded
locally as a foreign import.

In these circumstances there is a plain and pressing requirement for a re-incarnation of Christianity in the form
of these resurgent civilizations, the Oriental, the Near-
Eastern, the African. . . . In this way alone can the
Christian religion take root among the populations. It has
become part of our Western heritage only because it has
been incorporated into our cultural traditions; the concrete
thing called Western Christianity exists because there have
been such men as St Augustine, as Dante, Pascal or
Camoëns. In other cultural traditions, the story is entirely
different—they remain intrinsically and homogeneously
pagan. In such a case, Christianity can only be a foreign
body: as it has engendered no native cultural monument of
any value, it has no place in the tradition of the people. This
is of immense significance in missionary work; for it means
that Christianity is precluded from any influence upon just
those dominant social groups which maintain the distinctive

cultural patterns of any society; its impact upon the people can only be at the periphery; and conversion will inevitably be regarded as an act of treason against the national way of life. All this would be changed if Christianity were an essential element in that way of life. Thus it is clear that the civilization itself must first be christened before its leaders can be converted; and such conversions are an essential precondition of any lasting establishment of Christianity.

There is nothing extravagant about this vitally important process of evangelizing exotic cultures. Christianity is not essentially linked to any one form of cultural tradition; it is not even a product of civilization, but an historic act of God. The fact that its development has chiefly taken place in the Western world does not mean that it is a Western phenomenon. The revelation was in any case first bestowed upon a people of semitic origin and language. Christ was an Aramaic-speaking Jew. The preaching of the Gospel to the Greco-Roman world represented a first translation of the Word of God into terms of another civilization. Today we need another translation. There is nothing extraordinary about this, as the Popes have recognized in their insistence upon the need for native clergy.

But although the process is perfectly normal, it is none the less enormously difficult, as will appear when the formidable problems involved are fairly examined. In the first place, the cultures in question are never found in the pure state, as simple human structures, but always impregnated with religious elements of an idolatrous or other non-Christian kind; so that they are incapable of absorption into Christianity without being first purged of this dross—which takes a long time. The immediate reaction of a native convert is to abandon his traditional aesthetic and intellectual categories along with the paganism they enshrined: he takes his Catholicism as he finds it, from the West. He would be shocked to think of building a Christian church to look like a temple, or singing hymns to our Lady with melodies taken from the repertory of heathen incantations. It was just the same in the earliest days of Christianity: the first generations of Western converts rejected the whole body of Greco-Roman culture together with its pagan implications. Centuries elapsed before the dross could be purged away, and the essential humanities refined out in an assimilable condition. Thus, at first, no Christian was allowed to teach *grammatica*, for Homer and Virgil were the pagans' catechism. By the seventeenth century, children could be taught classics without fear of their worshipping Diana or Aesculapius: but it had taken a millennium and a half in the life of Christendom to reach this stage.

A second problem arises from the difficulty of idioms, and the question how to transpose the data of revelation from one cultural and linguistic medium into another. Christianity is by now so deeply rooted in the Western way of life, borrowing from Western sources so much of its theological and liturgical terminology, and its social patterns, that it seems impossible to disentangle them. Admittedly, this kind of transposition took place in the time of Christian origins, from the Semitic into the Greco-Latin tradition; but the operation was one of extreme delicacy and difficulty, and took centuries to complete. When St John rendered the Hebrew *dabar* by the Greek λόγος, it was a very bold thing to do, even though the Hebrew Bible had already been translated into Greek at Alexandria—itself an epoch-making event of limitless consequence for the future. These transferences could not be the work of a day. The term λόγος had over-tones of pantheism or rationalism, which had to be suppressed. The earliest Christian heresies can be regarded, for the most part, as a sort of revenge taken by the Greek language for the efforts made to force it to describe new things.

Finally there is the third question: is this very difficult enterprise worth while? Granted that one of the characteristic developments of our time is the growing-up into adult

nationhood of 'native' societies—is it possible to feel sure
that the new nations will be able to withstand the pressure
of an expanding Western civilization? Toynbee has enumerated twenty-two civilizations in the course of human history,
many of which have disappeared altogether—as, for instance, in Mesopotamia, the Akkadian and Sumerian; in the
Mediterranean basin, the Hittite, Aegean and Etruscan; in
America the Inca and the Aztec. Why should the civilizations of India, China and Africa escape? Perhaps the future
course of history will be in the direction of a single world-
wide extension of Western civilization: in which case the
current identification of Christianity with European culture
would represent a permanent reality. In favour of this
hypothesis it may be urged that, in the world as we know
it today, there is no civilization properly so-called but the
Western—the others serve merely to recall the lineaments
of an older world that has had its day: in the ordinary course
of things they must be expected to pass away.

Such views have been vigorously enunciated by Karl
Thieme. He links the Church closely with Western civilization, which he regards as, simply, civilization itself. His
method is as follows. He lays it down that there are two
essential, constitutive pre-requisites for the existence of
'history': first, the continuity of one and the same 'bearer'
(*Träger*) of successive events. For this continuity, geo-
graphy is not enough: the land of Canaan has long been the
site of a series of events, but with no single subject or
Träger, and thus no continuity. Secondly, there must be
changes which amount to a true transformation: so that, on
Thieme's hypothesis, there has been no Greek history since
the second century B.C., and no Egyptian history since the
fall of the Ptolemaic dynasty—and, by the same token, no
Chinese history before the sixteenth century A.D.

In Thieme's view, the necessary conditions have only
once been fulfilled, namely, in the case of Western civilization. In this solitary instance, we find a single continuous

subject of changes which successively transform the Roman empire into medieval Christendom, and this into modern civilization. So the West is the locus of history: and other races have progressively come to figure in history solely through contact with the West. Western history is essentially the whole of history, and Western civilization the whole of civilization. The highest representative of Western civilization was the Roman Senate; after its fall in the ruins of the Roman empire, the Church took over this function of a supreme court, which it still has. The Church proves to be the heiress of Senate as well as of Synagogue, the residuary legatee of both secular and sacred history. In this two-fold capacity, the Church is a source of culture no less than of sanctity—the Elect Event, the mysterious heart of all history.

There could be no stronger affirmation of the identity of history itself with the development of our own civilization: nor is the argument devoid of solidity. It is undeniable that Western civilization has, as a matter of fact, obtained a position of unique ascendancy in the world, and that, on its merits, it has rendered unique service to those ideals of justice and freedom that are of the essence of all truly humane society. But for our own part, we would be chary of linking together too intimately the Church and the *Imperium*, the Roman theme and the Latin theme. In this part of his work, Thieme does less than justice to the Eastern world—whether of Byzantium or of Benares. We remain convinced that there is such a thing as Eastern civilization—and Eastern history, too. Admittedly these systems fall short of their proper stature, so long as they are deprived of those principles of truth that the Church alone can dispense: but they have the same propaedeutic value as the Greco-Roman systems. Thieme's point of view is too exclusively European; there is no room in his picture for the theology of the Mission.

We can now formulate certain conclusions. We start from

the belief in a fundamental unity in the spirit of man, which underwrites the truth of scientific and metaphysical judgements. Western achievements in this way belong to the common inheritance of mankind. The differences of idiom between one people and another can only affect methods of enunciation, which derive from special patterns of mental habit—they cannot affect the truth of statements, which is universally valid. In the particular case of Christianity, it is of course obvious that, after two millennia of Western history, this religion, as it exists today, cannot be properly understood without some prior understanding of the Western way of life; but this does not by any means imply that Christianity may not in future materialize in altogether different shapes. The great Chinese Benedictine, Dom Lou, shows a fine understanding of this point, in a book whose title epitomizes a whole programme of education: *La rencontre des humanités*—'Humanities in contact'. Granted that a Chinese will have to learn Latin in order to gain a real knowledge of Christianity, he argues that in future this ought not to be a one-way traffic; more Western Christians must learn to appreciate the worth of Oriental culture. For in time to come, the Latins in their turn will find in a Far Eastern Christendom sources of unsuspected wealth. For this reason (if for no other), one of the best ways in which intellectuals can serve the interests of religion is to specialize in Oriental or African studies: in such directions their work can effectively help to catholicize the Church.

Here, then, are two distinct points of view, in the convergence of which it becomes possible to find the objective solution of a very difficult problem. First, as we have seen, the Church is not to be identified with any single race, culture or society; just as Christianity, whose original idiom was Aramaic, absorbed in time the culture of the Hellenes and finally the social structure of Rome, so now the Church must grow to be Chinese in China and Indian in India—all things to all men. . . .

But secondly, the Church, in its freedom from any permanent attachment to a particular civilization, derives an imperishable enrichment from each of the cultures with which it is united: and equally—to take a particular example—China can welcome Catholicism, and allow it to take root in Chinese culture, without repudiating the capital value of its existing investment in Latin forms, which would indeed be a ridiculous act of xenophobic self-impoverishment; the new accretion represents for the recipient a gain beyond all human expectation. The true Church is no more Greek or Latin than Chinese or Indian. The Church of the future will have passed through all history and incorporated every variety of human civilization, in order to wear that wedding dress, 'a robe of rich embroidery',[1] for the eternal union with the Bridegroom.

In the second of these two complementary points of view, it is clear that the Church is characterized for ever by its Semitic origins—the word of God is always the message that was originally given in Hebrew. It is equally clear that the Church has ineradicable connexions with the Latin culture, and with the historical circumstances of Petrine Rome; but it is also true that the Church can never lose its tincture of Hellenism. This last point deserves to be emphasized. The Church was born in Judaea, but grew up in Hellas: the Church's liturgy and theology are radiant with the traces of this education. Pius XI has said that we Catholics are spiritual Semites—we are spiritual Hellenes, too. As the great orthodox theologian Florovsky excellently says:

Hellenism has come to stay in the Church, as an integral component, being in fact a permanent category of Christianity. This has of course nothing to do with racial types, or with any particular geographical delimitation of Hellas—still less with modern Levantine realities. Our concern is with Christian antiquity, and in that field with Hellenism in doctrine, liturgy

[1] Ps. 44: 15.

and art. In the liturgy in particular, will be found the definitive formulation of the typical Hellenic devotion to the holy
mysteries—so much so, that it is practically impossible to appreciate the inwardness of liturgical praxis without some initiation into the mystique of Hellenism. It is wrong to think of the
Church as having passed through a Greek phase: any theologian who falls into this way of thought, setting aside the
Hellenistic categories as though they were obsolete, is simply
drifting out of the main stream of Catholic communion. Theological catholicity presupposes Hellenism.

The persistent Hellenism of the Church is evident in the
form of the liturgy: 'baptism' and 'eucharist' are Greek
words, and in the *Kyrie Eleison* of every Mass we repeat one
of the most primitive prayers of Greek Christendom. The
permanent structure of Christian theology is even more
profoundly Hellenized, for it was born in the Greek-speaking world. The very word 'theology' symbolizes the blessed
union of Christian thought with the language in which it
came to maturity. Its earliest formulation was in the expressions and categories of Plato and Aristotle, giving it a
character it can never lose. The same is true of spirituality,
where 'ascesis' and 'mysticism' are Greek words again: and
despite Nygren and others who regard it as a mistake, there
is nothing more wonderful than the definitive linking of the
Greek 'eros'—the Platonic nostalgia for the world of ideas
—with the Christian 'agape', the wholly free gift of the love
of the Blessed Trinity which over-abundantly fulfils the
deepest longings of mankind.

It may be said that this Hellenism belongs to the Eastern
Churches, that it is no concern of ours: but that is what I
strongly dispute. It is our Hellenism. It belongs to the whole
catholica. The cultural divergence between the Eastern and
Western Churches, which eventually led to doctrinal
schism, need never have happened if the matter had been
rightly understood. Dom Olivier Rousseau has lately drawn
attention to the happy days when a friend of St Jerome's,

called Gerontius, used to celebrate the holy mysteries alternately according to the Roman and Byzantine rites—and needed no particular authorization for this: the Byzantines were not supposed to have a monopoly of Greek; it belonged to the universal Church. Dom Lou's idea is the same: there should not be a Chinese Church in China and a Latin Church in Italy, but a Church in China that is Latin as well as Chinese, while the Church in Italy should be Chinese as well as Latin. That is what is meant by Catholicism—that is the true 'reunion': and one contribution towards it is for us to re-awaken the spirit of Hellenism in the heart of the Roman church.

The fact that Christianity has been embodied in Western civilization is a great and lasting achievement, part of the Divine scheme of redemption, a splendid tradition commanding our undivided loyalty. For all that, we must never forget that this is only one incarnation of Christianity: the Christian message transcends all cultures and all forms of society; the Gospel must be received by all the peoples of the earth; and so long as the Christian religion has not been deeply rooted in every civilization, so as to find expression in its native language, its dialectic, its philosophy, its art— so long as Christianity has not exploited and hallowed the hidden cultural treasures of every people, we must recognize that something is wanting yet.

These are the principles at stake in the grave problems of unity and catholicity. The Church cannot but be *ecclesia una*, one true Church because there is one God, one baptism, one Christ: but this unity cannot but be a catholic unity, the divers peoples and cultures being one in the Church without prejudice to their distinctive properties. There is always a temptation to turn the idea of unity into that of uniformity; in matters of organization, to think of unity as meaning centralization, and in matters of doctrinal expression to think in terms of terminological identity. On the contrary, there is no real unity without catholicity, which implies a continuing diversity of mentality, culture and civilization, within the single round of one faith, one Church, one dogma, one Eucharist. That is how the Church takes possession of the world to hallow it for God's acceptance. Just as Christ was incarnate in the Jewish race, so the Church must become incarnate in every nation in order to redeem it. The problems of unity and catholicity impinge at this point and in this manner upon the task of the Mission, namely to make known throughout the world the Church's message.

From this point of view, too, the present time is thus an exceptional period in church history: for it is in our own day that the essential requirements we have described have come to be most clearly recognized, now that the great non-Western civilizations are growing up, and properly insist upon being treated no longer as children but as equal kinsmen with a right to live their own lives. The consequences of this development are far-reaching. Pius XII showed his awareness of this more than ten years ago, when he declared that we must no longer think only of the contribution the West could make for the benefit of the coloured races: that we have now to live in a world where the relationship of various Churches is mutual; that the West will expect to learn from the Christendom of China, or of Viet-Nam, or of Africa, no less than these Churches may learn from the West. This ideal of equal fellowship in the enjoyment of a commonwealth is at once essentially catholic and essentially missionary.

We cannot all be said to have really grasped it yet. Indeed, we may be approaching the matter from the opposite angle, feeling a scandalized astonishment at the variations of Catholicism, instead of admiring its inexhaustible wealth. The missionary approach, which we have to cultivate, is not just a tolerant acceptance of the distressing aberrations we have to put up with; it recognizes and welcomes a state of affairs which in the wonderful providence of God helps towards the enlargement of the frontiers of his kingdom, embracing diversity in unity. We must put away all narrow insularity of views, as well as every trace of xenophobia; we must recognize in the infinite variety of the Church one of her best titles to our affection.

CHAPTER THREE

CONFUSION OF TONGUES

IT is clear from the opening pages of the Bible that the speech-barriers between peoples are a factor of some significance in the religious history of mankind, for they are there represented as a consequence of sin. The eleventh chapter of Genesis tells us that the Lord 'said, Here is a people all one, with a tongue common to all'.[1] But when they decided in the pride of their hearts to build a tower at Babel, that is Babylon, that should reach to Heaven (symbol of world-domination), Jehovah determined to 'throw confusion into the speech they use there, so that they will not be able to understand each other'.[2] This linguistic disruption of the human family was a favourite subject for theological commentary in former times, both among Jews and Christians: it was considered in the context of a belief that each nation had its own angel.

Let us examine first a passage in Origen's *Contra Celsum*. On both sides in the controversy it was agreed that God had divided out the earth among angelic powers, each of whom had received for his share a portion of territory with all its inhabitants. But Origen interpreted the principles of the arrangement differently from Celsus. The pagan writer regarded it as a primordial and invariable decree. Origen objected that, on this view, the distribution must be purely arbitrary, or a matter of mere chance; whereas, of course, his whole system requires, and depends upon, the intrinsic relation of all inequality, whether among angels or among men, to the antecedent merits or deserts which involve these consequential rewards and penalties. It was therefore neces-

[1]Gen. 11: 6.   [2]ibid. 7.

sary for him to find an intelligible justification for the apportionment of peoples to angels.

His solution goes back to the Tower of Babel. Mankind was at first one people. They lived in one part of the world, in the East. They spoke one language, Hebrew. They were ruled by Jehovah. But they came out of the East, and settled upon the plain of Sennaar: and there determined to conquer Heaven. For their punishment God handed them over to angels of greater or less wickedness, who gave to each people his own language, and took them away into various lands according to their deserts, some to the tropics, some to the regions of snow and ice. Israel alone, which had not left the East, kept the original tongue, and remained Jehovah's people.[1]

The argument presupposes an established body of doctrine on the subject of national angels, considered as acting in obedience to the will of God, faithful to the role with which he has entrusted them in guiding the destinies of men: it is not to be confused with the doctrine of the fallen angels, who also play a part in national history. Its analogies are rather with the accounts given of angelic influences in nature, upon the cosmic scale. Thus in both cases the angels themselves, whether of the nations or of the heavenly bodies, are not to blame for any idolatrous worship they receive—this is all the fault of men. St Paul's words about the 'robbing' of the angelic principalities[2] require a similar background of doctrine: the rule of the powers is not, in his conception, evil, but obsolete, like the Mosaic law itself, since the coming of Christ. With Origen, the whole system is explicitly and formally developed, along Christian lines.

Seen in this light, these speculations prove to be of universal application, as part of the general Christian theology of history: for they furnish an interpretation of one of the paradoxes of the current epoch, namely, the co-existence in one world of the pre-Christian system of nationalities simultaneously with the single world-wide system of Catholic

[1] *Contra Celsum* V: 30–31.   [2] Col. 2: 15.

unity—corresponding respectively to the angelic governments, and to the Kingship of Christ. The same theory also
indicates a line of convergence with modern scientific researches into the origin of myths, since it is in the subconscious tendency of social collectivities to personalize and
deify their national ideals that the psychologists of religion
now find the solution of their problem. On the other hand,
this tendency can equally be regarded as the national
idolatry of tutelary spirits.

Here, Origen echoes a Jewish theological tradition, which
is exemplified in the following passage:

> And do not forget the Lord your God . . . who was chosen by
> our father Abraham when the nations were divided in the
> time of Phaleg. For at that time the Lord . . . came down
> from his highest heavens, and brought down with him seventy
> ministering angels, Michael at their head. He commanded
> them to teach the seventy families which sprang from the
> loins of Noah seventy languages. . . . But the holy language,
> the Hebrew language, remained only in the house of Shem
> and Eber, and in the house of Abraham our father, who is one
> of their descendants. And on that day Michael took a message
> from the Lord, and said to the seventy nations . . . 'You
> know the . . . confederacy into which you entered against
> the Lord . . . now choose today whom you will worship, and
> who shall be your intercessor . . .' Nimrod . . . answered . . .:
> 'For me there is none greater than he who taught me and my
> people in one hour the language of Kush.' In like manner also
> answered Put, and Migraim, and Tubal, and Javan, and Me-
> sech, and Tiras; and every nation chose its own angel . . .
> But . . . Abraham answered, 'I choose and select only Him
> who said, and the world was created . . .' Then the Most High
> dispersed the nations and allotted to every nation its share and
> lot . . . Only the house of Abraham remained with his Creator.[1]

It is clear that this narrative contains much that is also
to be found in Origen: the distribution of the nations among

[1] From a late Hebrew *Testament of Naphthali*, in Charles, *Apocr. &
Pseudep.* II: 363.

the angelic powers; the angelic origin of the national languages; the preservation by Israel alone of the primitive speech, Hebrew: the status of the chosen people, being the reward of faithfulness. There are also points of difference. Thus the Jewish account is in two stages: first the linguistic separation, even before the project of Babel, and secondly the physical dispersion, consequent upon the nations all, except Israel, taking their angels for gods—Abraham here representing the chosen race. Another feature that does not appear in the passage we have quoted from the *Contra Celsum* is the coming of the seventy angels: but Origen alludes to this elsewhere, in a difficult passage of the *de Principiis*, when the 'seventy men of Israel who came into Egypt[1] are a figure of the coming of the seventy holy fathers [that is, angels] into the world, as God allowed, for the instruction of men'.[2] This obviously refers to the *Haggada* of the *Testament of Naphtali*.

Each of these themes is more or less commonplace in the old Jewish tradition. The allocation of the nations to angelic rulers appears in the Septuagint version of Deuteronomy: 'When the Most High divided to the nations their inheritance . . . he set the bounds of the people according to the number of the angels of God.'[3]

Equally traditional is the coming down of the angels to earth, to take up from God their commission to govern the peoples—something altogether different from the expulsion of the fallen angels from Heaven: it appears in the *Book of Jubilees* (IV: 15).

The figure seventy for the number of tutelary angels is given in the eighty-ninth chapter of Enoch. The special position of Abraham at the time of the dispersal of the nations is described in the first-century *Liber Antiquitatum*, formerly ascribed to Philo (VI: ed. Kisch, 1949, pp. 126 *et*

[1]Gen. 46: 27. [2]*de Princ.* IV: 24.
[3]Deut. 32: 8 (the Vulgate has the last words: *filiorum Israel*).
L.H.—E

seq.). The interpretation of nature-myths, particularly in
the form of astral cults, as an idolatrous worship of angels,
has a long history (Wis. 13: 2; Col. 2: 16). Even the connexion between tongues and angels is attested in Scripture
(1 Cor. 13: 1). The idea of a divine origin of Hebrew is
found in *Jubilees*, XII: 26.

But even the peculiarly Origenistic conception of a puni-
tive mission of angels, on the occasion of the Tower of
Babel, to disrupt the communications of men and to scatter
them abroad, can be paralleled in Philo of Alexandria. The
context relates to the passage in Genesis, dealing with the
confusion of tongues: 'It would be well to go down and
throw confusion [*descendamus, et confundamus*] into the
speech they use there'.[1] The use of the first person plural
is open to a polytheistic construction, and was in fact
sometimes so construed: as in Flavius Josephus—'the gods
sent out the winds to bring down that tower, and gave to
every man his separate language'[2]—and in Abydenos.[3]
Philo argues, against this interpretation, that Jehovah was
not speaking to gods, but to angels. 'God is one, but he has
around him numberless Potencies, which all assist and
protect created being, and among them are included the
powers of chastisement.'[4] But some men, dazzled by the
brightness of these Powers, took and held them for gods.[5]
It seems plain that this refers directly to a tradition, represented for us by Josephus and Abydenos, in which the confusion of tongues was attributed to gods. Similarly, Philo
goes on to mention the opinion of certain literalist interpreters who would derive from Babel the source of 'various
Greek and barbarian idioms'.[6]

[1]Gen. 11: 7.   [2]*Antiq. Jud.* I: iv, 3.   [3]Eusebius, *Prep. Ev.* IX: 14.
[4]*Conf. Ling.* (trs. Colson & Whitaker, 1932): xxxiv. 171.   [5]ibid. 173.
[6]190, 38. The connexion between speech-barriers and war, which
Philo examines in *Conf. Ling.*: 4, 10, is also mentioned in the text of
Abydenos: 'Mankind, which hitherto had but one tongue, received from
the gods a diversity of speech, after which there was war between
Saturn and the Titans' (Eusebius, *Prep. Ev.* IX: 14).

The special interest of this passage of Philo is in the way
in which the esoteric doctrine of national angels is used,
from the first, to account for the fact of national polytheisms
in the face of Jewish belief in one God. Philo was confronted
with various syncretistic systems, all more or less tainted
with polytheism: and indeed the whole of his treatise *De
confusione linguarum* is directed against the tendency
visible, for example, in Abydenos, to adapt the Old Testament narratives in terms of pagan mythology; not that he
rejects the syncretistic tradition *in toto*, but constantly recti-
fies it in accordance with Jewish orthodoxy. In the instance
now under discussion, he may have been the first to infer an
allusion to angels in the story of Babel, for his own doctrinal
purpose, or he may have followed an earlier tradition on this
point: he is in any case the first known authority for this
interpretation.

To return to Origen, the next question is to know
whether he found the legacy of Jewish traditions for himself in the written *apocrypha* (with which he was certainly
familiar), or orally from rabbis (with some of whom he was
personally acquainted): or whether, on the other hand, this
was something already incorporated into the Christian
sources at his disposal. In favour of the latter hypothesis it
must be said that there is solid evidence, from the earliest
days of Christianity, of a developed Jewish Christian theology among the converted rabbis of Palestine, and that
much of the Judaic tradition—particularly in the field of
angelology—was thus assimilated into Christian thought.
Traces of this work are to be found in such texts as the
Gospel of St Peter or the *Ascension of Isaiah*. The same
primitive development is represented in the oral traditions
reported by Papias, Irenaeus and Clement as deriving from
presbyters of the Apostolic period—presumably, as we have
said, converted rabbis. And it persists in those heretical
aberrations of Judaeo-Christianity known to us through the
pseudo-Clementine writings.

These last-mentioned works furnish certain parallels with the account given by Origen. In the eighth of the pseudo-Clementine Homilies, angels come down to earth to take care of mankind; here, too, appears the idea of angelic incarnation, which is also found in Origen. Again in *Recognitiones* I: 30, the Hebrew language, which God gave to mankind, is said to have remained in use as a single common speech until the sixteenth generation, when the sons of men left the East, and took possession of separate territories, which were denominated by each group in its own tongue. It will be observed that this account, like that of the *Testament of Naphtali*, differs from Origen's in that it does not connect the separation of nations and languages directly with the Tower of Babel.

The two themes—of national angels, and of the distinction of tongues—appear in conjunction in the eighteenth *Homily*, 4: 'According to the number of the Children of Israel when they went into Egypt, which was seventy, the Father determined the frontiers of the nations by seventy different languages. He gave his Son, who is called the Lord, the Hebrew nation for his portion, and proclaimed him the God of gods, that is of the gods to whom the other nations were allotted. All these gods gave laws for their own, that is the gentile nations: but the Son gave the law that runs among the Hebrews.' In *Recognitiones* (II: 42), also, the seventy (or seventy-two) nations are divided up among the angels, whom their subjects mistake for gods, though the angels themselves make no claim to divine honours.[1] The former of these two texts may be usefully compared with what Origen wrote in the *de Principiis* about the seventy men who went down into Egypt, symbolizing the seventy angelic instructors.

In conclusion, it may be said that the Jewish tradition exhibits practically every element in Origen's doctrine of

[1]On the fluctuating figure (70 or 72) given for the total number of distinct nations, see J. Daniélou, *Sacramentum Futuri*, p. 138, n. 2.

nationalities. It is true that Origen goes further than any one of the sources we have examined, in particularizing the linguistic activity of the national angels; the most detailed development is as follows: 'In Genesis, when God says— doubtless to his angels—"Go to, let us go down, and there confound their language", is it not clear that different angels have given mankind a diversity of language and dialects, one giving his people the speech of Babylon, . . . another the speech of the Hellenes?'[1] It is also true that Origen emphasizes the penal character of speech-barriers, to a greater extent than the *haggada*. But there is no means of deciding whether, even in these points, Origen was elaborating his material for his own purpose, or simply drawing on traditional sources that are no longer extant. Either way, his account represents the supreme attempt of all to analyse and define the particular phase of humanity denoted by the confusion of tongues.

But the state of affairs so described was ordained to be totally disorganized by the coming of Christ, who inaugurated a new régime: the Word of God incarnate took upon himself, without intermediary agencies, the government of the universe and the supreme direction of history. The angels were removed from the place they had occupied, under the providence of God, in the old order. Among several Pauline allusions to this theme, the most important is in the Epistle to the Colossians 'the dominions and powers he robbed of their prey, put them to an open shame, led them away in triumph, through'[2] his cross. These are the principalities that ruled over the nations: 'in those childish days of ours we toiled away at the schoolroom tasks which the world gave us. . . . Formerly, you had no knowledge of God; you lived as the slaves of deities who were in truth no deities at all. Now you have recognized the true God, or rather, the true God has recognized you. How is it that you are going back to those old schoolroom tasks of yours, so

[1] *Hom. Num.* XI: 4. [2] Col. 2: 15.

abject, so ineffectual, eager to begin your drudgery all over
again?'[1]—that is, the old régime, when mankind was
subject to the rule of angelic governors: a régime that was
abolished when God exalted Christ 'high above all prince-
doms and powers and virtues and dominations, and every
name that is known, [and] . . . put everything under his
dominion'.[2] It is a disputed point of exegesis whether these
defeated powers should be understood as good or evil. For
Cullmann they are evil, for Benoit good, for Cerfaux ambivalent. On the one hand it was a providential order of
things that was abolished in the dispossession of angelic
governors: but as this constitution had been corrupted
through the work of the fallen angels, the catastrophe
wears, on the other hand, also the appearance of Christ's
victory over the insurgent powers of darkness.

Origen was perfectly aware of this duality. He was
prompt to show how the good angels welcomed Christ's
coming to their aid, and freely proffered him their services:
'It was a great joy for those who had charge of men and
nations that Christ came into the world'.[3]

According to Cerfaux, the thought was already in St Paul:
'The angels preserved inviolate their original delegated
powers in relation to creatures, and submitted themselves
freely and unreservedly to the kingly role of Christ.' But
it was otherwise in the case of the fallen angels: 'In Christ
was fulfilled the word of Scripture, that "Thy seed shall
possess the gate of his enemies". . . . Thus the angels who
held the nations in subjection were consumed with anger
to see Christ's coming to take away their power: as it is
written "The Kings of the earth . . . and the rulers
take counsel together, against the Lord, and against his
anointed".'[4] Nor was it only their tyranny that Christ came
to destroy, but also their intellectual delusions and pseudo-
science: 'When the princes of the nations saw that the Lord

[1]Gal. 4: 3, 8–9.   [2]Eph. 1: 21–22.

[3]*Ho. Luc.* XII. Cf. Eusebius, *Dem.* IV: 10.   [4]*Ho. Gen.* IX: 3.

was come into the world to ruin the doctrines of their so-called learning, they set traps for him.'[1]

The question remains to know what shall be the effects of this dispossession of the angels upon the dependent social and political structures: are these abolished in reality, along with their spiritual prototypes? Is the whole diversity of peoples, cultures and tongues to disappear, along with polytheism? The several answers proposed for this question correspond to differing eschatological theories.

One point, however, is established beyond doubt: Christ inaugurates a new phase of existence, in which former lines of demarcation have vanished. Instead of the old order, based on the separation of races, languages and cultures, there is one new world in Christ. This unity was symbolized by the Pentecostal gift of tongues—the converse of the Tower of Babel—re-establishing the means of communication between the various families of mankind. The nations have re-discovered a common speech. At the same time they have come under the leadership of one Shepherd, the prince of Shepherds. In this respect, Cullmann's observation is sound, that the kingly government of Christ is already effectual, and embraces the whole range of human existence.

But if we consider the meaning of Christ's monarchy in relation to the kingdoms of this world, we find two contrary principles of interpretation. The first is represented by Eusebius, who considered the unification of the world as something already achieved, even at the level of material and political consideration: the separate individuality of nations being conceived as abolished together with polytheism. The Christian Empire had effected the unity of the whole world; the imperial monarchy was the visible manifestation of monotheism. In this view, the kingship of Christ is not merely ecclesiastical, and does not have to await the last day for the fullness of its realization in human society: it is a fact of contemporary politics and civilization.

[1]*de Princ.* III: 3.2.

The doctrinal background of this thesis is obviously to be found in a strict identification of political organization with the régime of the angels: so that the dispossession of the angels necessarily involves the disappearance of nationalities, which were but the visible effect of their government. Similarly, monotheism involves as its normal expression, world-monarchy; which in turn must bring peace, since wars only occur between separate nations. The *pax romana* was thus simply identified with the *pax messianica*. Roman civilization was to absorb and homogenize the variety of cultures and tongues, brought into the world by the spiritual Principalities at the confusion of Babel. As the Logos conquered the powers of heaven, so his vice-regent, the Emperor, conquers the nations of the earth.

Such was to be the theory of Byzantium and the Holy Empire. Over against it stands the contrary position, adopted by Origen, for whom the perfect fulfilment of world-unity is a matter of eschatology; now, and for the rest of time, this unification is realized only in the Church, which knows no frontiers within itself, but co-exists with a world of national autonomies. The dispossessed Powers retain until the Second Coming a certain measure of influence. There will always be this contrast between the kingdom of God and the kingdoms of the world, because in the current provisional phase of human development the separation of nations and cultures remains an integral feature of the natural order.

*   *   *

Speech-barriers, like national frontiers, are to be reckoned as belonging to the fallen state of mankind, not to the primordial destiny of the race; the obscure stirrings of an urge towards unification have, in this sense, the quality of nostalgia. But it is no less true that the distinction of tongues has its origin in the will of God. This condition of society is

appropriate to the intrinsic requirements of man as he is,
providing a natural medium well suited to his limitations.
In this matter as in others it is dangerous to ignore the
balance of nature. There must always be something equi-
vocal about any human attempt to restore an effective
linguistic unity of mankind: it is a sort of parody of the
original Paradisal unity, and is apt to incur a chastisement.
God alone can bring mankind together again in one people,
but that ideal is not for this world any more: it belongs to
the renewal of mankind in the heavenly Paradise; its fulfilment awaits the end of time, when men 'from all
nations and tribes and peoples and languages'[1] shall praise
the Lamb with one voice. Yet there is already a mysterious
beginning of the ultimate unification, through Christ who
has already opened Paradise to men. The sign of this unity
was given at Pentecost, the antitype of Babel, when the
Apostles, 'filled with the Holy Spirit, . . . began to speak
in strange languages', and the multitude 'from every
country under heaven . . . was in bewilderment; each
man severally heard them speak in his own language'.[2]

At Babel, the confusion of tongues signified the fragmentation of mankind through sin: the restitution to the
human race, through Christ, of unity in the Spirit was
tangibly signified when men were enabled to understand
each other again. But this was only in a figure. The new
unity of mankind remains a hidden reality. 'We are sons
of God even now', says St John, but 'what we shall be hereafter, has not been made known as yet.'[3] The Church is the
outward and visible sign of this unity; the common liturgical
languages, Latin, Greek, Old Slavonic, represent it in the
linguistic field: but the life of men is none the less conditioned by the confusion of tongues. The victory over sin
has been won, but the consequences of sin, whether death
and disease or speech-barriers, will not be destroyed until
the resurrection day.

[1] Apoc. 7: 9. [2] Acts 2: 4–6. [3] 1 John 3: 2.

It is now possible to define the distinctively Christian
position in face of this complex of questions, from speech-
barriers to internationalism. The Christian believes that the
final achievement of linguistic and political unification is a
matter of eschatology; he finds something sacrilegious in
every imperialistic or syncretizing programme of standardi-
zation or *Gleichschaltung*: but this does not require him to
adopt an attitude of passive resignation towards the her-
metic sealing-off of communication between the peoples of
the earth, each isolated in its private world. This, for a
Christian, would be an impossible dereliction of responsibility: his creed, on the contrary, includes belief in one
fellowship of man; but not in an external uniformity that
would abolish distinctions ordained by Providence. The
Christian notion is of a community, in which every member
is the complement of the others, and they of him.

The existence of civilizations altogether unlike our own
is thus by no means something to be resented, or extin-
guished as far as possible by the imposition of a Western
way of life. On the contrary, we have to recognize our own
essential need of such a complement to our system. Nothing
could be more unintelligent than insularity. The full beauty
of mankind would be diminished by the loss of China's distinctive contribution, or that of the Arabs or the Negroes.
Every race and every tongue gives expression to some irre-
placeable aspect of humanity. Each language, in particular,
has its own genius, its special capacity for handling certain
ideas. For Christianity, this means that the one Gospel message, transmitted through the diversity of cultures as
through a prism, reveals more adequately first one and then
another of its perfections. The Church is that Bride,
clothed in 'her robe of golden cloth, a robe of rich embroidery;'[1] the Church takes up the best in every civilization,
to consecrate them all to the Blessed Trinity.

[1] Ps. 44: 14–15.

CHAPTER FOUR

EXILE AND HOSPITALITY

ORCIBLE transfers of populations are one of the most
shocking symptoms of the cruelty of the modern
world. We have seen Hitler's Germany uprooting the
Jews of Poland from their homeland, and removing them
to concentration camps; Stalin's Russia substituting Slav
colonists for German natives in East Prussia; and Israel
driving nearly a million Arabs out of their own villages to
make room for Zionist immigrants. In every country nowa-
days there will be found colonies of exiles or refugees,
whether from Lithuania, perhaps, or Armenia, or Russia, or
elsewhere, living among—or rather, beside—the inhabitants
of their temporary resting-place, reproducing in our own time
the kaleidoscopic spectacle of the folk-migrations of antiquity.

These racial shifts appear new and strange to us only
because they have begun to disrupt the superficial tranquillity of a world whose peoples seemed to be settled, even
embedded, in their peculiar habitations. But from a re-
moter point of view, as in the perspective of biblical ideas,
the modern phenomenon is only an acute phase of the permanent instability of mankind; while the more inflexible
structures of civilization are seen as a fragile top-crust, like
the thin layer of solid lava on the surface of a volcano. The
events of the present generation are symptomatic of the
fundamental condition of fallen man, which is a state of
dispersal. We have tried to regain the benefits of a home-
land in the rigid mould of nation-states—the fractures ap-
pearing in the mould remind us that we are all really state-
less persons, sojourners: we rediscover no less than the basic

truth about our life on earth, through these crimes of contemporary society.

In the Bible, as we have already seen, the fragmentation of mankind into nationalities is recognized as a feature of the condition of life under sin. It is described as a consequence of the particular sin of Babel. Hence, immediately, that ambivalent quality in the situation, which points to the inward mystery of the phenomenon of deportations.

On one hand, the existence of separate nations is something that has been ordained; God 'divided the nations apart . . . giving to each people its own home'.[1] From this point of view, forcible expatriations run counter to the ways of Providence. Though it is no part of the primordial destiny of man that he should take root in a particular soil, this is nevertheless an integral characteristic of the lot decreed by God for sinful man. The balance of nature is not to be disturbed with impunity. Any policy of internationalism based upon the theories of the unity of science, or upon the religion of humanity, must incur the sentence passed upon the men of Babel; for it implies idolatry, and a rejection of the divinely-established order. Such a policy, seeking to reconstitute through human means the sort of unity that God alone can bestow, necessarily achieves nothing but disturbance and chaos. In this world, nation-states represent the normal framework of human existence. So too, mass deportations are not only inhuman, but also a direct infringement of God's law, violating 'the homes of each people' that were given by God himself when he put his angels in charge of the nations of men. This is the formal guilt of all who commit these crimes: for they break one of God's commandments, in violently removing men from the places and homes which it has pleased God to give them. This was the sin of the kings of Babylon, who took the people of Israel away from the land the Lord gave them, leading them captive to the banks of the Tigris and

[1]Deut. 32: 8.

Euphrates: and Babylon fell under a curse for breaking the commandment. 'On all the gentiles that fell to and feasted on lands of mine, marked them down for pillage, my jealous love pronounces doom.'[1] And finally, these deportations are not only a wickedness in their perpetrators, but also a great evil to the sufferers. Once they have been torn away from their natural environment, they become a proletariat, a restless factor of unrest, a corrosive solvent of all established order.

Yet this brutal disruption of the normal conditions of human life, wicked and dangerous as it is, may be the occasion of an even greater good. It is true that the spiritual activity of mankind must be exercised, as a general rule, within the context of a *patria*, but this natural frame of reference can also be a barrier. The deeper a man's roots lie in his native land, the more easily he may forget that patriotism is a secondary and conditional virtue, while essentially his most intimate allegiance is common to all humanity. Deportation, removing him from the home of his earthly fathers, may lead him to a clearer understanding of the fact that he has here no continuing city: 'our spirits are exiled from the Lord's presence so long as they are at home in the body'.[2] So the anonymous second-century author of the *Epistle to Diognetus* found a wonderful formula for the Christian attitude: 'Every foreign country is a home to them, but they are foreigners in every man's country' (V: 5). Wheresoever he may be exiled or deported, the Christian man finds his true home in the Christian fellowship, the figure of his heavenly fatherland: and even when he is settled in the land of his fathers, he knows that this is not where he finally belongs. But in case he might forget it, the experience of these mass-deportations is there to recall to mind his highest destiny, by showing the fragility of all the rest.

This salutary example is pointed out, in the Bible,

[1]Ezech. 36: 5.   [2]2 Cor. 5: 6.

through the story of the Babylonish captivity. The Prophets, first of all, gave the theological interpretation of this event as a punishment for the sins of the chosen people: 'Strange that this people of mine should forget me, and resort to vain sacrifices . . . I will sweep them away . . . as the east wind sweeps all before it.'[1] But this was not all: at the same time, Jehovah broke the ties which bound the hearts of his people to their earthly promised land, so as to awake in them the expectancy of spiritual possessions. This idea finds expression in closely related passages of Deuteronomy and Jeremiah: 'the Lord will make an end of you, scattering you over the world, and leaving but a few of you to live in a land of exile. . . . There, if thou wilt have recourse to the Lord thy God, if thou wilt but have recourse to him with all thy heart, in the bitterness of thy tribulation, thou wilt find him again.'[2] 'So the day shall dawn, the time be ripe at last . . . when Israel and Juda both together shall come back, weeping as they hasten on their journey to find the Lord their God . . . they will come back, and bind themselves to the Lord by an eternal covenant, never to be forgotten.'[3]

Even this does not exhaust the potential gains of the Captivity. There is a remarkable passage in Tobit, showing how the deported Jews were to be apostles of Jehovah, so that the captivity appears as a mission—the means of making known among the heathen the name of the Lord: 'if he has dispersed you among heathen folk who know nothing of him, it was so that you might tell them the story of his great deeds, convince them that he, and no other, is God all-powerful.'[4] Thus, by a strange reversal, the crime of forcible expatriation becomes a positive source of spiritual value. In the first generations of Christianity, the missionaries were sometimes Christian slaves, or soldiers, displaced persons in effect, who brought about the conversions of their masters; but going further still, there have been mission-

[1]Jer. 18: 15, 17. [2]Deut. 4: 26–27, 29. [3]Jer. 50: 4–5. [4]Tob. 13: 4.

aries who chose to go into exile of their own free will, to bear witness to Christ in foreign lands—as the Irish and Anglo-Saxons did in the Dark Ages, or the French colonists in Canada in the seventeenth century, or the lay missionaries of our own day.

Nevertheless, though exile may be productive of good, even though it may be freely chosen as a mode of the apostolate, the fact remains that the dispersal of mankind is one of the consequences of sin: mankind is essentially one community. On the other hand, this union which is required by the nature of man is something other and more than any alliance or federation of states, or any scientifically designed supra-national collectivity. Its realization is in the gathering together of all men in Christ at the last day, when the primordial unity of mankind shall be restored. This is the condition of life for which man was created, before the dispersal of the nations; but it cannot be re-established through human resources, or for human ends. It consists in the order of the communion of saints, whose brotherhood comes from one common paternity. St John, in one of the very few passages of the New Testament that refer to the subject, declares how the restoring of unity depends upon Christ's cross: 'Jesus was to die . . . not only for that nation's sake, but so as to bring together into one all God's children, scattered far and wide.'[1]

Thus. while individual historians are free to put their own gloss on the phenomenon of deportations, we may stand by the view that it represents one distinctive element in the *mysterium*, the inwardness, of contemporary historical development; and that those responsible are but blind tools in the hands of God, who 'moves in a mysterious way' to produce unsuspected good out of obvious evil. The Jewish people, says Butterfield, 'provides us with a remarkable example of the way in which the human spirit can ride disaster and wring victory out of the very extremity of defeat. We

[1]John 11: 51–2.

have had an opportunity in recent years of picturing to ourselves the chilling horrors associated with the displacement of populations, and some of us may have made for ourselves a vision of such a tribulation as almost a kind of living death. Such things apparently took place amongst the grim empires of the ancient world, to the cruelty of which our own world has been fast reverting. Yet . . . the Old Testament people . . . showed that by resources inside themselves, they might turn their very catastrophe into a spring-board for human achievement.'

In the measure in which the deportations of our own time have reproduced some of the conditions of the ancient *Völkerwanderungen*, so they have re-introduced the currency of the ideal of hospitality—the very counterpart of that social instability in which we live. Now this whole question of hospitality is something which the Christian West (to put it bluntly) cannot face. I recall the experience of a Chinese pilgrim, who made his way from Pekin to Rome on foot. The nearer he came, unfortunately, the less hospitality he found. In Central Asia there was no trouble at all; his journey through the Slavonic territories was fair enough: but once he got into the Latin countries he had, as they say, 'had it'. Here is a somewhat painful reminder that our Western Christian world is rather deficient in this particular virtue at the present time.

Yet hospitality, apart from all other considerations, is a priceless human asset. The Greeks recognized it as one of the criteria of civilization, so that, from one point of view, the measure of a community's approach towards a fully civilized polity was given by the theory and practice of hospitality maintained therein. Some idea of the real value of the moral achievement represented by the very notion of hospitality may be gathered from the curious fact that many languages have only one root for the words 'guest' and 'enemy'. The two categories have as their common basis the single undifferentiated notion of 'stranger' or 'foreigner', the outsider, not belonging to the same tribe or race, not a member of the same social or biological group; such a one may either be enemy or guest. It is thus a triumph of civilization, or even the supreme triumph of civilization, to have made a foreigner a guest instead of an enemy; for this is essentially the brotherhood of man. Before this step was taken, packs of men were at war with one another, like the wild creatures in the primeval forests. From the moment when a stranger is taken in as a guest, no longer an object of execration but one of peculiar respect, a new thing has come into the world.

I have spoken of linguistic roots, and must now give my references: in Latin, a guest is *hospes*, while an enemy is *hostis*; the two words have a common ancestry. An hotel in German is *Gasthaus*, *gast* representing the same root. These observations are highly significant, because philology records the development of society. The Greek word for 'stranger' or 'foreigner', ξένος, may be used pejoratively, as in 'xenophobia', but also in the contrary sense of 'guest'; 'hospitable' in Greek is φιλόξενος, 'loving strangers'. No doubt the same kind of development can be traced in other linguistic systems as well as in the Indo-European group.

The primordial condition of the 'outsider' is described in the tragic words of Cain, at the dawn of human history: 'I shall . . . wander over the earth, a fugitive; anyone I meet will slay me.'[1] The normal, appropriate reaction, on finding a refugee, a wanderer, an outlandish man, is to kill him. To take him in instead, as a guest and a godsend, is, simply, revolutionary. It will be of interest to notice the workings of this revolution within two great cultural systems from which our own civilization is derived—the Greek and the Semitic.

Taking the Greeks first, their exalted conception of the value of hospitality dates from a remote period of history, as may be seen from the wonderful passages devoted to

[1]Gen. 4: 14.

hospitality in the Homeric poems; and especially in the episode of Ulysses, on his return to Ithaca, arriving home in the guise of a stranger, and being taken in as a guest by the swineherd Eumaeus, and by Penelope. Here we may recognize the theme of the mysterious guest who is something more than he seems: the unknown visitor, whose identity will eventually be declared, as a superabundant recompense to his hosts.

On another plane, there is a paragraph in the *Laws* of Plato, about the status of guests in Greek society, which is one of the fundamental texts for any understanding of the Hellenic culture. Plato has dealt with the mutual obligations of his citizens, and turns to the subject of foreigners:

> as regards the alien, we must remember that compacts have a peculiar sanctity; indeed, offences by alien against alien, we may say, compared with sins against fellow-citizens, more directly draw down the vengeance of God. For the alien, being without friends or kinsmen, has the greater claim on pity, human and divine. . . . What anxious care, then, should a man of any foresight take to come to the end of life's journey guiltless of offence towards aliens.[1]

To read a text like this is to understand what the Greeks understood by φιλοξενία, hospitality, namely that all men whatsoever are worthy of respect. It is, furthermore, to understand the meaning of civilization, namely that state of human life in which individual man is accorded his due of respect and of love, being loved the more in proportion as he may be defenceless, lonely, or unlucky. Thus it appears that any condition of society in which the contrary applies, where weaklings and outsiders are undervalued, discarded, or liquidated, is not civilized at all, whatever its degree of technological achievement. We must be clear about civilization, that it is not a function of material progress, but a stage in the emergence of humanity: and

[1] *Leg.* 729 d–730 a. (trs. Taylor, 1934).

hospitality is one of the oldest and most reliable tests of humanity.

The Semitic peoples, and particularly the Arabs, share this tradition with the ancient Greeks: it is a commonplace that their inherited customs of hospitality are sacrosanct for them above all others. The Bedouin of the desert treat their guests as their ancestors did in the second and third millennia B.C. Once a man, even an enemy, has set foot in the threshold of their tents, he is a guest, something sacred: the fellowship of hearth—and still more the fellowship of board—is enough to bestow this special quality, so that any manner of violence or contumely that might be offered him would be a kind of sacrilege. It was even so in the tragic story of Sodom in the Bible, when an angel in human shape was taken in by the Sodomites, and then exposed to threats of infamous treatment: the divine punishment of destruction fell upon the city that thus offended against the law of hospitality. For the reverse of the picture, the due practice of this virtue, it is impossible not to recall another passage of Scripture, describing the conduct of Abraham in the plains of Mamre—a passage which corresponds to the narrative of the homecoming in the Odyssey. 'He had a vision of the Lord, too, in the valley of Mambre, as he sat by his tent door at noon. He looked up, and saw three men standing near him; and, at the sight, he ran from his tent door to meet them, bowing down to the earth. Lord, he said, as thou lovest me, do not pass thy servant by; let me fetch a drop of water, so that you can wash your feet and rest in the shade. I will bring a mouthful of food, too, so that you can refresh yourselves before you go on further' [Gen. 18: 1–5]. Then we see Abraham hastening to Sarah in the tent, for three measures of meal; running to the byre, to fetch a calf, and giving it to his servant, 'who made haste to cook it'. When all was prepared, 'he stood there beside them in the shade of the trees' while they ate.

The actions of Abraham, bowing down before his guests,

washing their feet, giving them bread to eat and milk to drink, embody the immemorial outward expressions of hospitality. Washing the feet, as the first service to be rendered to a guest, has been adopted into the Christian liturgy of Maundy Thursday; and in the ancient rites of Baptism all the ceremonies that follow the administration of the sacrament itself seem to constitute a pattern of hospitality— the feet of the new Christian were washed, his head was anointed with oil, milk and honey were set before him. Along with water for the way-worn feet, and with the sharing of food and drink, the application of unguents to refresh the weather-beaten, sunburnt head and face was one of the sacramental rites of hospitality. The liturgy makes use of these simple actions, just as they were practised in the beginnings of the Hebrew civilization, to signify the supreme hospitality of the divine host receiving a stranger into his Church.

Christianity has thus consecrated these ancient practices, by conferring upon them a quasi-sacramental status; but this is not all: Christianity has also developed and transformed the very spirit of hospitality, and brought it to a new perfection. In the earliest ages of the Church, great importance was attached to hospitality as one of the essential Christian virtues. (It had to be said, earlier in this chapter, that the absence of hospitality in the modern so-called civilized world is proof of a real want of civilization: in the same way, if contemporary Christians are inhospitable, their Christianity can hardly be more than skin-deep.)

Among the early Christians, hospitality was not merely a private virtue, but a feature of the public life of the organized hierarchical community. The bishops who governed the churches were required, among other things, to be actively hospitable: this was already mentioned in the First Epistle to Timothy—'A bishop, then, must be one with whom no fault can be found; faithful to one wife, sober, discreet, modest, well behaved, hospitable'[1]; and again in

[1] Tim. 3: 2.

the second century, by the popular Roman writer Hermas, when he speaks of the trees giving shelter to the sheep, in his symbolic description of the Church: these are 'hospitable bishops, who have gladly at all times received into their houses the servants of God without hypocrisy'.[1] This was then a regular feature of the Primitive Church: any Christian stranger would find hospitality awaiting him in every parish—or bishopric, for in those days the bishop corresponded rather with our idea of an average parish priest, not even the rector of a big metropolitan parish, who might have been an archbishop. The traveller had only to find the bishop to be taken in, 'gladly, without hypocrisy'. It must be emphasized that this early Christian hospitality was strictly an institution, maintained by the whole body of the Church under the superintendence of its local ruler. In modern times, we compound for this obligation through the establishment of 'hospices' or 'hostels', which have come to be nothing but a kind of 'hotel', with a charge for admission, organized on an economic basis. The debasement of the word 'hotel' is an indication of what has become of the idea of 'hospitality'. We could profit, in this field, by the example of our Protestant brethren, whose Salvation Army, for instance, does a great work: an institution like their rescue homes for girls bears effective witness to the true Christian ideal of hospitality.

And there are two sides to this question, for hospitality involves a receiving as well as a giving, and this exchange of values is an aspect of the communion of saints: it means opening and broadening the narrow circles in which we live and move, establishing channels of human communication, through which the life-giving spirit of Christ may freely flow. Thus we cannot fulfil our obligations merely by taking in strangers who come our way: we must sometimes be strangers ourselves in the way of others. This is the link between hospitality and the mission. The early Christian

[1] *Sim.* IX: 27.2 (trs. Hoole, 1870).

missionary, who had forsaken everything for the Gospel's sake, lived on the hospitality of his hearers, to whom in return he gave the good news entrusted to him: 'When you enter a house, say first of all, Peace be to this house . . . Remain in the same house, eating and drinking what they have to give you . . . and tell them, The kingdom of God is close upon you.'[1]

These words reveal the true significance and inwardness of hospitality, which had been adumbrated even among the pagans, in the figure of the stranger who came to Ithaca and proved to be other than he seemed; and again in Abraham's guests, who were really angels. So in the Epistle to the Hebrews, the first Christians were exhorted: 'do not forget to shew hospitality; in doing this, men have before now entertained angels unawares.'[2] As with Abraham, the stranger-guest may turn out to be an angel. There is always a mystery about him, for he is the unknown— except that we Christians now do know, since Jesus has told us, that he is always Jesus. We are told that in the last judgement, Jesus will say to the blessed: 'I was a stranger, and you brought me home', and they will say: 'When was it that we saw thee a stranger, and brought thee home?' and the King shall answer: 'When you did it to one of the least of my brethren here, you did it to me.'[3] Elsewhere in the Gospel he says: 'He who gives you welcome, gives me welcome too; and he who gives me welcome gives welcome to him that sent me';[4] and again, according to St John, 'the man who welcomes one whom I send, welcomes me; and the man who welcomes me, welcomes him who sent me.'[5] So we receive Jesus in each of our guests, always and only Jesus. He has identified himself for ever as the guest, the stranger in this world who knocks at our door: 'See where I stand at the door, knocking; if anyone listens to my voice and opens the door, I will come in to visit him, and take my supper with him, and he shall sup with me.'[6]

[1]Luke 10: 5, 7, 9.   [2]Heb. 13: 2.   [3]Matt. 25: 35, 38, 40.
[4]Matt. 10: 40. [5]John 13: 20. [6]Apoc. 3: 20.

The mystery of hospitality is thus seen to consist in an inversion of values: the real gainer is the host rather than the guest. The exercise of hospitality is itself a blessing, a grace. A household at Benares reckons it an honour to take in any pilgrim or devotee, young or old, among the voluntary mendicants who live on hospitality alone: when they come begging a handful of rice for the daily meal, they are made welcome with every mark of the kindest respect. The Christian conception is even more exalted, as may be seen in that faithful mirror of primitive tradition, the Rule of St Benedict, the text in which we find perhaps the truest expression of early Christian hospitality: for there it is explicitly laid down that a guest be received as the Lord Jesus himself. Those of us who have ever knocked at the Black Monks' door, with or without previous notice, will know what real hospitality means, and what a 'guest house' should be.

In this world, Jesus is the guest we receive into our houses; but we know that he is also the host who will receive us in the end. Today, he is with us as a stranger: he comes among men and men receive him not. But in the end we shall be the strangers in another world; rounding the promontory of death, adventuring into uncharted places alone, with no friends and companions, no kith and kin to help us; then we shall know with a vengeance what it means to want a home. How will it feel, then, to hear a well-known voice saying to us: 'Come, you that have received a blessing from my Father . . . for . . . I was a stranger, and you brought me home'? And when we say: 'when was it that we saw thee a stranger, and brought thee home?' he will reply: 'when you did it to one of the least of my brethren here, you did it to me.' If we want the perfect host to take us into his eternal home when we come to knock at his door, he has told us himself what we have to do: we must be ready to open our own door to the earthly guests that come our way. That shows the value and importance of our hospitality—it is simply the criterion that Jesus will use when he comes to judge us among the living and the dead: it is the key of paradise lost.

CHAPTER FIVE

MARXIST AND SACRAMENTAL HISTORY

IN former times, 'the Christian Missions' were exclusively concerned with propagating the gospel among such communities of men as were geographically outside those territories which had been evangelized already. But latterly there has come into existence a new kind of civilization, common to the whole human race, and alien from all the civilizations that have so far received the Gospel. The distinctive achievement of the nineteenth century, the fruit of technological advance and of the industrial society which this led to, was the establishment of new communities of men, standing outside all the old social categories, but themselves drawn together by an identity of conditions and interests, to constitute new urban collectivities around the towns and cities of the old world—the working-class districts. For although the recent structural changes in society affect all mankind, their primary manifestation is in the working-class, which owes its very existence directly to them.

The reaction to this new world has followed the pattern of reactions to the ancient non-Christian cultures. The first move was an attempt at colonization, an endeavour to annex and assimilate the workers to the constituted forms of bourgeois Christianity—just as Christians once tried to impose their Western traditions upon the Far East. When this failed, as it was bound to do, efforts were made to start a Christian working-class movement, over against the secular working-class movement: but, as always happens, this only took in a fringe of the working-class; the core and the leadership were untouched. For Christianity to take root in any society, it must be embraced by the leaders, the accredited trustees of its ideals.

So we have eventually arrived at a third position, equally appropriate to the working-class world and to the Far East: a recognition that we must ourselves belong to a society, whatever its faults and failings, before we can think of implanting the Gospel in it. In the words of Albert Dominique:

> The idea of any return to 'Christendom' (which is, in any case, a somewhat imprecise and mythical conception, constantly eroded by historical criticism) is going out of date: the Christian's aim is now rather to set about his business of being a man, in a true-hearted spirit of partnership with anyone who is trying to build a decent world for men to live in, and with a sincere respect for the worth and autonomy of human ideals. Words like 'conquest' imply the enrolment of the masses into Catholic organizations, or the growth of a Catholic party at the expense of other parties: instead of these words, there is a growing use of such significant expressions as 'gospel witness', 'missionary spirit', conveying the idea that a Christian's function is to 'be there', on the job.

This means that the problem of establishing Christianity on a solid basis in the working-class society of the future has at last been stated in adequate terms: the requirement is for authentically class-conscious workers, fully committed to the cause, and at the same time Christians. But the very definition points to the elements of tragedy in the situation of these working-class Christians, which is indeed the common lot of Christians in the world, only in an exceptionally acute form. For the working-class is, on the one hand, a moment in the creative process; it represents a valid ideal in conflict with obsolescent institutions, and as such fulfils God's purpose. But it is none the less a heathen society, worshipping a new idol, in place of the old gods of the Gentiles, namely man himself, exalted by the new discovery of his own quasi-creative power.

The Christian worker has, and must have, two loyalties:

he cannot deny the claims of either. He must be true to his class, even though the working-class movement, as it exists in fact, is anti-Christian. But, within the movement he must keep clear of any complicity with its idolatrous tendencies. Without this absolute intransigence, which is required of him, his position is meaningless. The combination of these two attitudes in the working-class Christian may well be called incomprehensible, self-contradictory, or just impossible. But that is the way he has to be.

And after all, it is no wonder: for this is simply the Christian way of life, in the limiting case. Who ever supposed Christianity was a viable arrangement, except people who have grown accustomed to worshipping God and Mammon —and what do they know of Christianity? The normal condition of Christians is described by St Paul: 'It seems as if God had destined us, his apostles, to be in the lowest place of all, like men under sentence of death; such a spectacle do we present to the whole creation, men and angels alike . . . we have no home to settle in, we are hard put to it, working with our own hands. Men revile us, and we answer with a blessing, persecute us, and we make the best of it. . . .We are still the world's refuse; everybody thinks himself well rid of us.'[1]

Such is the lot of every Christian, but particularly of the working-class Christian in our own day, who thus typifies the apostolic ideal. He is rejected on all hands—by Christendom instinctively, because he is committed to a hostile movement; and by the Marxists, who will not indefinitely tolerate his deviations from their idolatry. 'Filth', 'offscouring', he is 'made a spectacle . . . to angels'; jetsam in the strongest cross-currents of a world in travail. He is a contradiction in terms, standing for something that does not exist in reality. His affirmation is meaningful only as a prophecy; but that is the point of it: he embodies the future. He asserts the impossible as a fact, for he is himself the rough draft of a Christian working-class society.

[1] Cor. 4: 9, 11–13.

He is in a position to make personal trial of the solidity of those working-class values, which are the preparation, as it were the toothing-work, for the building of Christianity in time to come. There are three experiences in particular, belonging to the working-class, the taste of which is enough to cure a man of bourgeois tendencies for good, on pain of treason against himself. The first is poverty—not playing at poverty, as some Christians like to do, when they have something solid to fall back upon; but the pitiless insecurity of the wage-earner, 'haunted by the inexorable spectre of a gap between purchasing-power and the cost of living, obsessed by the fear of partial or complete unemployment, or of sickness in the family'. To live like that is to belong among the countless multitude of the world's poor: and 'the poor', as Fr Desroches expressed it, 'are the privileged objects of the Saviour's providence'. In the bowed figure of a Russian serf, Péguy discerned the tragic immemorial supplication of Oedipus; the invariable pattern of poverty embodying man's supreme acknowledgement of God.

Then there is the experience of a brotherhood of man. Bourgeois society is built upon a framework of lines of demarcation, whether between nations or between classes; but there is no longer anything in the realities of working-class life to correspond to these artificial divisions of mankind. This elimination of boundary-lines is a world-wide development: 'one integral feature of the modern unification of the globe is the emergence of a single world-wide proletariat, consisting of all the toiling masses of every race, colour, language, and type.' Here is another of the structural prefigurations of future Christianity. 'There is something providential in this development of a social homogeneity throughout the world, in parallel with the growth of a spiritual ideal of "one world". Our present generation faces a critical moment in the apostolic mission.'

Finally, the working-class, as such, is consciously transforming the life of the world. Our planet, as we know it today, is one vast building-site. 'The delicate equilibrium in man, between his involvement in the world of nature and his private personality, is shifting, under the pressure of conflicting developments on both sides; the human race is undergoing a painful mutation, with a sort of growing-pains, as it were of adolescence or a sloughing-off of its old skin. The workers of the world are at the epicentre of an earthquake; they represent the lava-flow that issues from the eruptive activity of modern technology. The trans-formation of personality corresponding to the physical changes is represented by the working-class movement. There may be much exaggeration in the myth of a mes-sianic proletariat, but there is no disputing the decisive influence of the working-class movement in shaping the future of civilization. Its essential functions are to ensure that the new world of the industrial revolution shall not be impropriated by any privileged caste, and to promote the interests of the great mass of mankind by raising the workers' standard of living in proportion to the progress of technical advance.'

Well: but these factors in the working-class situation, each of which intrinsically belongs to the Christian social order of the future, are also obstacles in the way of its accomplishment. The justifiable complaint of the wage-earners against capitalist exploitation has been translated by Marx and his disciples into a denial of all transcendental authority, which was considered to be a form of exploita-tion, simply because the truths of religion were regarded as standing or falling with their associated social structures. The unity of the working-class is in competition with the unity of Christendom: 'It must be acknowledged that Com-munism has taken the lead, in many parts of the world, in promoting the ideal of workers' solidarity'—an advantage which it is not slow to realize. And the very consciousness of man's new powers and enlarged field of control in the physical universe has resuscitated the temptation to be 'as gods', to create mankind anew merely by altering the material conditions of human existence.

The class-conscious worker who is also a Christian has to live in the point of intersection of these contrasts—he must always be on both sides of the fence at once. In this position he exactly reproduces the situation of the Primitive Church among the heathen. The Constantinian phase of Christian history is coming to an end: the old Christian world, or worldly Christianity, is breaking up under the irresistible pressure of new and vital forces. The Christians who see this most clearly are those who bear the heat and burden of the workers' day: they feel a much closer affinity with the early Church than with medieval Christendom or with the Age of Reason. Albert Dominique brought out this point in the article from which I have been quoting: 'Equally significant is the strong appeal of the first period of Christianity, the centuries before the growth of Cesaropapist ideas, and the persistent attraction of biblical and liturgical origins.' And this also furnishes the complete explanation of something else, a development which I take to be peculiarly characteristic of our own time, namely the re-entry of contemplatives into the active life of the world. For in the early days of Christianity, the holy virgins and the men of prayer lived their daily lives as part of the one Christian community in full contact with the world of paganism. The flight into the desert was a revolutionary innovation, dating from the fourth century, when St Anthony inaugurated the age of monks, the withdrawal of the contemplatives from a world in which Christianity was compromised, into the solitudes where they might keep alive the faith of the martyrs. That age is passing—St Anthony is coming back from his desert; there is no need for flight now that the Church is once again an army of martyrs, in the midst of a heathen society. 'My factory is my desert.'

For a Christian who has to live among men whose pre-occupations, under Marxist influences, are exclusively materialistic, the main difficulty will be to preserve his faith in moral and spiritual values. Marxism interprets the historical process as a transformation of mankind through economic change. The social mechanism of progress is class-war: the rising class, which conforms to the economic infrastructure of the future, struggles to displace the exploiting class, which belongs to an earlier state of the economy. In order to exist, a man must take part in this struggle, he must be engaged in the historical process. And the Christian answer to all this is too often only an inverted copy of Marxist social doctrine. For want of any serious analysis of the authentic Christian solution of the question on the spiritual plane, the debate is conducted in Marxist terms.

But the right answer, as we understand the matter, should be sought from the other end, in the dedicated life of Christianity, especially through the sacraments: there is no reason why Christians should feel like refugees whenever they practise their religion; on the contrary, they are then in the vanguard of the historical process. To prove our point, we will examine a series of situations showing (despite all preconceived probability) that the highest and deepest supernatural aspects of Christian life, and in particular the sacraments, furnish the best solution of contemporary problems. Thus it will appear that these eternal realities, far from being a side-issue, belong to the innermost structure of our life in the world: practising Christianity is not merely an optional arrangement to secure good relations with almighty God, but means committing oneself utterly, and for good.

The modern mind is habituated to an evolutionary, or historical, conception of reality. This universal attitude is partly due to the rapid growth of human knowledge, which has automatically familiarized us with the notion of progress, and partly to the scientific recovery of the pre-history of mankind. No system of thought which fails to take account of the time-process, as one of its dimensions, will survive criticism today. If Hegel was the first to give philosophical form to this attitude of mind, it has been increasingly fortified since his time, and particularly by the Marxists.

But the Marxist formulation of the position is curiously restrictive. The basic idea of Marxism is that history consists in a dialectical process whereby man creates himself—that is, progressively attains to the full stature of humanity, by successive changes in the economic conditions of his existence. Consequently the men who really count, the heroes of modern history, are the scientists and the manual workers: poets, artists, philosophers and saints rank lower; they are not, in the Marxist system, indispensable—as the scientist is, for the methods of material progress, and the worker, for its achievement. It is obviously a stimulating doctrine for these two categories of people, that they are the essential factors in history-making: that history really consists of a succession of industrial processes—the Iron Age, the ages of fire, steam, electricity, or atomic energy—that everything else is only superstructure. The whole mechanism of human progress is comprised in the techniques of production, and the improvement of these techniques is the only way to a better world.

The compulsive force of this position comes from the fact that it is not simply an intellectual account of reality presented for men's acceptance, but invites an engagement of the will by exhibiting a morally valid reason for activism. The system is not just a brute materialism, but a kind of humanism; its conception of mankind is certainly atheistic, but supremely exalted: it is in fact a religion, or cult, of man. As such it is the absolute contradiction of Christianity; it finds man's highest good in man himself; it posits man as his own creator. For a Marxist, any recognition of God represents a loss of human status and dignity, so that true humanism must be fundamentally godless.

In these circumstances it is quite useless for Christians to put forward any more or less half-hearted form of Christian humanism in competition with the Marxist doctrine.

Christian thought is always and inevitably at a disadvantage
in this field, unless it holds fast to the essential principles of
Christianity, which are the religious worship of God, and
the recognition of God in history. The product of history,
in the Christian view, is not only a certain social organization of mankind, but primarily mankind's fulfilment of
God's will. Our only hope of defeating Marxism depends on
our conviction that Christianity is the real maker of history.
The crucial conflict in our time is between these two philosophies of history: for Christianity, like Marxism, is basically
historical—it is not at all, and never has been, a system of
ideals to be superimposed on a different and more or less
refractory world of real life. Its interpretation of the entire
historical process is final.

The structural pattern of history, as the Christian under-
stands it, is given by what is called Sacred History, that is,
the temporal succession of works whereby Almighty God, the
Creator, proceeds to the building of the eternal city of mankind. Thus the interpretation of Christian history requires
more than an understanding of outward and visible events;
it must take account of what happens in the hearts of men,
which is revealed to us by the Holy Spirit—and chiefly in
the Scriptures, the chronicle of the mighty works of God,
wherein his ways are made known to us, and the characteristics, so to say, of his creative policy and methods. Our
discovery and comprehension of God's universe will be no
more than proportionate to our acceptance and assimilation
of the Holy Scriptures as containing the fundamental realities of life and truth.

The Bible starts with the historical record of creation, and
proceeds to exhibit the continuous effect of God's action in
the course of events. God makes choice of Abraham to be
the Head of his people, and enters into a covenant with him.
Thereafter, he guides his people in his own ways. But at
once we find a new and important set of considerations: this
sacred history which is accomplished through God's creative

activity, stands in contrast with another kind of history that men would fashion for themselves (and leave available for Marxist research). All through the record, there are these two contrasting sequences. On the one hand, man's efforts at history-making through pride, ambition, the lusts of the flesh, a succession of empires and conquests, down to the struggles of our own generation between the rival great powers, each seeking to determine the course of human history: a bloody chronicle of war, persecution, and enslavement. Many people know no other meaning of the word 'history': but all the while God is making history in his own way, shaping the lives of men towards the establishment of his kingdom. The Old Testament furnishes us with a typical instance of this duality, in the narrative of conflict between the prophets—representing the Christian conception of history, through the spiritual illumination whereby God revealed to them the reality of man's eternal destiny—and the principalities and powers of this world by whom they were invariably persecuted.

At the nodal point of history, the Son of God himself became incarnate, came down to earth to take upon him the nature of mankind, purifying and perfecting it in his own person through the shedding of his precious blood, setting man free from death and sin, to inherit the Father's kingdom for ever. For it is indeed freedom that the human race requires, and release from the burden of captivity; but this enslavement is spiritual, not economic. Original sin is not capitalism, wrongly regarded by Marxism as the root of all evil: even if all mankind could be rid of poverty and oppression and economic distress, they would still be by nature the wage-slaves of sin. Marx was mistaken in thinking that when men were once delivered from economic bondage, the world would be happy; for the horrors of spiritual destitution remain. It may be that the people of Soviet Russia have achieved economic freedom, but the depth of their spiritual despair is unmistakable.

L.H.–G

Thus the activism of the Marxists is superficial, it does not get to the roots of man's unease. It is certainly our duty to attack social wrong and economic distress, but these are only the symptoms of a more deep-seated evil, the work of the devil: and from this real captivity there is only one deliverer, Jesus Christ. The purport of history, according to Marxism, is the liberation of man; we would entirely agree, but add that it can only be achieved by Christ and his followers. Apostolic and contemplative souls are the real saviours of mankind. So long as we fail to appreciate this, so long as we are content with a social programme which is merely an alternative to communism, instead of following out into practice the essential principles of our religion, we cannot escape an inferiority complex. For us, social and economic policy is not the whole story: we have a deeper and more important concern, to further the work of Jesus Christ for the salvation of men.

Marxists, for their part, are not strictly obliged to deny the worth and beauty of historical Christianity, or to minimize its revolutionary consequences: but they maintain that its work is done, that the crisis of dissolution is upon it, that a new era has begun; mankind has progressed beyond Christianity towards a religion of the future. The Christian answer to this contemporary challenge is a confession of faith: there is no superseding Christ, he is the fulfilment of all things, he is Alpha and Omega, the last end of the world as he is the spring of its eternal youth. In him all things are made new, and the word 'beyond' has no meaning in relation to him who is the consummation of all. His coming is the completion of the human story; therefore we look for no progress, no development comparable in importance with that which we already possess in Jesus Christ. He has given us infinitely more than any technological advance or social revolution could offer.

The Marxist conception of history is open-ended: his pre-occupations are with the future. For Christians, the structure of history is complete, and its decisive event, instead of coming last, occupies the central position. Nothing can ultimately go wrong. The acceptance of final justification and salvation as a gift, not as of our own making, is simply a reflexion, in the eschatological plane, of that sense of utter dependence which characterizes, and indeed constitutes the basis of, all religion. But this does not mean that we have no more to do; after the central, decisive event, the task remains of ensuring that all men come into effective possession of the gift once secured in principle for all mankind. Sacred history is thus also the history of our own time.

In this later current period of time the outstanding events are those of the sacramental life. This is something vastly more important than the achievements of modern thought, or the discoveries of science, or victorious wars, or successful revolutions, all which things make up the tissue of recorded history, but leave no trace at the deeper levels where real history is enacted. The greatness of these mighty works belongs to the intellectual and the physical world, but the mighty works of the spiritual world, in the order of charity, are the sacraments. 'Jesus Christ made no discoveries', wrote Pascal, 'but he was humble, patient, holy, holy in the sight of God, terrible to evil spirits.' For want of a thorough-going conviction of this truth, we are too easily apt to be impressed by intellectual and physical achievements, and to forget that we ourselves hold the secret of God's own plan of love. In our false sense of values we make to ourselves idols of the things men revere—science, money, history, the State— though the first of the commandments is 'thou shalt worship the Lord thy God and serve none but him.'[1]

The working of God's power among us is through the sacraments. As we have seen, there is a worse captivity than the economic enslavement of the workers through capitalist exploitation: it is the captivity of men, 'slaves of sin',[2] and exploited by the powers of darkness. From this servitude the

[1]Matt. 4: 10. [2]Rom. 6: 17.

only deliverance is through holy baptism. Jesus Christ alone
sets us free from the bondage of sin: Jesus Christ, who went
down into the kingdom of death and sounded the depths of
human suffering; Jesus Christ, who rose again, victorious
over death and hell for ever, and opened up for all mankind
the way of salvation. Baptism, in the words of St Paul,
means dying with Jesus Christ in order to rise again with
him, and reign with him for ever on the right hand of the
Father. In the primitive liturgical context of the Paschal
vigil, baptism is recognizably a continuation of the mighty
works of God whereby he saved his people in the first Passover, from bondage in Egypt, and in the second Passover
delivered his son from the bondage of hell. So, too, the third
Passover, the Mass, not only commemorates but effectively
continues the one reality of the former two.

The significance of baptism is not only a liberation, but
a creation. St Paul calls it παλιγγενεσία,[1] regeneration, 'a
new Genesis'. In the beginning the Spirit of God moved
upon the face of the waters, and there was brought forth in
them the physical life of the first creation. The same Spirit,
according to the Gospel, overshadowed Mary, that she, in
the power of the Most High, might bring forth the world
of the second creation, the world of grace, wherein men
become sons of God; the world whose orientation is towards Christ, the eternal sun-rising. Baptism is this same
new creation of every living soul. That which comes out of
the stream of living water, 'water and the Spirit'[2] regener-
ated, new-begotten, born again in Christ, belongs thereafter
to the new creation. In the Marxist myth, man is the demiurge of mankind, through a continuous 'creation' which consists in economic change. But just as Marxism is incapable of
setting man free from the worst of his servitudes, so it cannot
really produce a new kind of man, for Jesus Christ himself,
'the man who came afterwards',[3] is alone *homo novissimus*.

[1]Tit. 3: 5.   [2]John 3: 5.   [3]1 Cor. 15: 47.

CHAPTER SIX

TEMPORAL WORKS AND THE MARXIST MYTH

GRANTED the data of the previous chapter, we have
still to meet the question implied in the title of
Father Montuclard's book, *Dieu pour quoi faire?*
'Why God?' See the contemporary hardships of individuals
and communities, between the disasters from which they
have just escaped and those which already threaten their
future—is there nothing that Christianity can do to alleviate
this tragedy, we ask? How can we be deaf to this cry? It is
true that our Lord Jesus Christ refused to be accepted by the
people as a magician, who should provide for the satisfaction
of their temporal needs: yet, for all that, 'he had compassion
on the multitude', and *he did give them bread*. The Christian's due recognition of eschatological values, his rightly
exclusive concern with eternal salvation, can never make
him callous or indifferent towards the sufferings of mankind
in this world; this is the tragedy that moved Fr Montuclard,
and moves us today.

There remains room, however, for an independent commentary on his solution of the problem, and particularly on
what he has to say of the role of Christianity in the world of
economic and social affairs. After showing, in his book, that
Christianity is not designed to secure earthly benefits for us,
but to admit us to a share in the divine mysteries, he continues: 'It is for us to plan the earthly paradise in which no
man shall be exploited by another, it is for us to work towards this end, patiently, yet boldly, through an ever-
increasing understanding of the principles of sociological

evolution and progress. At the present time, it is true, we cannot fully realize the ways in which human activity will be developed through the progress of sociology, scientific socialism, psychology, medicine, pedagogy, and the rest of the social sciences. But we can at least be sure of this, that we are promised a boundless hope.'

If we understand the author's argument correctly, this means that, apart from the saving of souls, there is an 'earthly paradise', 'a boundless hope', founded upon the extraordinary scientific extension of mankind's natural potentialities. In this 'boundless hope', there is included the possibility of a 'transformation of the life of man'. The prospect is open to Christians—despite the communists, who exclude the eschatological dimension from their programme: that is their error; but the temporal prognosis is sound. The Christian parts company with the communists because of his belief in God, but he can share their belief in the capacity of mankind to transform itself. There are two distinct spheres of Christian action, which must be considered separately: in temporal affairs, the Christian is neither more nor less than a man among his fellow-men; but another field of operation is open to him as well, in the life of the spirit.

This solution of our problem is admittedly attractive at first sight. We all know the kind of Christian socialism that claims to produce the Christian answers to social and economic questions, but in practice succeeds only in debasing Christianity to the level of a party programme (which does not work). From the weariness of spirit caused by such misdirected efforts, there is a real refreshment in going back to a proper discrimination of categories. It remains to be seen whether this discrimination itself has perhaps been imprudently exaggerated into a discontinuity: but the first point is worth making, namely that the Christian has both a spiritual calling, to await the world to come, and also a duty in this world to improve his brethren's lot.

Yet the notion of 'improvement' in this context still

requires analysis. It may refer simply to the limited practical humanitarian measures we can take to alleviate the pressure of economic laws in the world as we know it. Christians have always played a part in this kind of work, just like other men, with more or less success. We are not in the habit of emphasizing this particular aspect of Christianity, and certainly we do not regard it as a thing of primary importance; but for what it is worth, the evidence is overwhelming, from medieval times onwards to the present day, and cannot honestly be disputed. Christian humanitarianism has suffered from a twofold limitation—the want of effective zeal among Christians, and the resistances implicit in humanity itself.

Why is it so often said that Christianity does not work? 'You have been on the job for nearly two thousand years in this world: what is there to show for it?'—so runs the familiar accusation. The results that we are alleged to have failed to achieve are something quite different in kind from the limited progress which, as suggested above, has actually been attained. It is a fact that mankind has become increasingly aware of human potentialities, especially during the last couple of centuries, the period in which scientific developments have most remarkably extended the scope of man's activity. This has gradually reinforced the visionary hopes of a radical change in the conditions of human existence, to be effected through a modification of the material circumstances of life. Hence the myth of man as his own demiurge, and the theory of an earthly paradise, a classless society, to be achieved by man through his own unaided efforts.

This is what is commonly understood today when people talk of an improvement in the lot of humanity as 'a boundless hope'. This is what Fr Montuclard appears to find perfectly compatible with Christian ideas, apart, of course, from the atheistic corollaries of its Marxist context, and without prejudice to the status of hope as a theological virtue. On

this hypothesis it is fair to complain that Christianity does
not work, because Christianity has not enabled man to re-
cover the earthly paradise for himself. Fr Montuclard himself puts the crucial question, in another passage: 'How can
you maintain that salvation, all salvation is through Christ
alone, when you insist that Christians in the world must
work for the material betterment of living conditions? This
sort of progress is itself a form of salvation—the salvation of
mankind by man, over and beyond the salvation of mankind through Jesus Christ.'

That is exactly the point. All Christians agree in recognizing the reality of sacred history, which records the sequence
of events in the salvation of men. On the other hand there
is no denying, as a fact, the contemporary acceptance of a
view of profane history, according to which the progress of
technology, taking over from biological evolution, is in process of making man. How are these two forms of history
related? Fr Montuclard starts by affirming that belief in
progress 'affords to those who have no religious affiliations a
kind of faith and hope, a certain conception of life and
reality, which may be inchoate and dim, may fall short of
any full understanding of the range and scale of what is involved, but which does nevertheless call for a measure of
self-sacrifice and an exacting standard of conduct'. In short,
faith in progress works like a rudimentary form of religion:
but what is its essential significance for those who are
Christians already? Fr Montuclard, who has the great distinction of being the first to analyse correctly this temporal
development of sacred history, arrives at the following
conclusion: 'The Church's main concern must be to recognize this species of history and to revitalize it from within,
though God has begun to write it outside the Church, and
without her visible or direct co-operation.'

There will be many to whom this solution of the problem
must appear strangely optimistic and inadequate. Optimistic
it is indeed. Belief in progress may in some cases represent,

albeit improperly, an act of faith in the Absolute: but when, as in the case under discussion, it amounts to a positive dogma of 'salvation of mankind through man', surely we must recognize the essential negation of all religion—the great distinctive heresy of modern times. Accordingly, another school of thought maintains that the religion of progress is actually the besetting sin of our generation, and the chief obstacle to conversion: technological man is intoxicated with the sense of his own power. Kraemer writes: 'It cannot be denied that the material progress achieved in modern civilization has entitled man to feel himself as it were the creator of his own world; but the first consequence of this instinctive reaction has been restrictive: the history and the life of mankind are regarded as exclusively immanent, wholly explicable in human terms.' Marxism is the precise formula of this intuition of a creative humanity, so understood as to exclude all transcendent activity or influence. In Kraemer's penetrating words, again, 'what makes the situation apparently hopeless is not so much the bankruptcy of man in his projects for a new society and a new world, but his stubborn refusal to acknowledge failure'. The sickness of the modern world does not consist in its recurrent political and economic crises, which are merely symptomatic, but in its obsessive idolatrous persuasion of self-sufficiency.

Gabriel Marcel has explored the metaphysics of this delusive pretension. He observes, first, that technology is itself morally indifferent and cannot be regarded as inherently wrong—'a condemnation of Technique would be meaningless verbiage'. He then proceeds to show that what is wrong is 'the transition from Technique itself to the sacrilegious attitude that makes an idol of it. Along this line of analysis it will appear that the primary deviation into idolatry determines a further step down into autolatry, self-worship'. Here Marcel confirms Kraemer: the danger of the cult of technological progress lies in its tendency to restrict and confine mankind within the adoring contemplation of his own creative power. Thus technology may lead to a substitution of the means for the end, losing sight of 'the irreducible, inviolate mystery of Being'. Technique, in itself a thing indifferent, neither good nor evil, becomes a 'technique of sin'.

It follows unquestionably that the religion of progress and the dogma of 'salvation of mankind through man', so far from being a rudimentary form of real faith, is on the contrary the real sin of our contemporary world. When people talk of 'efficiency', if they mean the production of results commensurate with the idea of progress so understood, then indeed Christianity is not 'efficient', does not work: but that is because this kind of 'efficiency' does not exist. It is only by a hoax on the grand scale that a vast number of our contemporaries have been brought to believe in the real possibility of an earthly paradise, and consequently to accept the suggestion that a religious system which falls short of any such promise is a failure—'does not work'. What is extraordinary is that appreciable numbers of professing Christians are ready to endorse this idea; for, indeed, the conception of 'efficiency' that underlies it is the most obvious nonsense, and Christianity is well advised to have no part in it: the special distinction of our religion is a rigid refusal to deceive mankind—it is better to forgo the prospect of proselytes than to feed men with lying promises. That is not to say that Christianity rejects the idea of a transfiguration of mankind, body and soul, and of the whole creation: on the contrary, Christianity is obstinately optimistic—but this is in respect of God's intervention, and on the eschatological plane; the Christian hope is not of this world, because the essential definition of the Christian life is in terms of transition from one stratum of being to another.

The scope of progress in this world must always be limited. Christians are undoubtedly obliged to work for the betterment of the conditions of human existence, and against the common disasters of sickness, war, and want.

But on the one hand, mankind itself opposes against these efforts the blank wall of finite human nature as it is, with all its innate predetermined and ambivalent tendencies: there is no panacea for moral disorders and for the misery they lead to. Death itself may be deferred by the aid of scientific discoveries, with no better result than the indefinite prolongation of human misery—as Simone de Beauvoir pointed out in *Tous les hommes sont mortels*. And in any case there is, on the other hand, an unwarranted pre-supposition in all theories of a new earthly paradise, namely that the machinery of economic and social progress will be employed in beneficial directions: whereas Christians know that sin will last as long as the world lasts, and that human history will always wear two faces. Indeed there is reason to fear that what is in prospect for us may be a more dreadful earthly inferno, seeing the equivalent potentiality of evil in all the elaborations of science.

What is wrong with the 'boundless hope' of humanity, the chief defect of it—in spite of its capacity to evoke the sort of generous, even heroic, response which understandably makes a profound impression on Fr Montuclard—is its radical unreality. The Marxists call Christianity a hoax, but they are themselves the hoaxers. The real 'opium of the people', distracting men's minds from their essential task, is the communist myth of an earthly paradise: because this orientation of working-class action towards a world revolution, with promise of a perfect classless society, necessarily involves the neglect of all the limited objectives, towards which—alone—human efforts may be effectively directed, the practical alleviation of remediable distress and the righting of corrigible wrongs. This is the 'idealism' rightly classed by Sartre as a worthless hypocrisy—throwing away, for the sake of and in the name of a meaningless ideological cause, all the limited, but real and realizable, fruits of practical work.

Even so, this is not the whole story. Certainly we must

first get rid of the illusion that Christianity is a means of obtaining earthly happiness. Christianity does not make a perfect world; no one can, for there is no such thing. The tragedy of the world's pain and sorrow is still there, a pain and sorrow that cannot be altogether done away, since it is all part of the present state of human existence; not indeed 'man's lot' essentially, as Sartre wrongly held, but his present lot. Yet this pain and sorrow can be alleviated in some degree. After all, Christ himself did give the multitudes bread to eat in the desert. So the question remains, whether our faith in God is relevant to this human task.

Once again, it is not the purpose of our religion to improve the standard of living; but there is an influence of religion on social ethics. I am not referring to the secular activities of Christian people, but to the effects of religious faith as such. As a matter of simple fact, the civilizing consequences of Christianity have not been achieved through any turning aside from spiritual concerns in order to attend to material things; on the contrary, they came about because Christianity was true to itself. Christianity has not abolished the relationship between master and man, or put an end to war; these matters lie outside its scope; but the incontestable fact remains, that wherever Christianity has been solidly established it has helped to make slavery impossible, to improve the worker's lot, and to create a comity of nations. The discontinuity of the religious and secular planes is not such as to preclude the possibility of interaction. It is right to insist on the difference between the natural and supernatural orders, but it is also true that nothing is outside the order of Providence.

The influence of the Christian religion upon civilization has not completely transformed the structure of social life, but that is because, as we have repeatedly urged, such a transformation is nothing but a myth. The effectiveness of human activity is limited by conditions which are outside human control. A proletarian revolution can secure the redistribution of the fruits of production; but it cannot alter the basic conditions of the means of production—for example, it cannot simply abolish sub-standard conditions of underground employment in the mining industries, where progress depends on scientific developments, which will be no more rapid in a collectivist than in a capitalist society. The deceitful, lying aspect of Marxist communism is the suggestion that the social revolution will transform conditions of labour. In fact, the lot of the working-class is everywhere more or less alike: the nearest equivalent to the Russian labourer's life is the life of an American labourer.

What can be done is to make the existence of man more human, within the possible and practical limits of real life. In this context, there are certain identifiable human values, not peculiarly Christian, which nevertheless flourish only in a Christian setting, and tend to wither away when Christian influences are withdrawn. With the removal of Christianity, men lose their religion, but also in a measure their humanity. We should be the last to exaggerate the value and importance of the civilizing aspects of Christianity, especially in comparison with its essential other-worldly significance. And we are satisfied that non-Christian civilizations have their own values, which are not to be depreciated. But when we consider the universal constant work of civilization, which is the defence of mankind against necessity, or fate, we remain convinced that civilization's most reliable ally is Christianity, though the essential purpose of Christianity is something entirely different.

Even so, this does not exhaust the function of the Church in the matter of history-making. The formula we quoted earlier, from the pen of Fr Montuclard, would suggest that history belongs to human society, while the Church, as a supra-temporal institution, acquires historical status only by reason of its socialization. But Christianity itself is historic; indeed, the historical approach to reality was originally a Christian discovery; and even today, it is only in virtue of

Christian presuppositions that history can attain to its proper standing, because Christianity alone represents a positive and irreversible increment. So it is true, as Fr Montuclard says, that Christianity must 'revitalize' the passing forms of civilizations as they come and go, making Christendoms of them: for 'Christendom' is not to be identified exclusively with medieval institutions, and Fr Montuclard's phrase about the 'retreat of the Church' since the Middle Ages reveals a complete misunderstanding of *bourgeois* Christianity in the ages of reason and enlightenment. That is one aspect of the Church in history; but it is also true that Christianity is itself the archetype of the historical process, and imposes its own pattern on the development of civilization. It is this latter point that Fr Montuclard failed to bring out.

Thus secular history is taken up and assimilated into sacred history.

The whole of this development is of course something essentially secondary. Emmanuel Mounier shows a want of proportion when he defines the progress of the Church exclusively in terms of 'sanctifying the new shapes of the world'; and again when he accuses those who oppose a 'liturgical cosmos' to 'the scientific and rational cosmos' of confusing 'the eternal essence of the religious act' with 'outmoded forms of representation'.[1] Even those of us who are least disposed to set much store by the preservation of obsolete forms, may hesitate to believe that the introduction and substitution of new and living patterns in Christian worship, however desirable or necessary, makes up the whole matter of sacred history in our time. Fr Montuclard makes the same disputable point when he writes: 'it is obvious that the progress of the Church cannot be left to the mystics'. If the expression 'progress of the Church' is defined in terms of an adaptation to successive patterns of social organization, then indeed this is not the saints' affair: but such a definition is excessively superficial; it is on the

[1] *Be Not Afraid* (trs. C. Rowland, 1951), p. 69.

plane of Marxist communism. In this conception, progress takes place essentially in the infrastructure of economics, and the Church can do no better than to follow suit. But that is not really history at all, as we have been trying to show. The real progress of the Church is the deliverance through baptism of souls in bondage, and the greater glory of God in the holy Eucharist: and the protagonists of this history are in truth the saints.

CHAPTER SEVEN

A BIBLICAL INTERPRETATION OF MODERN
HISTORY

MUCH has been written in our time by philosophers and theologians about the interpretation of history. Their work is always subject to the suspicion that they may be twisting the facts to fit into the particular system which they favour. Professional historians tend to take all these large generalizations with a grain of salt. There is the germ of a conflict between the 'academic historians', concerned only to establish truths of fact, and scrupulously avoiding any kind of interpretation, and the theologians, who interpret the facts, perhaps without paying enough attention to the question whether they are fully established. For the resolution of this antinomy, we need the witness of a professional historian who will address his mind to the possibility of a valid interpretation of history: exactly as Professor Butterfield has done in his short but remarkable book on *Christianity and History*.

Butterfield is quite clear that 'academic history' is not self-sufficient; plainly, as he appreciates, there must be an interpretation. It is the merest hypocrisy to pretend to be writing 'pure' history. The simplest arrangement of facts presupposes an act of judgement. This does not mean that all historical writing is irremediably subjective: one can pass beyond the stage of mechanical enumeration without necessarily forsaking science in favour of prejudice. There are certain criteria of truth in 'academic history' to ensure the correctness of the record, and there are equally valid criteria for its interpretation. It remains to be seen what they are:

but although they are obviously something other than the rules of historical criticism, they must be no less strict and of equally probative force.

The aim of Butterfield's book is to discover the principles of a right interpretation of history. He starts from an examination of the wrong interpretations. Considering the Protestant historical schools of fifty years ago, he observes with a certain friendly sharpness that 'the unanswerable Pope was some Professor—a system more inconvenient than that of Rome, . . . because the seat of authority might change overnight and be transferred to a new teacher who had never been heard of before'.

The result is to encumber men's minds with a mass of preconceived ideas, wrongly mistaken for observed facts. Instead of seeing 'things as they really are', we tend to see them 'in the categories which historians have created . . . attributing things to the Renaissance when the Renaissance is a mere label that historians have chosen to apply to a generation of people'.

It is bad enough that any dogmatic system should be interposed between the minds of men and the reality of their experience, but the worst of it is that the systems actually distort our perceptions. Butterfield shows the frightening influence that particular notions of history can have in shaping men's minds—a far more powerful and graver influence than that of the corresponding notions of physical science, because historical ideas have to do with human life and conduct. One danger of this sort is the tendency to regard the history of mankind as a prolongation of biological evolution, so that it is only the development of the human species that counts. 'This attitude is more understandable, more dangerous, and more likely to recur than many people realize.' Contrariwise, a first principle of interpretation will then be to preserve the distinction between history and the natural sciences, always considering humanity as a separate world.

L.H.—H

The Marxist vision of history is another preconception, concerning which Butterfield's ideas are interestingly complex. He starts by acknowledging that there is a great deal of truth in the Marxist view of the importance of social conditions as a factor of human life. But he detects an illusion, common to all systems which presuppose a direct relationship between technical and moral progress, namely, the erroneous belief that living conditions modify the nature of man. This error arises from the correct observation that certain social forms do in fact produce a certain standard of conduct, called civilization. But these conventions are essentially nothing but mutual arrangements in restraint of self-interest; they do not eliminate it. As soon as any crisis weakens or destroys the pattern of restraints, the natural barbarism emerges at once from behind the deceptive façade of civilized manners.

No technical advance or social progress has any effect on human nature. 'No man has yet invented a form of political machinery which the ingenuity of the devil would not find a way of exploiting for evil ends.' Nothing is more dangerous than a failure to understand this truth: worst of all is the kind of optimistic idealism which persuades people of one culture that they are the privileged possessors of absolute social and ethical values, and thereby entitled to judge their inferior contemporaries in the light of this monopoly: 'situations become more frantic and deadlocks more hopeless because of man's universal presumption and self-righteousness'.

Hence follows another essential principle of historical interpretation, not to have faith in human nature. It is impossible to understand history unless you start from the conviction of universal sinfulness.

On this observation, which is the key to his book, Butterfield establishes a connexion between the two points of view, that of the pure historian and that of the biblical theologian. He shows that any really objective historian, honestly scrutinizing the record, must come to the conclusion that all the mistakes as well as all the crimes in history derive their origin from the sin of self-righteousness; while the basic axiom of revelation, in the Bible, is that no man is righteous, but all men are sinners: this is the essence of the dogma of original sin. 'Though history does not carry these questions to the searching depths at which the theologian may make his judgements and expose the fallacy of our pretended righteousnesses, it seems to me that even at his own level, even in the realm of observable historical happenings, the historian must join hands with the theologian.'

The conclusion is plainly one of far-reaching importance. We are not dealing with an extraneous rule of interpretation, superimposed upon the results of historical reflection, deriving its validity from the private judgement of the individual critic. On the contrary, the historian himself, objectively inspecting his material, is compelled to this particular conclusion—admittedly a negative conclusion, ruling out the possibility of any constructive theory of interpretation: but coinciding in this with the biblical view of reality. The ground-work of the prophetic message was similarly a denunciation of all human attempts to arrange history in the interests of mankind. The scepticism of the historian and the prophet's pessimism have a common origin: for the biblical interpretation of history is not simply a theological construct, not just another arguable theory, but a demonstration of the inadmissibility of any human theory of history, an absolute denial that history has any meaning or direction at all, other than mystical, and as may be divinely revealed.

The speculations of Christian theorists are no more valid than those of atheists. In his most interesting chapters, Butterfield discusses some of the ecclesiastical interpretations of history. Self-satisfaction is just as hypocritical among Christians as among communists. It is false to claim that the Church is responsible for social progress and enlightenment.

As a matter of fact, the working-class movement, led by communism, has achieved much more than the Church in the way of social justice (though that does not mean that communism is progressive). But then it is not the function of religion to save civilization, but to convince man of sin, and to teach him that it is only when he acknowledges his sinfulness that he can hope to be saved.

How does history look in the light of the dogma of original sin? When Butterfield has disposed of bogus ideologies, whether of Christian or non-Christian inspiration, he addresses himself to the constructive aspect of the case. It has never been easy for an observer of historical trends 'to see that morality itself was part of the structure of history, a thing as real and as drastic in its operation as the material strength of principalities and powers'. At first sight *realpolitik* seems to be universally triumphant, whether in the case of Napoleon, or of Bismarck (or, some would add, of Gladstone). But the very absurdity of this conclusion from outward appearances should indicate that we are looking for interpretations at the wrong level. We must recall to mind the mystical intuition of Isaiah: national triumphs in the realm of temporal affairs are no proof of the divine favour, as is falsely supposed in the dream of political messianism. These things only mean that God is using the nation as an instrument of his judgements; the instrument itself is expendable.

If anything is certain about the Christian view of economic and political values, it is that these are entirely relative. To treat them as absolute is a form of idolatry. The fundamental mistake in communism is the belief that communism is good and capitalism is evil; and the capitalist's mistake lies in holding the contrary belief. Collectivism and capitalism are both half-truths. If people understood this, they would not turn policies into ideologies; for there is no such thing as a mystique of politics: mysticism belongs to the revelation of God in Jesus Christ. It is the intrusion of mystical attitudes into political questions that leads to fanaticism, and to ideological wars, which are conflicts between false gods. The Christian's duty is to denounce these group-idols. There is no possibility of peace in the world until everyone recognizes that his own way is only a half-truth, so that instead of trying to exterminate other people, he must love them for their share in the truth.

If external prosperity affords no assurance of God's blessing, it must be extremely dangerous to derive moral satisfaction from the circumstance of temporal success. Self-abasement would be a more appropriate attitude. But the lesson must be taken further. The inward reality of history is not to be understood as consisting in an onward march of civilization, where particular nations or classes, successively co-operating in the general progress, assume in turn the role of providential agents. In actual fact 'every generation is equidistant from eternity'. The real purpose of history is to achieve—through the mill of temporal vicissitudes—'the manufacture and education of human souls'. The real measure of history is not to be sought in the level of technical attainment, but in the more or less effective production of personalities, 'which represent the highest things we know in the mundane realm'.

From this point of view it becomes clear that historical disasters may be as richly productive as historical triumphs, and often more so. Once again, Butterfield recalls the history of Israel. He shows that it was 'amid disasters and predicaments more permanently hopeless than those of' any peoples of the present-day world, that 'the ancient Hebrews, by virtue of inner resources . . . turned their tragedy . . . into one of the half-dozen creative moments in world history'. In the days of their prosperity they were content with a grossly material conception of life; but in the period of their tribulation they found their way to a deeper stratum of human experience than man had ever sounded before, in the idea of the redemptive power of love, as it is unfolded in the Deutero-Isaiah. 'Only in a world where suffering is possible . . . can human beings measure the heights and depths of love and reach the finer music of life.'

In sum, the quality of an age is not determined by its material characteristics or by its ideological colour, but by its fruits of human and spiritual experience. What counts, in the end, is the response of personalities to circumstances; the circumstances themselves have neither value nor demerit of their own. Adversity is not itself a creative force, but it may call forth a response from the depth of men's souls, whereas prosperity is apt to leave men content with the surface of life as they find it.

This, then, represents the accumulated experience of a first-rate historian, which he has chosen to record for us after many years spent in the exploration of past time, and after discovering for himself the unreality of all the myths that obfuscate the various modern interpretations of history. The lesson of his experience is that a plain Christian man may understand more of the inwardness of history than highly-educated scholars whose vision is impeded by pretentious intellectual systems: 'Even in the study of history a kind of acquired simplicity is needed just to see things as they really are.' So seen, with the undisturbed clarity of the simple mind, the protagonists of visible history lose the prestige of their apparent importance, and take their rightful place in real history, which is the record of God's formation, in this world, of eternal souls destined for his kingdom. God makes use of those historic figures in the execution of his design, but they have no intrinsic value of their own: real history is not concerned with them. God made the world for his saints; it is through these, and on their account, that history, too, makes sense.

One of the key-words in Butterfield's book, highly expressive of its particular human and spiritual atmosphere, is 'judgement'. For one thing, the word sums up the mature, reflective wisdom of the experienced historian, who knows what he is talking about, and presents us with a true picture of the facts. That makes his book worth reading as an intellectual production. But the word also indicates a divine perspective; for Judgement is the revelation of things as they are in God's sight—that is, as they really are. In this light the pomps and vanities fade away, for all the brave show they make in human chronicles, and in their stead appear the things of real worth, the hidden glories of charity. This judgement is veiled from the eyes of the world, but it is discernible by faith. It is proclaimed in the *Magnificat*: 'He has put down the mighty from their seat, and exalted the lowly'.[1] Mary rejoices to see this, because it means putting things in their right place.

This is the Judgement that really illuminates human history; and the great merit of Butterfield's book is to have shown that history is meaningless without it. For those of us who are convinced that the most dangerous tendency of the modern world is the way in which bogus theories are given the force of dogma—as that technical progress is good in itself, or that a particular class or nation has a messianic function—for us, the book is like a gust of fresh air to clear away all these poisonous fogs. Seen through all the false, pretentious trappings of theory that it habitually claims to wear, here is the nakedness of history, and it is in the likeness of everlasting sin. Only so long as history acknowledges the truth of this likeness can it find its place in real history, the history of salvation.

Butterfield's interpretation is endorsed in a truly extraordinary fashion by the author of another book of the same period—not an historian, this time, but a philosopher, starting from an entirely different position.[2] Mr Löwith's question is to ascertain whether *historia*, defined as research into the facts of human behaviour in the past, is reconcilable with the theology of sacred history: can we find in sacred

[1]Luke 1: 52.   [2]Löwith: *Meaning in History*, Chicago, 1949.

history a valid interpretation of empirical history? It is a question that has exercised the minds of Christian thinkers for some two thousand years, and may be said to have remained unanswered: though it is true that some have tried to impose a 'providential' form on the succession of civilizations, in the shape of a tendency towards the evolution of a Christian civilization. Löwith pays particular attention to Bossuet, in this connexion; but it should not be forgotten that Eusebius of Caesarea had already developed the same theory when he characterized the *imperium romanum* as a providential preparation for the Constantinian monarchy. It may also be remarked that Toynbee, at the other end of the Christian era, arrives at a similar conclusion, by identifying Christianity as the latest form of civilization.

What is ordinarily called the philosophy of history derives its origin from this Christian conception of design in profane history. It begins with Voltaire's substitution of the idea of enlightenment for that of Providence; his interpretation amounts to a theory of indefinite progress in civilization. The supreme exponent of this optimistic philosophy was Condorcet, rightly appreciated by Löwith as a figure of primary importance. Hegel added a tough metaphysical framework to support the theory: history is rational throughout; mind directs it irrevocably towards fulfilment. Nothing but the restricted scope of our understanding prevents us from recognizing this logic in events. After Hegel, it only remained for Marx to provide a dialectic of economics, in order to present the theory as a rigorously scientific system.

But in fact this philosophy of history falls a long way short of the scientific precision claimed for it by such writers as Comte and Marx: for it has never succeeded in overcoming the basic difficulty that vitiated the 'providential' theory (from which it derives, through a process of secularization). It is still a hybrid between the positive analysis of facts, and a value-judgement, an act of faith. The act of faith has some foundation for those believers who can base it upon the word of God; but for the positivist, it is in the air. Thus the doctrine of progress, in the secular philosophy of history, is a pure myth. The only valid conception of history that can be derived from a factual study of events is Burckhardt's vision of man at odds with various sociological data, displaying his greatness by overcoming his environment. But this greatness is no less sublime in the age of Pericles than in the Napoleonic period. Empirical history affords no evidence of progress in the scale of human values.

If we turn to the 'providential' theory, this proves equally invalid. It has a solid basis, indeed, in the Word of God: but this word has to do with the things of faith. Attempts, like those of Eusebius and Bossuet, to interpret the history of the empires in the light of revelation, are thus necessarily misleading. Here Löwith's criticism coincides with Butterfield's. The growth of empires, economic change, social progress—these things seem to be unrelated to the coming of the kingdom of God and the course of sacred history. The former have no effect upon the latter; and conversely, the effect of Christianity on civilization does not amount to any structural modification, but only (as Orosius saw in the fifth century) to such measures of reform as the ethical requirements of Christianity may necessitate.

Thus profane history and sacred history appear to be perfectly independent of each other; at all events we cannot establish any relationship between them. Our knowledge of them derives from two incommensurable sources, since profane history is known by research, *historia* in its ancient meaning, while sacred history is only known by faith. There is no common ground for a philosophy of history, whether religious or secular: 'More intelligent than the superior vision of philosophers and theologians is the common sense of the natural man and the uncommon sense of the Christian believer. Neither pretends to discern on the canvas of human history the purpose of God or of the historical process itself. They rather seek to set men free from the world's oppressive history by suggesting an attitude, either of skepticism or of faith.'

The conclusions of the philosopher Löwith are startlingly like those of the historian Butterfield. Both are in reaction against optimistic theories of progress, which Butterfield unanswerably convicts of pharisaism. Both are also in a most salutary reaction against the secularization of the biblical conception of history, as they plainly declare that the ultimate meaning of history is a matter of theological faith and not of empirical research. It is, no doubt, also true that they both go rather too far in the direction of pessimism when they make an impassable gulf between sacred and profane history. We should prefer to say that although the latter is meaningless in itself, it makes sense as part of the former. The history of peoples and minds all belongs to the universal picture in the mind of God. But it remains true to say that the relationship of human events to sacred history lies wholly in the field of mystery, and defies every attempt at formulation.

CHAPTER EIGHT

THE HISTORY OF RELIGIONS:
AND THE HISTORY OF SALVATION

ANY investigation of the great non-Christian religious systems—Hindu, Mohammedan, Confucian—forces the student to consider how these stand in regard to Christianity. In looking at this particular question, I am not now concerned directly with the content of the other religions themselves, or to expound the nature of the Christian religion, but to see what is the relation of the former to the latter. It is a problem of some contemporary importance. Books and periodicals everywhere abound for the dissemination of Indian, Islamic and Jewish literature; adherents of these great systems rub shoulders with us daily. Whether in books or in personal contacts, we are constantly impressed by the deeply religious quality of what we find. This can be, and often is, disturbing.

Tritheistic speculations, or the symbol of the cross, found in Indian traditions, invite us to think about the fundamental relationship between these things and the Christian dogma, or sign. We can hardly acknowledge the good we get out of reading a Buddhist or Mohammedan mystic without wondering about the distinctive character of Christian mysticism, recalling perhaps Simone Weil's provocative formula: 'In practice, mystics belonging to nearly all the religious traditions coincide to the extent that they can hardly be distinguished.'[1] But granting all this, what becomes of the unique transcendence of Christianity? And if

[1] *Letter to a Priest*, Routledge & Kegan Paul, 1953, p. 47.

we are still sure of it, can we justify our conviction? First of all, what is it?

Here we have to avoid two errors. One is to regard all non-Christian religions as gross superstitions or aimless speculations. We must, on the contrary, fairly allow the genuine spiritual worth that is in them. Pius XII, in the encyclical *Divini praecones*, said that 'the Church has never despised pagan teaching, but rather freed it from its errors'. In Péguy's characteristic phrase, there is no need to run down Sévère in order to set up Polyeucte: we can appreciate Christianity without belittling other creeds—in fact, it will only stand the higher for a due recognition of the stature of all that it surpasses.

But the opposite error is more harmful still. On every hand, among our contemporaries, we hear arguments tending to minimize the transcendent quality of Christianity, or denying it altogether—obliterating the frontiers that mark its distinction from all other religions. Sometimes it is made out to be merely one element (and not even the most indispensable element) in a single stream of 'religious tradition'. Again, it is seen as a stage in the religious evolution of mankind, and as such doomed, maybe, to make room for others in the future. In another order of ideas, the suggestion is made that dogma is of secondary importance, and that it is possible in any religion to achieve the essential 'spiritual experience'. Or, pragmatically, we are advised to sink our domestic differences, and combine our 'spiritual energies' in the common struggle against the rise of materialism.

These are obviously unacceptable ideas. But they are all around us; they make a certain impression; we hardly know how to refute them. The problem, simply expressed, is this: given the real worth of the pagan religions, what exactly is the superiority of the Christian religion?

*   *   *

The first characteristic of Christianity is belief in an event, the resurrection of Christ, which represents an incursion of God's action into the historical process, a radical change in the conditions of human life, an absolutely new thing. Here is a fundamental difference from all other religions. This was what René Guénon missed, when he saw no more in Christianity than a particular form of the original religious tradition—he left out just what is original in Christianity itself. The great non-Christian religions know of an eternal world over against the world of time; but they know nothing of an irruption of one into the other, giving substance and form to the flux of time, making it into history.

Greek thought furnishes examples, in the Platonic theory of ideas, and in the Stoic theory of eternal recurrence. But I am more concerned now with living religious systems. Mircéa Eliade has noted the 'revolt' of primitive religions 'against concrete, historical time, their nostalgia for a periodical return to the mythical time of the beginning of things'.[1] The aim of primitive ritual is to get away from the small change of common life into the single eternity of first things: it is the 'abolition of time through the imitation of archetypes and the repetition of paradigmatic gestures. A sacrifice, for example, not only exactly reproduces the initial sacrifice revealed by a god *ab origine*, at the beginning of time, it also takes place at that same primordial mythical moment.'

It follows from this view of things that no particular occurrence has any permanent reality, and that the historical process pays no dividends. Real value is only to be found in re-presentations; to quote Mircéa Eliade again: 'reality is acquired solely through repetition or participation: everything which lacks an exemplary model is "meaningless".' And this reality is achieved in and by the abrogation of normal, everyday time. 'No event is irreversible,

[1] *The Myth of the Eternal Return* (trs. Trask, 1955), p. ix.

and no transformation is final. In a certain sense, it is even possible to say that nothing new happens in the world.' The contrast is evident with the opposite, Christian idea of the particular occurrence of the Incarnation—an irreversible fact, of supreme value, wholly a new thing.

In Indian religious thought, time is even further cheapened, though in another manner. The notion of time is highly developed, in the theory of *yuga*, or cosmic cycles, manifested in regular procession. But the appearance of progress is deceptive: the succession of *yuga* amounts in the end to destruction and renewal. If time is cyclical it is not irreversible—we are back in the eternal recurrence, the myths of periodical destruction and creation. As Eliade has said elsewhere: 'seen against the higher Time, all being is precarious, insubstantial, illusory. History proves impermanent, not fully real. Ontologically, temporal existence is a kind of non-existence.'

So that here the aim will be not to revivify temporal existence, as in primitive rites, by returning to the beginning of time, but simply to escape from time itself. The whole technique of *yoga* is designed for this escape out of time, not only through a conviction that time is unreal, but positively through the practice of a timeless trance. Once more, there is a diametrical opposition between this and the content of Biblical revelation: for the prophets, time is neither unreal nor evil; it is the framework of God's plan, within which the body of Christ is built up. And, as will appear, this fundamental contrast involves a contradiction between the two corresponding ideas of contemplative ecstasy.

Islam is no different from the rest, which is the more extraordinary because of its Biblical tradition. Yet the fact is certain (and provides evidence of the regressive character of this religious system). Joachim Mubarak has shown, in an important article, that the basic idea of Islam consists in a primitive, or original, type of monotheism, constantly subject to corruptions, restored successively to its pristine purity by the three prophets, Abraham, Jesus, Mohammed. Here again the temporal process is mere debasement, there can be no valid aim but reversion to a perfect beginning. Hence what M. Massignon calls 'instantaneism': 'Mohammedan thought has no place for continuous duration, recognising only discrete moments of time (ânât)'.

There is a measure of truth in these notions of time. They represent for mankind, more or less faithfully through all the aberrations of paganism, one plane of reality, the plane of natural religion. The Epistle to the Romans acknowledges this measure of truth: 'men have caught sight of his invisible nature, his eternal power and his divineness, as they are known through his creatures.'[1] God is revealed in the alternation of seed-time and harvest, his witness shown to all nations, spoken of in the Acts of the Apostles.[2] In the natural order, we do believe in the inherent stability of things—we cannot conceive an evolutionary transmutation of structures. Guénon is thus far right. But then Christianity establishes a different order.

Here we do indeed find something that is new, for God here breaks in upon history. Christianity is first and foremost an historical event, the Incarnation of Jesus Christ. Thus the substance of the Christian revelation is not in a knowledge of God's existence (which other religions have as well), but in the perception of his activity on the scene of time, his effective interventions in the world of human history. From the Creation to the Resurrection, by way of the choosing of our father Abraham, the Christian revelation is a sacred history, the chronicle of the wonderful works of God, a documentary narrative: alone among sacred books, the Christian's Bible is not a collection of doctrine but a story.

* * *

So much for our first point, that Christianity means belief in God's coming into the world as the man Christ Jesus.

[1] Rom. 1: 20.   [2] Acts 14: 17.

Now we proceed to a second statement, namely that this divine act alone can save mankind; there is no salvation but in Jesus. This truth is contrary to another of the syncretistic notions we have been considering, the idea that all forms of mystical experience amount to the same thing: a broad view, which has its attractions for those who are repelled by the intransigent claims of Christianity. But if religious mystics are all alike, this means that salvation is brought about by the practice of detachment from creatures, and by the efforts of man to achieve union with God, rather than through the work of Christ's cross. Once again, we must recognize a fundamental contradiction.

To avoid possibilities of misunderstanding, let it be said plainly that we do not undervalue the instances of a truly interior life and spiritual detachment that are to be found among non-Christian religions. From China, we have received a wonderful rule of wisdom, in the teachings of Confucius, to govern the dealings of men with one another. India furnishes the example of a society attuned to the highest ideals of the ascetic and contemplative life: the masterpieces of Indian religious literature, from the Bhagavadgita to Aravinda, powerfully inculcate an impression of the vanity of earthly goods, and the supereminent values of the unseen world. In the West, at a time when the exploitation of natural resources absorbs men's whole attention, under the Marxist illusion that human nature can be changed by a variation in the material conditions of life, it is no wonder if the message of the Indian sages appeals to people whose souls are athirst for silence and recollection.

But these aspirations presuppose that it is possible for man to attain to God through his own efforts, which Christianity absolutely denies for two reasons. The first is the solid fact of original sin, cutting man off from God. Man cannot cancel this separation: he is imprisoned, he cannot get out by himself. It is of no use simply to say that men having taken the wrong road by pursuing outward appearances, need only turn away from corporal things in order to regain that life of pure spirituality which is their true life. In any case Christianity does not regard the body, or the world of matter, as the root of all evil. But the whole man, body and soul, is cut off from God, and God alone can set man free by grace from captivity.

And, secondly, our God is, absolutely, unattainable, so that he alone can confer upon man that participation in himself which we call supernatural life. If the soul is supposed to be essentially divine (as in fact it is, in the Hindu and in the neo-platonic theodicy), the mere elimination of extraneous obstacles is enough—the soul finds God in awareness of self: but this does not follow if there is a radical distinction between the uncreated God and the spiritual creature. Indian mysticism is based on a kind of pantheism. The Christian profession of faith, on the other hand, begins with God the creator, that is, with the radical distinction between him and man. God alone can raise man up into that sharing in his own life which constitutes our supernatural existence and culminates in mystical union. It is unattainable by human effort.

From this position, several consequences flow, each of which emphasizes the singularity of the Christian religion— and first of all this: that salvation comes through faith in Christ Jesus our Saviour, not through works (as St Augustine triumphantly maintained against Pelagius). What a man must do to be saved is to acknowledge himself a sinner and open his heart to receive the grace of God. Thus humility is essential for salvation, and pride, particularly the pride of worldly wisdom, the chief impediment. Whereas from the syncretist point of view, all those who lead the interior life are saved, regardless of their religious affiliation, the Christian vision is exactly the opposite—those who believe shall be saved, regardless of their progress in inwardness: an infant, or an overdriven labourer, given faith, can take precedence before heroes of asceticism. 'We are not great religious figures,' as Guardini excellently said, 'we are servants of the word.' Christ himself told us that there had been no greater man than St John the Baptist, 'but he that is least in the kingdom of heaven is greater than he'. There may be great religious figures outside Christianity— it may well be that the greatest religious figures are to be found outside Christianity—but this is of no consequence: what matters is obedience to the word of Jesus Christ.

It is in the light of these considerations that we may see the difference between non-Christian mystics and Christian mysticism. For the former, union with God is the term of an ascetic process whereby the soul strips itself of all extraneous attachments, to find at last its own true being, which is God himself. The emphasis is on technique— recollection, singleness, etc. Christian mystics may make use of these methods; but then they are matters of secondary importance, and they cannot be effective in themselves: for our God is a living God, the all-highest, not to be encompassed by any technical proficiency. He grants his favours and himself to whom he will, freely and as he chooses. Mystical experience is not subject to the rules of method. Divine grace smote down Saul the persecutor on the road to Damascus, and flooded the soul of Marie de l'Incarnation as she worked among the wine-casks on a jetty by the Loire. The spring of grace is simply divine love, sovereignly free. To be ready to win it and receive it is not so much a matter of psychological training, as rather a religious disposition of the soul. Abdication of the will, conformity to God's good pleasure—this is the language of all Christian mystics. Thus, too, it will be found that all mystical favours are independent of any typical patterns of the contemplative life, of outward silence and sensible recollection; they are compatible with the most exacting of apostolic labours. St Francis Xavier, storm-tossed in the ship that took him to Japan, was carried away by a torrent of heavenly consolations.

The same contrast can be described in another way, by saying that the difference between the Christian and the non-Christian religions is the difference between saints and heroes. The ascetic achievements of the Indian sages are admirable, indeed: they may be said to mark the limit of human possibility. But the saints are not like that. Humanly speaking they are often cowardly and weak, yet they undertake hard things, superhuman tasks, relying on the power of God. So it was with the early martyrs: so it was for Jean Brébeuf, who admitted he had not the courage to prick his own finger with a pin, and went to preach the Gospel to the Iroquois in the knowledge of hideous tortures awaiting him. This explains how a saint can remain personally humble in the performance of heroic deeds; and how martyrdom and sanctity constitute a proof of the divine origin of Christianity. If the evidential value of martyrdom consisted simply in proving that Christianity can inspire the highest kind of self-sacrifice, it would be reasonable to object that men have been willing to die for other causes, too. The real point is that martyrdom as such exhibits the power of God even in the absence of any exceptional human generosity. Heroism shows what man can do: holiness shows what can be done by God. Holiness is independent of all particular human characteristics. Holiness depends on faith alone.

Origen and St Augustine saw this clearly enough. They accepted martyrdom and sanctity as proving the pre-eminence of the Christian religion, because these facts demonstrated the working of a divine δύναμις in the world. It is St. Paul's formula for the Gospel: 'God's power (δύναμις), that brings salvation to all who believe in it, Jew first and then Greek'.[1] 'Our preaching to you did not depend upon mere argument; power was there (ἐν δυνάμει), and the influence of the Holy Spirit.'[2] Thus we come back to the essential point of our argument: Christianity does not

[1]Rom. 1: 16.   [2]I Thess. 1:5.

consist in the strivings of man after God, but in the power of God, accomplishing in man that which is beyond the power of man; human efforts are merely the response called forth by the divine initiative. This, then, is the second mark of the unique transcendence of Christianity.

*   *   *

So far we have been mainly concerned to point out how the Christian religion is characterized as an immediate act of God. Its transcendent quality is equally visible in the content of dogma, despite that third group of syncretist theories, claiming to trace in other religions the outlines of the chief tenets of Christianity (the Trinity, the Redemption, and so on). There is in fact a certain number of these parallels. They have been shown, over and over again, to be quite superficial; no instructed person can really take them seriously: but they have enjoyed a wide publicity, and still serve to introduce into people's minds a kind of ambiguity, debilitating the force of conviction. To this extent they deserve consideration. As it happens, Simone Weil made a collection of these talking points in her *Letter to a Priest*. It is extraordinary that anyone with such powers of penetration as she showed in other contexts should be so uncritical; but her example could easily be enough to resurrect this theme. Her text may therefore serve as our starting-point.

She relates Christ's words 'I am the true vine' to the Dionysiac cult of the fruit of the vine. These are, as is well known, two different ideas: one, Palestinian, of the vine symbolizing the chosen people (Isa. 5: 1); the other, Greek, of the vine symbolizing immortality, through the notion of drunkenness. She finds parallels for the motherhood of the Blessed Virgin in the various mother-goddesses of antiquity; but it is matter of proof that the Christian worship of our Lady derives from the fact of her share in the historical process of human salvation, and not from any sublimation of womanhood, comparable with the development of nature-cults. Again, Christ's death upon the cross is related to the crucifixion of the world-soul in the *Timaeus*, whereas, obviously, the Christian cross derives from the instrument of our Saviour's passion, which was T-shaped—and not from the multidimensional symbolism of other religious systems.

Simone Weil quotes the Greek and Hindu triads in parallel with the Christian doctrine of the Holy Trinity—but this teaching has plainly nothing in common with any dialectical process, it is rather in direct conflict with human reason; our God is not revealed as primal unity in separate manifestations, but as three Persons subsisting eternally in one Nature. 'St John,' she says, 'in making use of the words Logos and Pneuma, indicated the profound relationship between Greek stoicism . . . and Christianity.' But there is conclusive proof that the Johannine λόγος is the Hebrew *dabar*—the word as creative of what is spoken: it has no point of connexion with the Stoics' λόγος, 'reason'. And πνεῦμα in the New Testament is the Biblical *rouah*, the image of God in a strong gale of wind—not the common Greek πνεῦμα, 'a breath', the figure of incorporeity.

The formulae of Christian liturgy are often borrowed from the rites of natural religions. Thus in the third century, Hippolytus of Rome develops the cosmic symbolism of the cross.[1] From the fourth century onwards, the terminology of the pagan mysteries is used in connexion with the sacraments. In the catacombs the vine symbolizes immortality. Within the last few years, Abbot Monchanin has proposed the use of the term *saccidananda*, which denotes the Hindu triad, for the mystery of the Holy Trinity.[2] All these developments are secondary, matters of cultural acclimatization. Christian dogma starts by being a new thing.

[1]See the *Paschal Homily*, derived from Hippolytus, printed in P.G. 59: 735–46, esp. 743 (ed. Nautin, 1950, pp. 176 et sqq.).
[2]*An Indian Benedictine Ashram.*

This is not to deny that natural religion possesses a measure of God's truth—we have already seen that it does, and that 'from the foundations of the world', as St Paul tells us, 'the invisible nature' of God is 'known through his creatures'. Before Abraham was, 'God left us some proof of what he is', men could learn in some degree what to expect of him, and something of his infinite perfection. But that was all. The non-Christian religions, then, could arrive at such knowledge as it is in the power of unaided human reason to attain—the knowledge of God *ab extra*, of his existence, and of his perfections in so far as these are made manifest through his activity in the world.

But beyond the reach of all human reason there is something else, an inaccessible threshold, an impenetrable cloud, the secret of God's private life: the inscrutable mysteries of the Holy Trinity, which no man can fathom, which could be revealed only by the Son of God. In the words of St John: 'No man has ever seen God; but now his only-begotten Son, who abides in the bosom of the Father, has himself become our interpreter.'[1] This is the heart and core of the irreducible originality of Christianity, that the Son of God came among us to reveal these two intimately related truths: that there is within God himself a mysterious living love, called the Trinity of Persons; and that in and through the Son we men are called to share this life of love. The mystery of the Holy Trinity, known to us through the Word made flesh, and the mystery of the deification of man in him—that is the whole of our religion, summed up in one person, the person of Jesus Christ, God made man, in whom is everything we need to know. Here we put our finger on the essential distinction, the specific element of Christianity, the ultimate reason of its unique transcendence: it is Jesus Christ, son of God, our saviour. The religions of nature bear witness (and this is the measure of their real worth) to the natural tendency of man towards God: Christianity is God's

[1] John 1: 18.

approach towards man in Jesus Christ, taking possession of man to bring him to himself.

The reality of the Biblical revelation being radically different from the content of the other religions, the former cannot be regarded simply as one form, even as the supreme form, of the natural religious instinct. Nevertheless, as we have before insisted, the nature-religions are not destitute of positive values. They represent an authentic manifestation of true religion, the representation of God through the regular procession of cosmic events, corresponding to the covenant with Noah. But when a new and better covenant was made, the former covenant was superseded. And not only so, but the religion of nature is invariably found, in the several non-Christian religious systems in which it exists as a matter of historical fact, to be more or less corrupt. This was St Augustine's point when he deplored the example of Socrates, the very model of the pre-Christian sage, who came so near the Truth, and yet asked that a cock should be sacrificed to Aesculapius before he died.

Are we at all concerned in these survivals of a former dispensation? They enshrine something of absolute worth, the relics of a primitive revelation: would it be no loss if they were to disappear altogether? Simone Weil felt this anxiety: 'were these other traditions to disappear from the face of the earth, it would be an irreparable loss. The missionaries have already made far too many of them disappear as it is.' Notwithstanding the finality of the revelation of Jesus Christ, our understanding of this revelation is progressive, and can be furthered by these other categories of insight. In his encyclical, *Divini praecones*, Pius XII gave an exact definition of the Catholic position in this matter (in a sentence which we have already quoted in part), and of the respect that is due to the genuine worth of the natural religions: 'The Church has never despised pagan teaching, but rather freed it from its errors, perfecting and crowning it in the light of Christian wisdom.'

It is to be observed that the Bible itself affords instances of this method. The chosen people lived in a world of other religions, rich in myths and cults of their own; rejecting these inadequate and faulty Gentile creeds, the Hebrews nevertheless constantly borrowed from them. The authors of the first chapters of Genesis controverted the very Babylonian or Canaanitish nature-myths, from which they derived their own patterns of representation. The Mosaic liturgical practices reflect the rites of Egypt under the Pharaohs. The apocalyptic writers took over much of their eschatology and angelic lore from Persia, but assimilated it into their own notion of history.

The Sapiential books are especially characteristic from this point of view. Throughout the Near East, in both Semitic and Greek-speaking lands, there was an immemorial tradition of sages, giving utterance to the wisdom of popular experience. There is mention of one Daniel, in a passage of Ezekiel: the excavations at Ras Shamra reveal this personage as a Canaanitish sage, the typical 'wise man' of a people that inhabited Palestine before the Jews. Arikah, who appears in the book of Tobit, has been identified as a sage of Babylon. Job was an Edomite, but the Scripture puts into his mouth some of its sublimest teaching. The Egyptian Amem-em-ope offers many parallels to the Book of Proverbs. Greece had her Seven Sages.

The Biblical revelation brought with it a new and better wisdom: as the Third Book of Kings has it, 'Wisdom, too, God gave to Solomon . . . For that, no king of the east or of Egypt could vie with him, of all men the wisest; wiser than Ethan the Ezrahite, or Heman, or Chalcol, or Dorda, that were sons of Mahol'.[1] Christ was to teach a yet more perfect wisdom, which to the wisdom of men would seem folly: 'a greater than Solomon is here'.[2] But the utterances of the rabbi of Nazareth, no less than the Sapiential books, will be found to preserve the best of the wisdom of

[1] 3 Kings 4: 29–31.   [2] Matt. 12: 42.

the Gentiles, re-animated with a new inspiration. So the Church in her turn 'does not despise pagan teaching, but sets it free, fulfils and crowns it'.

This formula contains an excellent summary of the Christian position. The spiritual values contained in the pagan religions are not under-estimated; but they need, in the first place, to be purged of error and corruptions, especially idolatry. Conversion therefore always involves an abjuration—there is no gradual evolution from paganism into Christianity. And secondly, Christianity perfects and fulfils, in the light of Christian wisdom, the incomplete truths that are to be found in paganism. It takes over the religious capital of the natural man, and sanctifies it. In the first ages of Christianity, the riches of Greek philosophy were thus purged and assimilated. It may be that in future years Christianity will similarly cleanse and incorporate the treasures of Hindu asceticism and the wisdom of Confucius. The mission of Christianity, rightly understood, involves no destruction of pagan religious values, but liberation and transfiguration. Christ came not to destroy, but to fulfil.

CHAPTER NINE

STRENGTH AND WEAKNESS
OF RENÉ GUÉNON

THE work of René Guénon, who died in 1949, was surely among the most original productions of our time. It stands so completely outside the boundaries of modern thought, and is so sharply at variance with the most inveterate habits of the modern mind, as to seem like a foreign body in the intellectual world of the present day. But then the strength of Guénon's position was this absolute independence of all contemporary prejudice, and the austere discipline of mental solitude in which he worked. By common consent, his subject-matter included the most critical problems of the age: technological civilization and its inherent dangers, and the whole question of the economic and political organization of society. His treatment of these topics was penetrating, disturbing: he cannot be ignored. There was truth in much that he had to say, but there were short-comings which made his position untenable for a Christian.

A first service to truth was his rehabilitation of symbolic understanding in opposition to scientific epistemology. This was perhaps his most violent departure from modern habits of thought. For men trained in the methods of the exact sciences, as chemistry or astronomy, any idea of a return to alchemy and astrology is a monstrous absurdity. Guénon held, on the contrary, that the whole direction of modern thought was hugely astray: he found more of the substance of truth in the childish fancies of the astrologers than in all the technical achievements of scientific astronomy. The two

122

things are not on the same plane. Science enlarges the dimensions of the cage in which the mind of man is imprisoned, but all the science in the world will not get him out of it. But in the intuitive perception of symbolism, the mind reaches out from material reality to grasp another reality beyond: this is an enlargement of the spirit.

To avoid misunderstanding, it should be said that Guénon was not concerned to re-establish the popular pseudo-scientific conceptions of astrology and alchemy. His point was that mankind's interest in stars, or metals, as symbols lies deeper than any consideration of their mechanical utility or of their physical structure. In a lovely passage of his *Roi du Monde*, he tells of the emerald that fell from Lucifer's brow, the stone from which the Holy Grail was cut. An emerald has a certain commercial value, which is what interests the jeweller, or the rich man who keeps the gem in his safe. Again, it has certain physical properties and characteristics which concern the student of inorganic chemistry. But what really matters about an emerald is its colour and its hardness; and these are what the alchemist cares for.

It is the same in other departments of knowledge. Thus astronomy teaches us the mechanics of the heavenly bodies; but this is a superficial knowledge. The stars are full of meaning, which is much more important. Guénon knew well enough that there could be no question of regarding the stellar motions as determinants of sublunary events; their significance would be rather as symbols of a higher order of reality. Here we are reminded of Mircéa Eliade, who has shown that the devotees of astral cults do not in fact worship the stars themselves, but a spiritual reality which is made known through the hierophany of the visible heavens. This is obviously poles apart from the conceptions of popular astrology, according to which the stars exert an influence on human life.

The same critical principles are applicable to geometry

and the science of numbers. Geometrical figures are of
interest, apart from their mathematical properties, for qualitative reasons; they are the basis of all pictorial symbolism.
Guénon was particularly concerned, in this connexion, with
the form of the cross, as we shall shortly see. Arithmetic is
in the same position as geometry, for there is a symbolism,
as well as a science, of numbers. Guénon pointed out that
the special importance of the numbers seven and forty in
the Bible is not fortuitous; they are part of a significant
language; and this not merely by an arbitrary convention,
but because of the intrinsic qualities of the numbers themselves, just as in the case of the figures of Euclid and the
constellations.

For it must not be overlooked that the symbols found in
the various racial and cultural traditions are identical, or at
least similar. It will hardly be admissible to explain this
phenomenon by the hypothesis of unbroken tradition from
a common source; though Guénon, in some of his less satisfactory passages, seems to have inclined towards such an
explanation. Mircéa Eliade seems to be on much surer
ground in attributing the fact to the intrinsic characteristics
of the symbol-objects themselves on the one hand, and those
of human intelligence on the other: the mind of man is so
constituted that it will always spontaneously find the same
symbols in the same objects. On this hypothesis there is
bound to be a natural, universal pattern of symbolism, such
as actually appears in the historical traditions. That does
not mean that the pattern is invariable, for symbols have a
life of their own in the group-mind, which is as yet largely
an uncharted sea.

Guénon sees Christian symbolism as an element in the
universal tradition. He compares the significance of the
cross in the Hindu and the Christian systems. He notes the
number of the twelve apostles, as a parallel for the twelve
signs of the Zodiac. The Pope's white cassock is part of the
evidence for the special regard paid in all religious systems

to the colour white. Undoubtedly there are analogies between Christian and other symbols: Guénon proceeds from this point to conclude that Christianity is one manifestation of the primordial human religious tradition, and consequently to restrict his attention to that which Christianity has in common with other religions. Here we begin to part company with him.

Of course Christianity recognizes the existence of an authentic natural symbolism, which belongs to natural religion, and to the revelation of God to all mankind through the world of creation, which we have already discussed. But Christianity itself is just not that at all: it is something else, something entirely new, an invasion of history by the creator of the world. The cross is important in Christianity, not primarily because of its symbolic qualities, but because Christ was put to death on a particular kind of wooden gibbet. The historical event came first; it was later that liturgical development, seizing upon the approximately cruciform shape of this instrument, enriched it with all the natural symbolism of the cross, the figure of the four dimensions, or of the four cardinal points, illustrating the universal value of Christ's redemptive suffering. This is all secondary, in comparison with the historical facts.

Guénon completely failed to appreciate the special position of Christianity as the religion of a new thing: and it is no wonder, for a wholesale repudiation of history was one element in his system. This is the second aspect of his work that we have to consider. Here again we find a strange mixture of admirable and worthless material. Taking the best first, he is profoundly satisfactory in the unparalleled vigour with which he castigated modern ideas of progress and evolution, or historicism. Not content with the belief, which we share, that it is absurd to look to scientific developments for a qualitative transformation of human nature, Guénon went further: he insisted that this folly is symptomatic of a decadence which has been progressively marked since the sixteenth century. This raises a serious question. Ought we to conclude that science itself, not only the criminal abuse of science, but the whole tendency of science to usurp the due prerogatives of human wisdom, is bound to involve the world in catastrophe? Guénon's opinion may be thought too drastic, but the question admits of no simple optimistic answer.

We must not underestimate the full force of Guénon's courageous assault on some of the most deep-rooted and pernicious of modern prejudices. It is the fact that, by looking to science for salvation, mankind inevitably turns away from the true saviour; and all those who foster this delusion, be they Marxists or liberals, incur responsibility for the unhappy state of the world today. It is unquestionably true that the conceptions of scientific development and of biological evolution have no relevance for the life of the spirit. It is equally true that an exaggerated and exclusive preference for the methods of the experimental sciences tends to disqualify our contemporaries for the intellectual exercise of philosophical judgement. And it is true that, in the order of nature, the lapse of time affords no substantial increment of human values, for substantial values belong to the timeless world of metaphysical reality.

In the order of nature there is no real innovation. But this rule does not hold good for Christianity, which consists of a series of events effectively transforming the life of man in a perfectly new way. The most superficial inspection of the writings of St Paul cannot fail to reveal his preoccupation with novelty, the new creation, the new man. This points to the existence of something that was not to be found in the earlier tradition, a positive advance, a step forward— corresponding exactly to the transition from a knowledge of God through his visible creation to the new intimate revelation of the divine nature in Jesus Christ. With this new thing, this actual qualitative change, we find that which alone fully deserves the appellation of history. Guénon had no idea of it. He never admitted that Christianity was in a privileged position, as indeed he showed plainly enough by turning Mohammedan before he died.

These considerations lead towards a third and last aspect of Guénon's work, dealing with the inter-relation of science, wisdom and faith. In this field, as elsewhere, the author's positive contribution is what first claims our attention. In despite of relativity and pragmatism, Guénon insisted upon the primacy of the speculative intelligence, both in the temporal and in the eternal orders. The highest reality is in the world of incorruptible Ideas, whereof material things are only a transient reflection: so the highest activity of man is in the understanding of these essential principles. Thus Guénon reproduces the Platonic theory of contemplation. Then, secondly, it is only through the knowledge of eternal truth that human affairs can be wisely regulated; the possessors of such knowledge constitute Authority in the spiritual sphere. So Guénon, by restoring the basis of an hierarchical society, offended against another modern dogma, namely the universal law of democracy and manhood suffrage. Spiritual authority derives from the guardians of tradition. It belongs in an eminent degree, archetypically, to the *roi du monde*. It is visibly embodied in certain human characters, one of whom is the Pope. Hence Guénon's championship of the authoritarian aspect of Catholicism, contrasting with his denigration of Protestantism as a perversion of true Christianity.

Authority consists in the trusteeship of tradition; and the tradition in question consists of intellectual principles, primarily those of the Hindu philosophy, in the Vedanta, which was the subject of Guénon's first book. This is rather a dubious position, even from a narrowly philosophical point of view, for the Hindu philosophy is notably inadequate in such essential chapters as the transcendence of God, the immortality of the soul, and the creation. What is worse is the very postulation of philosophical truth as a supreme reality: while religion, and particularly the monotheistic tradition of the Mediterranean basin, is presented as a compromise between pure metaphysical principles and the affective demands of human nature, which require mystical and liturgical satisfactions. This inversion of the relationship between metaphysics and revelation is the great weakness, the fundamental flaw in Guénon's work.

Here is the point of insertion of the theory of esoterism, which occupies an important position in the system. Esoterism may mean either of two entirely different things. Within a single religion, there may be a group of doctrines which are held to be too mysterious for indiscriminate promulgation, especially to neophytes: for instance, in the case of Judaism, such matters as the interpretation of the Song of Songs; or, in the case of Christianity, the teachings of mystical theology. There is no difference in kind between the content of these esoteric doctrines and the substantial truths of religion, but only in degrees of spiritual penetration. Thus, for St Paul, gnosis—knowledge—is the unilinear continuation of faith. Nothing could be more repugnant to the ethos of Christianity than a segregation of first- and second-class Christians. The sacrament of baptism is sufficient once for all; the regenerate need no second initiation into the ritual and dogmatic mysteries.

The other meaning of esoterism, which was Guénon's, implies the existence of a secret body of doctrine behind and beyond the varieties of organized religion, but intrinsically common to them all, and attainable through a distinct initiatory process. Such were the gnostic heresies of the first centuries of Christianity. In this conception, the common people and the initiates have actually differing objects of faith or knowledge. The content of the secret doctrines is something other than the public teaching, something that is not Christianity at all as understood in the catechism. Defined dogma may be a symbolic representation of this esoteric doctrine, but the true hidden meaning of the doctrine is known only to the initiates. And in Guénon's system, the relation of exoteric to esoteric teaching corresponds exactly with the relation of religion to philosophic wisdom—the wisdom that alone affords salvation.

It is obvious by now why Guénon's work is at once so important, and so disappointing. He compels attention by concerning himself with things that are really interesting in themselves, and by his bold denunciation of fallacies that seem to us, as they seemed to him, to be ultimately responsible for the decadence of the modern world. But his constructive system proves, upon examination, to be fundamentally incompatible with Christianity; for he has eliminated the very substance of our religion, in denying the privileged status, the absolute factual unicity of the event of Christ's resurrection.

CHAPTER TEN

SYMBOLISM AND HISTORY

IT is a fact of experience that symbols have an important function in all religious life and thinking. Theological expression draws largely, in the normal course, upon images taken from sensory perception, in order to deal with spiritual realities: this is equally true of Biblical theology, and of the theology of the sacraments, as of mystical theology. Yet we have to recognize that there is something disturbing, for the modern mind, in this mode of intellectual activity. People conditioned to think in terms of efficient causes are inclined to feel that the notion of exemplary causality must imply a lower standard of comprehension, better suited, perhaps, to poetry than to scientific knowledge, and falling short, at all events, of the strict criteria needed for full conviction. This line of criticism must be taken seriously, for it involves a kind of rebellion against the symbolical element in all theological teaching.

It is a comparatively recent aberration, and one with which the theologians of former times had not to reckon. Even apart from scriptural texts, which are obviously full of symbolism, patristic and medieval theology clearly made generous use of symbols: the *de Divinis nominibus* of the pseudo-Dionysius, which belongs in a sense to both periods, is a kind of *Summa* of symbolism, resuming from this point of view the teaching of the Fathers and preparing that of the scholastics. It is our intention in the present chapter to show that this symbolic theology is not to be regarded as a survival from a supposed 'pre-logical' phase of mental development, and thus as something of purely archaeological interest, but on the contrary as a permanently valid category of religious thought.

Let us first consider the facts. The use of visual images to represent the realities of religion is universal throughout the Jewish and Christian traditions. Already in the first verses of Genesis the creative power of God is likened to a great bird hovering over the surface of the waters, eliciting the first stirrings of life: this was, no doubt, the picture that first prompted the image, in the New Testament, of the dove descending over the river Jordan, as the Holy Ghost elicited the first-fruits of the new creation. Again in the closing chapters of the Bible, St John describes the new creation in terms of cosmic symbolism: there will be no need of the sun, 'for the Lord God will shed his light on them'[1] and 'no more sea',[2] for this represents the kingdom of death, and the habitation of the Dragon.

The Christian liturgy has taken over these images. At Christmas, after the winter solstice, when the days begin to lengthen once more, the Church celebrates the nativity of Christ as the eternally rising sun of the new world, of whom the prophet Zacharias said 'Here is one takes his name from the Dayspring'.[3] The new fire kindled in the Paschal vigil symbolizes that column of fire by which the Jews were guided in their wanderings in the desert, as it was said: 'He who follows me can never walk in darkness.'[4] The sacramental rite of baptism, immersion in the font, recalls the symbolism of water in the Bible; it is a going down into the deep waters of death, where Christ went down before us, to accomplish the baptism he had to be baptized with.[5] A whole corpus of 'death and resurrection' symbolism surrounds the theme of water, from the Creation to the Last Judgement, through the Flood, and the Atonement, and the laver of regeneration.

Granted the facts, what is the real importance of all this?

[1]Apoc. 22: 5.   [2]Apoc. 21: 1.   [3]6: 12.   [4]John 8: 12.
[5]Luke 12:50.

A system of imagery which is authorized by the whole
scriptural and liturgical tradition can certainly claim the
tribute of reverence; but is it anything more than an in-
crustation, a patina of antiquity? The cosmic symbols in
question are clearly derived from obsolete general notions
of astronomy and physics. The theme of the 'waters of
death' belongs to an ancient Eastern belief in 'the waters
under the earth'; what meaning can it have for us today?
It was already superseded to some extent when Christian
thought first accepted Hellenic influences, the maleficence
of water being associated no longer with the Semitic idea of
the dragon, but with the idea of the turbulent passions of
men.

The difficulty is not to be lightly dismissed. Can we establish that certain material things are by their very nature
intrinsically and distinctly appropriate to 'signify' or symbolize this or that? or does the quality of 'sign' depend in
each case upon a positive attribution, extrinsically relating
one thing to another? In the latter case it is clear that symbols would have little or no cognitional value. In their illus-
trative function, they would have a certain significance derived solely from the meaningful reality which they serve
to indicate, but no distinct significance of their own at all.
The question being generally regarded as open, the value
of symbols, as a means of knowledge, is consequently dis-
counted: they are felt to be too imprecise and uncertain to
be trustworthy.

Admittedly, symbols are always liable to exhibit in fact
a multiplicity of signification. Night, for instance, can symbolize the world of death and evil, as well as the idea of
transcendence. The ocean is an image of destructive, as
well as creative, power. Hence the variation of symbolic
representations in different cultural traditions. The multi-
valence of symbols at least serves to elevate the technique of
symbolic interpretation above the level of elementary alge-
bra: and it must be remembered that such variations as

there are take place within definite limits. The range of meanings is not unrestricted, for every actual instance of symbolic representation is always related in some way to the natural qualities of the symbol. But it remains to be seen whether this relationship can be more exactly defined.

The comparative history of religions furnishes valuable evidence for the pursuit of such an inquiry, for it shows that identical patterns of symbolic imagery recur universally. Thus we find the sun representing creative power both in ancient Greece and among the American primitives; and the same symbolism in Christianity. Similarly the theme of destruction by water, the theme of the Flood, is found in African religions, in the ancient Babylonian religion, and the Old Testament. I am not now concerned with the qualitatively different acceptation of these symbols in the pagan, and in the revealed, religions. The immediate point to be noted is the identity of representative methods, which does not, of course, imply an identity of real content.

These parallels might be explicable as due to the influence of one system or another. Comparative religion has notoriously overworked this hypothesis: every traceable analogy between the Bible—in particular—and ancient Eastern religious traditions, or between Christianity and the pagan mystery-religions, has been attributed to an 'influence'. Unquestionably there may have been such direct influences in points of detail: but the theory simply will not bear the weight of the facts to be explained. Another school would interpret the worldwide conformity of symbolic representations as vestigial evidence of a single primitive tradition, more or less imperfectly preserved and corrupt. On this view the various Flood-narratives would represent the tradition of an historical event that must have taken place before the separation of men into distinct races.

All such explanations are quite inadequate. The only acceptable conclusion is that the existence of a common set of symbols in the various religions is due to the parallelism of mental processes; but this means that the objective reality of the symbols themselves must be common ground as well. The argument is set out in Mircéa Eliade's *Traité de l'histoire des religions*. Owing to the immense collection of historical data, it has become possible to relate patterns of ideas to groups of symbols. We find that the sky is always linked to the notion of divine transcendence; meteorological phenomena reveal God's power to create and to destroy; water symbolizes death and fertility; the moon is also connected with death and with life; trees support a congeries of interpretations—the axis of the world, tree of life, ladder of heaven.

On this foundation it is possible to construct a positive science of religious symbolism, because we are no longer restricted to a single culture, or theorizing in a vacuum, but handling observed facts, and over the widest field. A scientific method takes into account both the flexibility of symbols in actual use, and also the fundamental constants which represent an objective correlation of image and idea. The same method reveals a tendency for symbols to be associated together in groups, which recur in widely separated contexts; as for instance the moon, the serpent, and water: patterns of correspondence and assimilation, arising from mysterious affinities.

It is significant that the results of these historical researches are paralleled by the independent work of certain psychologists, notably Jung, and the colleagues of Fr Hugo Rahner in the *Eranos Yearbooks*. In Jung's view, pagan myths are not simply an indication of primitive mentality, but represent one of the permanent manifestations of the life of mind. They make up the world of *archetypes*, that is, the background of all psychic activity: they are the expression of the deepest psychological reality, below the level of consciousness; they belong to the structure of soul itself. The significance of the archetypes being thus necessarily inexhaustible, it follows that the use of archetypal symbolism in liturgy and theology provokes an intuitive response in the soul.

Whether by way of analysis of concrete symbols in actual religious systems, or by way of the analysis of the subjective function of myth in subconscious psychology, we are thus brought to the same conclusion, namely that symbols have a constant significance. Symbolism proves to be a definite, characteristic psychological attitude: it is substantially the effort of mind to extract the intelligible meaning contained within physical reality. This is not something purely subjective; the mind does not merely project its own pattern upon the world of things, but discovers a real content through the symbolic appearance: that which is revealed is from without.

The question remains, what is this reality which is known through symbols? Many writers would maintain that nature-symbolism refers only to a simple representation of nature itself in terms of archetypes, or to a primitive conception of nature. On this hypothesis, myths are a sublimation of the laws of biology, a picturesque formulation of the cyclical movement of the universe: symbolic ritual, so understood, has the function of perpetually renewing the actual life of every day by keeping mankind in touch with the rhythm of physical existence—the classical theory of nature-myths and its counterpart in psycho-analysis both point towards this conclusion. If it is sound, there can be no such thing as a cognitional value of myths: the mythical or symbolical interpretation of reality would still be an alternative to scientific method, but would offer no escape from the phenomenal world.

But in fact these theories fail to take account of the real significance of symbols, whose function is to afford us access through the visible world into a higher, transcendent plane of being. Rudolf Otto rightly observed that there are particular symbols, such as the boundless desert or the unfathomable night, whose echoes in the mind are specifically 'numinous', and irreducible to other types of experience. Mircéa Eliade has made masterly use of the same idea: he calls each of these individual phenomena an *hierophany*, a manifestation of the holy, so that one aspect or another of the divine being and activity is revealed in all of them— power in the storm, constancy in the circling of the stars, inexhaustible productive wealth in the rain and the sun- shine. That theory of nature-myths is at fault which would make of human symbolism nothing but a sublimation of created biology. That which is revealed to us through these symbols is something authentically divine.

There is an objective validity in religious symbolism which is rooted in the real nature of things. The difficulty we find in accepting the fact comes from a mental distortion which we suffer through paying attention too exclusively to causal relations and too little to relationships of type, idea or exemplar. Symbolism is no survival from a past, pre-logical mentality of man, but depends on the functioning of laws which never cease to govern the realities of mind and of nature. It is directed towards the discovery of analogies be- tween the visible and the invisible worlds, and towards the formulation of their meaning. It is a genuine mode of ap- prehension of the things of God.

*　　　*　　　*

We have so far been concerned with religious symbolism in the abstract, as one distinct phenomenon, and have de- liberately left aside the question of the various uses to which it is put, being thus enabled to consider under a single head- ing both Christian symbols and those of the non-Christian religions, myths as well as revelation; for there is in reality a measure of common ground in these two different things. On the other hand, the diversity between them is profound. In real life, there is no such thing as pure, undifferentiated symbolism, there are only historically attested particular systems of symbolism, exhibiting all kinds of transmutations and deformations. Our next task will be to examine these concrete historical situations, and to see the ways in which symbolism is employed in various religious contexts: more especially, we shall have to inquire what becomes of nature-symbolism in the case of the Christian revelation.

It has been established that religious symbolism is essentially a revelation of the divine through the things of the visible creation. This means that it belongs to the field of natural religion, to that religious capital, the patrimony of the human race, which is inexhaustibly exploited among all the perversions of paganism both before and since the coming of Christ. Nature-religions, as a class, are identified by this characteristic, namely, that they arrive at a certain knowledge of God through his creative activity and his providence, manifest in the visible work of his hands, while ignoring the fact of his interventions in the historical process—as to which there is no witness before Abraham. It follows that natural religion, so understood, is the appropriate field of application and development of religious symbolism.

Yet, as we have said, the continuity of a thread of natural truth in the religious order throughout all the varieties of paganism is everywhere distorted by unnatural deviations. St Paul expressed the matter exactly in his Epistle to the Romans: 'although they had the knowledge of God, they did not honour him or give thanks to him as God; they became fantastic in their notions . . . and exchanged the glory of the imperishable God for representations of perishable man, of bird and beast and reptile.'[1] It was possible for men to come through the visible creation to some knowledge of the invisible God, but in practice they have not been able to discern him; instead of worshipping him as he is revealed through the significant aspects of his universe, they debased their adoration by devoting it to these created signs themselves, in cults of the sun and of the

[1] Rom. 1: 21, 23.

moon, of animals, or of the dead. It is this debasement of
hierophanies into idolatry that constitutes the specific essence of paganism: a debasement of the natural revelation,
of the first Covenant, into the characteristic form of myth.

The distinctive feature of a religious nature-myth, from
this point of view, is that an hierophany is thereby frus-
trated; instead of leading up to an analogical apprehension
of the transcendent Godhead, the process is arrested at the
level of biological significance, and results in a mere ideali-
zation of physical events. Thus mythology represents the
worship of biological occurrences in their rhythmical regularity, instead of God, whose constancy is imaged for us in
this inevitability of nature. Every pagan system stumbles at
this threshold of truth, never getting beyond the notion of
the immanence of God, never distinguishing him from his
works. Whether more or less, they are all pantheistic. But
this condition of affairs is not an intrinsic quality of the
religion of nature as such: it is a falling away and a corruption.

Read in the light of these considerations, the opening
chapters of Genesis take on a special significance. It has
long been observed that they contain much that is common
to certain Babylonish and Canaanean myths—the opposition between the light and the waters of darkness, the story
of the Flood, and the generations of men before the Flood.
Now each of these themes belongs to the common stock of
natural religious symbolism, and is thus capable of two interpretations, one mythical, the other theistic: the narrative
in Genesis is written to controvert the mythical conception
in the name of the theistic principle. It is to be read as a
deliberate attempt to correct a deviation, by confuting the
erroneous mythical interpretations which the pagan traditions put upon these elements of nature-symbolism, and restoring them to their rightful function as expressing the
power of God, creator and judge of the world.

So far, the programme is not intrinsically original or new,

for it consists in a rectification of the true religion of nature, and a return to the true conception of its symbolic element. But beyond all this, the specific aim of Genesis is to bear witness to the historical works of God. Here was indeed a radical transformation, first in the order of observed reality, and consequently in the order of religious ideas. It meant that God is revealed not only in the rhythm of cosmic cycles, but also in the contingent singularity of historical events. There is, then, a sacred history of successive individual acts of creative power: the election of Abraham, the exodus from Egypt, the kingdom of David, the incarnation of Christ, and his resurrection, the sacraments of the Church, and the Last Judgement. In this wholly new point of view, the meaning of creation itself is altered, for it can now be seen as the first event in an homogeneous series of divine historic actions.

At first sight it might appear that this revolution of religious thought would leave no room for nature-symbolism, which, as we have seen, is essentially an intuition of the divine through the regular repetition of cosmic phenomena; whereas it is of the essence of historical events to be unique, unrepeatable, and new. They cannot be related to pre-existing universal forms or archetypes. And it is true, as Mircéa Eliade has shown, that the symbolic approach to reality always shows an inherent tendency to eliminate the individual peculiarities of things as they actually occur, being concerned exclusively with the repetitive aspects of its subject-matter. The climax of this tendency is reached when the temporal process itself can be interpreted as reflecting even in its own mobility, through the myth of eternal recurrence, the changelessness of eternity.

But in practice what happens is that the historical events themselves, which at first seemed altogether refractory to a symbolic interpretation, generate a new symbolism of their own. In the gradual unfolding of God's design, there appears a system of analogies between his successive works, for all their distinct self-sufficiency as separate creative acts. The Flood, the Passion, Baptism and the Last Judgement, are closely linked together in one pattern. In each instance, though at different levels, there is a divine judgement on the sinful world, and a divine clemency whereby a man is spared to be the beginning of a new creation.

Hence arises a new kind of symbolism, which is characteristic of the Bible. Its specific difference is historicity, for it denotes a relationship between various events belonging to sacred history. It is called *typology*, from the wording of two passages in the New Testament: one where it is said of Adam that he 'was the type (τύπος) of him who was to come'[1]; and another where baptism is called the 'type (ἀντίτυπος)' of the Flood.[2] This figurative sense of Scripture is grounded in the structural unity of God's design: the same divine characteristics are revealed in the successive strata of history. The typological interpretation of events does not in any way tend to ignore or mask their individual existence and value, but affords a frame of reference for intelligible co-ordination. It is also a groundwork of apologetics, being the very stuff of prophecy, wherein Christian thinkers, from the Fathers to Pascal, have seen the essential proof of the truth of our religion.

The real source and foundation of typology has sometimes been obscured in the course of theoretical discussions about methods of Scriptural exegisis. Aquinas defined it accurately when he showed that it is not a meaning of words but a meaning of things[3]—not a sense of scripture but a sense of history. It begins in the Old Testament, where episodes in the past history of Israel are presented as a figure of what shall come to pass in the end of time. It is thus originally and essentially eschatological. In the New Testament, Christ is shown as inaugurating the régime of the last days: it is in this eschatological view that he was prefigured in the Old Testament. The reality of the last things lives on in the

[1]Rom. 5: 14.   [2]1 Pet. 3: 21.   [3]*S. Th.* I: i, 10, *in corp. art.*

sacraments of the Church during the interim between Christ's ascension into Heaven and his coming again; that is, until the eventual fulfilment in Judgement, Resurrection and the world to come.

So understood, in the strictest sense, typology is an intrinsic element of Christian doctrine. It stems from the apostolic teaching; the New Testament is full of it; it was the basis of all sound scriptural interpretation in Patristic times; and it is freely used in the Christian liturgy, where the application to Christ of texts from the Psalter and from prophetic books is directly justified by their eschatological bearing. But this use of figure, this strictly historical kind of symbolism, is something altogether different from the use of allegory by such as Philo, and by some of the Fathers after him. The latter is a recrudescence of nature-symbolism, from which the element of historicity is absent.

From this point we may proceed to examine a final question, concerning the relationship between these two kinds of symbolism. Typology, being historical in character, is a new thing, depending on the occurrence, at given moments of time, of particular divine events in the historical process of redemption: but the cosmic process is not beyond its scope; on the contrary, typology is an interpretation of reality as a whole. In the new system, cosmology, which had been the exclusive medium of the natural revelation of God, now takes on an historical character: the creation is seen as the first episode in sacred history; in the person of Noah, the natural revelation passes over into the historical covenant. But, on the other hand, while the elements of nature-symbolism are thus integrated into the historical frame, it is also true that the events of sacred history are themselves natural phenomena of cosmic significance. The resurrection of Christ is the creation of a new world; baptism, no less than the Flood itself, destroys a world of sin in each regenerate soul; the incidents of the last day mean a new heaven.

The revelation of God in history, despite its absolute unprecedented novelty, does not in any way conflict (as Marcion supposed) with the natural world of the visible creation; there is no opposition, nor even a lack of continuity, but only a step forward, a new phase of the one divine plan. Furthermore, while the first phase, the natural revelation, considered by itself, appears non-historical in character, it acquires historical significance from the fact of being superseded by a second phase. Supersession is indeed the exact description of its status. As a result of the covenant with Abraham, and still more with the new covenant in Jesus Christ, the religion of nature, for all its intrinsic worth, has been superseded. This, then, is an additional characteristic of paganism in the present era—besides being corrupt, it is obsolete, even in respect of the good that is in it.

Neither the Mosaic nor the Christian dispensation, however, destroys the substance of the nature-religion; the old is incorporated in the new. The importance of this point, for our present inquiry, is that it serves to explain how the Bible makes a religious use of the symbolic elements in nature-cults, investing them with new significance. We have already noticed this aspect of the narratives in Genesis; there are other applications of the principle, for instance the Jewish festival commemorating the exodus from Egypt, which is set in the context of solar festivals associated with the springing corn. In the same way the festival of the resurrection of Christ is set in the context of the Jewish Passover. The very form of the liturgy announces the harmony and continuity of the three covenants. The vernal Pasch is both an anniversary celebration of the creation of the world, and a figure of the second spring, the new creation inaugurated by the risen Lord.

In the post-apostolic age, Christianity similarly took over Hellenistic forms of nature-symbolism. There is indeed nothing in common between the historical events of Christ's death and resurrection—which are the subject of Christian faith—and the theme of the dying god and his resuscitation in the mystery-religions, representing the biological rhythm of seed-time and harvest. Nevertheless Christianity took possession of certain elements in the mystery-religions, and endowed them with its own new meaning. Thus, although the birth of Christ was a single, irreversible event once for all in history, the liturgical celebration of this event takes place every year at the winter solstice: the sun of this visible world becomes a sign or sacrament of *Oriens*, the eternal sun of the invisible creation. Again, the cross of Christ was the squalid gibbet where, once upon a time, he was hung up to die. In its factual origin, it was quite devoid of symbolism. Yet the Fathers—and, it may be, St Paul before them—saw in the cross of Christ the four cardinal points, symbolizing the universality of redemption.

Another characteristic instance of this line of development is to be found in the cult of Mary. Paganism is full of virgin-goddesses and mother-goddesses. The cult of Mary owes nothing to these pagan cults: they simply represent an apotheosis of biological fertility, in the symbol of womanhood; whereas the cult of Mary is in no sense at all a sublimation of the feminine principle, but just the personal worship due to a particular woman because of the historic function she fulfilled in the sequence of events whereby mankind was saved. But when all this is said and firmly established, to the exclusion of any mythological interpretation whatsoever of the cult of Mary, it remains perfectly true that Mary sometimes inherited a sanctuary from Diana or from Demeter, and that her liturgy has taken over a certain amount of symbolism from pagan goddess-worship. There is a line in the office of the Seven Sorrows which is pure Virgil, with substitution of *Virgo* for *Dido*:

Quid tibi nunc sensus dum cernis talia Virgo.

One danger of this process, of taking over the formal symbols of nature-religion into the context of the religion of history, is that the historical structure itself may be lost in the limitless universality of the symbol. This is the characteristic defect of allegorism. Philo of Alexandria, contemplating the physical events recorded in the Old Testament, instead of recognizing in them a figure of eschatological reality, found an image of cosmic nature. Thus the Mosaic narrative becomes myth—a constructive reflection of the physical universe, or alternatively psychic ideality: in either case something other than a piece of history. This perverted view of the Old Testament has often tended to adulterate and discredit the authentic typological interpretation: whenever nature-symbolism thus re-encroaches upon historical symbolism, the whole symbolic reading of the Scriptures is in danger.

A not dissimilar situation might be said to exist in regard to the New Testament, for there is a tendency, especially among poets, to turn Christianity itself into a mythology. Guardini[1] has made the point that three poets in particular have transformed the Biblical revelation into myth, each of whom belongs to one of the three Biblical religious systems —the Protestant Hölderlin, the Catholic Rilke, and the Jew Kafka. So Pierre Emmanuel assimilated Christ to Orpheus, and the blood of the redeemer shed on Calvary to the symbol of blood which represents the vital principle in nature. Now it is true that Clement of Alexandria called Christ the true Orpheus, but he meant that the function of Orpheus was taken up into the work of Christ; the same idea is expressed in the art of the catacombs: for Emmanuel it is the other way about—the person of Christ is absorbed into the figure of Orpheus. Relations will always be strained between myth and revelation. The latter requires to make use of nature-symbolism, in order to incorporate the whole sum of creation within its comprehension; but must constantly take heed lest it fall.

This consideration brings us to one final aspect of the symbolic method, namely its tragic quality. The intuitions

[1] In a private conversation with the author.

of symbolism are always a victory over temptation: nature-symbolism must overcome the temptation of myth, and historical symbolism must transcend nature-symbolism. Within historical symbolism itself the tragic conflict re-appears, as the drama of faith. The things which are seen are a figure of invisible truth; things past are a figure of things to come. Through faith in what has happened once, the soul of man must declare for that which is not yet. Kierkegaard was right to take as his ideal pattern of a Christian philosopher the picture of Abraham as he leaves the home of his fathers, and journeys forth towards an unknown land that God will show him.

*   *   *

We are now in a position to judge the worth and meaning of theological symbols. The revelation of God, as made known in the Bible, is progressive. God was first known through nature, and afterwards revealed himself in successive historical events: but so that the later revelations, transcending without destroying the truth of the earlier, incorporated and continued it. Consequently the nature-symbolism through which men first came to a knowledge of God was adopted into the religion of Abraham and into the religion of Christ, being constantly enriched with new significance. Thus the water of baptism means the waters of the Flood, the divided waters of the Red Sea, and the deep waters of death into which Christ went down: the spring festival of Easter recalls the creation of the world in spring-time, the renewal of the chosen people at their exodus from Egypt, and the birth of a new world in the resurrection of Christ.

This is what gives Christian symbolism its unique theological character. Being grounded in the hierophanies of the physical universe, it is natural, and thus accessible to all mankind; but throughout the ages of sacred history it has not ceased to grow, with successive accretions of historical

L.H.—L

significance. It is because Christian symbols have this two-fold quality that they are exceptionally rich in mystical significance. Besides this, it is at the level of Christian symbolism that the interaction can be most clearly discerned between the natural and the supernatural apprehension of God. And finally the liturgy, whose very kernel is symbolism, thus becomes a form of theology—a knowing as well as a doing: a figurative contemplation of the living God, manifest in all his mighty works, in nature and in history.

PART II

CHAPTER ONE

MAGNALIA DEI

THE subject matter of sacred history is 'God's wonders'.[1]
As we approach the task of giving some account of
them, the first point to be observed is that the Bible
exists simply for the purpose of describing the *magnalia
Dei*: from Genesis to Revelation, it is nothing but a
chronicle of these privileged events. The Christian theology of history is all in the Bible. It is through the study of
this document that we may gradually come to understand
the ways of the living God, which are not our ways, being
the expression of a power, a wisdom and a mercy infinitely
beyond our conception.

We shall not follow the chronological sequence of events
in our description, because our aim is rather to explore the
character of sacred history than to trace its course. In each
moment of its development, it exhibits the same intrinsic
qualities, the same pattern of the divine action, which it is
our business to elucidate. Whether in the act of creation,
or in the resurrection of Christ, in the sacrament of baptism
or in the Second Coming, there is to be found at every stage
the evidence of an unchanging system, as it were the signa-
ture of God's design.

This evidence is manifold and complex, but certain indispensable elements of it may conveniently be distinguished.
Take for instance the category of creation. The Hebrew
word *bara* implies a divine action, irrespective of the particular object. This explicitly religious term can be applied
indifferently to the creation of the world, to the election of

[1]Acts 2: 11.

149

the chosen people, to the resurrection of Christ, to Christian baptism: and each of these acts is a work of creation. In the same way, the word for the covenant, *berith*, primarily designates God's definite testamentary disposition of his goods in favour of the chosen race: but the regular succession of the seasons is itself evidence of an original covenant, established in the promise made to Noah and guaranteed by the everlasting faithfulness of God; and the incarnation of the Word in Jesus Christ is the new, the supreme covenant, whereby the nature of God and the nature of man are indissolubly united for ever.

In this covenanted relationship, the living God reveals those attributes described in the Bible as his truth, his righteousness, and his love—words which must be interpreted in the light of Bible usage, if they are to preserve for us their original content. Thus the truth of God, in the Biblical sense, does not ordinarily imply a reference to the immediate intellectual apprehension of divinity, in the beatific vision of the *primum intelligible*: it means the faithfulness of the living God, in whom men may safely put all their trust. The assurance of faith comes, then, not so much from the nature of the evidence as from the quality of the witness; faith is symbolized in the Bible, not by the Greek metaphor of illumination, but by the image of a rock.

Again, the righteousness of God, *tsedeq* in the Bible, is not the righteousness, or justice, of mankind, which latter is based upon the rights of men, and upon correlative duties. If this were the appropriate criterion, then clearly a world in which children suffer, and the innocent are oppressed, would be an unjust world, and mankind would be entitled to indict God, as Camus did, and to bring in a verdict of guilty at the bar of humanity. But in God's sight nothing is due to anyone, and mankind has no rights to stand upon. The righteousness or justice of God consists in honouring his own undertakings and fulfilling his own promises. And in our own interest we might prefer to be treated in accordance with the righteousness of God and the justice with which he observes his own laws, rather than on the case we could make out for ourselves: for all the incomprehensibility of his ways, it could be wiser to rely implicitly upon this righteousness, which is simply love being true to itself, regardless of the loved one's infidelity.

Lastly, the supreme revelation of God in the Bible is love, objectively realized in the setting up of a stable relation of amity between the Lord and his people, called *hesed*. God is thus revealed in the Scriptures as an ally, one who has committed himself, one upon whom we can count —not, as in the Barthian conception, one whose illimitable freedom is incompatible with obligations. Our God is party to a fellowship, gives not only grace but an entitlement to grace: wherever this title can be proved, as in the teaching office of the Church, or in the sacraments, it will infallibly be honoured.

It is in the light of these conceptions that we may understand how the Song of Songs gives a Biblical basis and sanction for the theology of the Church, the Spouse of Christ. The Church can only be one, because monogamy is of the essence of the marriage bond, and the bridal status of the Church would be meaningless otherwise. The Church cannot fail, because fidelity is an essential element in marriage, and the espousals of Christ and his Church must imply faithfulness or mean nothing. The Church is holy, because marriage essentially requires a perfect community of possessions, and Christ endows his bride with all his heavenly goods. The spiritual wealth of the Church is not of her own bringing, but it is really and unalterably hers because she has it by an irrevocable gift from her Lord.

Besides all these indispensable marks of the divine action, we will now attend to another, a point in which the transcendence of God is most forcibly demonstrated within the ambit of history, and one, too, of the most mysterious, namely his wrath. For this purpose we shall simply expound a single text, the prayer of the prophet Habacuc, in which the matter is most directly set forth.

> I have heard, Lord, the tale of thy renown, awe-stricken at the divine power thou hast. Reveal that power in these latter days, in these latter days make it known once more! And though we have earned thy anger, bethink thee of mercy still. God coming near from Teman, the holy One from yonder hills of Pharan! See how his glory overspreads heaven, his fame echoes through the earth; the brightness that is his, like light itself, the rays that stream from his hand, masking its strength; pestilence his outrider, the wasting sickness in his train! There stood he, and scanned the earth; at his look, the nations were adread; melted were the everlasting mountains, bowed were the ancient hills, his own immemorial pathway, as he journeyed. I saw the Ethiop quail in his tent, the dwellings of Madian astir with terror.
>
> Is it the rivers, Lord, that have awaked thy anger; should it be the rivers? Or has the sea earned thy vengeance, that thou comest thus mounted on thy horses, on thy victorious chariot; that bow of thine brought into full play, which grants to Israel the assurance of thy succour? Earth is torn into ravines; the mountains tremble at the sight. Fierce falls the rain-storm, the depths beneath us roar aloud, the heights beckon from above; sun and moon linger in their dwelling-place; so bright thy arrows volley, with such sheen of lightning glances thy spear.[1]

The splendid vigour of this passage depends upon the concurrence and interaction of images belonging to two distinct categories, one group deriving from the phenomena of war, the other from meteorological disturbances. There is a constant alternation between the lightning and the spear, between the thunder and the tramp of hoofs. From one moment to the next, we are in doubt whether the picture is of an army on the march, or of the passage of a storm.

[1]Hab. 3: 2-11.

'That bow of thine brought into full play'

—here is a battle-image.

'Earth is torn into ravines'
'Sun and moon linger in their dwelling-place'

—this refers to a storm, and the darkening sky.

'So bright thy arrows volley, with such sheen of lightning . . .'

represents a fusion of the two strains of imagery: the lightning is the arrows of the Lord of Hosts, who marches out
from his dwelling-place in a triumphal progress throughout
the wide world. By another literary device, which is extremely characteristic of the Bible, natural and historical
disasters are depicted in parallel—on one hand the trembling mountains, the overflowing water, 'the depths . . .
roar aloud'; on the other, 'the nations adread'. The Lord's
triumphal world-wide progress subjugates empires and
elements alike: the former aspect is presented under the
image of an army on the march; the latter, as the breaking
of a storm.

There is nothing really surprising about the use of such
language. The imagery in this Scriptural text is all taken,
with modifications, from the pre-existing stock of religious
symbolism, the figures whereby the things of God are revealed through the visible creation. Not only the cyclical
regularity of the heavenly bodies, or the impenetrable
stability of the rocks, but the boundless sea itself and the
destructive violence of storms are all accepted signs of invisible truth; and among these hierophanies, the storm is
one of the most universally recognized, and one of the
plainest. Even today, when we have long outgrown the
forms of nature-cults, the crash of thunder affects our feelings in a way that is basically religious: it may be partly
superstitious, but the fact remains that a thunderstorm, in
our twentieth-century civilization, is still a kind of hierophany. This is the groundwork of human experience from

which the scriptural development originates, and proceeds to the reality behind the image, to a theophany of Jehovah.

The particular truth so revealed in this instance is the wrath of God—which immediately poses the same problem of interpretation over again. There is hardly anything in the terminology of religion that gives more offence to the pious (or prudish) ears of the modern world than this expression, the wrath of God. It was already something of an embarrassment to the Alexandrian Jews, who attempted, in discussion with the Greek philosophers, to water it down.[1] In our own day, Simone Weil, for example, finds it simply intolerable: for she, like Marcion of old, contrasts the New Testament God of Love with an Old Testament God of Wrath. Unfortunately for this position, there is love in the Old Testament, and there is wrath in the New—as Tertullian pointed out long ago. We have to reckon, whether we like it or not, with wrath as one of the divine attributes: and, what is more, for all its anthropomorphic appearance, this particular word may well carry a stronger charge of mystical significance than any other, and afford the deepest insight into the meaning of the divine transcendence.

Obviously it is necessary first of all to know what the word means. Any modern child may learn from his catechism that anger is a sin: so it is no wonder if he is shocked to hear of it in God: and similarly with jealousy. But this reaction is philosophically indefensible. The passion of anger is a creature, and thus far intrinsically good. Christ was angry with the traders in the Temple; Péguy wrote of Saint Joan's *grandes colères blanches*. Wrath is the emotional response of a sound personality to anything vile, low and mean. So Christ would not tolerate the making of his House into a den of thieves, or the laying of burdens on others by men who would not bear them, or the giving of scandal to children.

[1] Philo, *Post. Cain.* I: 1 and 4.

Essentially, anger is not the same as *Ressentiment*, the typical reaction of wounded self-love; but rather a refusal to have any dealings with what is beyond the pale. From this point of view, the wrath of God means the incompatibility between his purity and sin. Perhaps we ought to go further still, because the fundamental senses of θύμος and *ira* do not even imply reference to an object: the primary meaning concerns a person's own vitality and self-expression. One of the Hebrew words used in this sense comes from the same root as the word for the smoking muzzle of a bull. So that the innermost kernel of this idea of the wrath of God would be simply a mark of the intensity of his being, and the irresistible force with which his power may be manifested in creation, when he is pleased to give a violent reminder of his existence to a world that steadfastly turns away from him.

Wrath, so understood, is purged of every connotation of pettiness, meaning simply that intensity of existence which nothing whatever can withstand. It is a precious conception, because other, more abstract, ideas, while they afford us a knowledge of truth, may give us no measure of intensity, whereas the ideas of jealousy and wrath do convey some impression of the intense life of God. In this way, the word 'wrath', which looks so anthropomorphic at first sight, really points to the secret of that which is most transcendent in the divine nature. So far from representing God in the image and likeness of man, it brings us to an apprehension of just that in which he most of all excels us, namely the supreme and perfect intensity of his being, which is out of all proportion and analogy with our own.

There is perhaps no clearer way of expressing the truth of this matter than in the words of Christ to St Catherine of Siena: 'It is I that am; you are that which is not'; under the violence of contact with absolute being, mankind recognizes the nothingness of its own contingent being, its pitiful, ludicrous insufficiency seen in the light of the fullness, intensity and reality of God's existence. So mankind may experience in practice what it is to be a creature; but only so: only in proportion as we realize something of the essence of Godhead. An intuition of this sort, sounding the depths of one's own existence, carries its own compulsive conviction of overpowering reality: and wrath is the very definition of that irresistible force in the divine being.

Our contemporaries have almost no conception of what is implied in the idea of absolute being. In their incredibly exalted revaluation of humanity they have lost sight of the essence of creatureliness: while on the other hand they have evacuated the notion of God of all its substance, leaving the merest ghost of an abstraction in a thin air of metaphysics, so that anyone may understandably feel free to discard it at will, as an obsolete survival, irrelevant to the experience of real life. Indeed the liquidation of such a spectral deity is no great loss; but then he had not much in common with the living God, of whom it is said in the Bible that no man can see him and live. This latter sort of language, indicating the existence of God in terms of intensity, gets rid of the edulcorated sentimental detritus of pseudo-piety, and brings us up against the hard existential core of religious reality, the supreme reality of the absolute being. That is the true foundation of worship. People are still capable in our time of devotional feelings, but hardly of any deep-rooted conviction of the mystery of Godhead. There is a need in our churches of such a clearance as the Saviour effected in the temple of Jerusalem, a riddance of the clutter of secondary devotions, that block the way to the all-important central emptiness which is filled with the presence of God alone.

This is what the prophet recognized as the wrath of Jehovah in his irresistible progress through nature and history.

'God coming near from Teman, the holy One from yonder hills of Pharan'—

Jehovah is indeed 'he that cometh', ἐρχόμενος, a God who invades the life of men. The divine irruptions are the *magnalia Dei*, the very object of all prophetic vision: and the prophet's unchanging mission is to preach the lesson of conversion because God is coming. 'A cry, there, out in the wilderness, Make way for the Lord's coming; a straight road for our God through the desert! Bridged every valley must be, every mountain and hill levelled; windings cut straight, and the rough paths paved; the Lord's glory is to be revealed for all mankind to witness: it is his own decree.'[1]

When this message is repeated on the threshold of the holy gospels by St John, 'the voice of one crying in the wilderness, Straighten out the way of the Lord'.[2] we become aware of the basic reality of all preaching of repentance. We are required at all times to moderate our fleshly impulses in favour of aspirations towards a higher life, but penance means more than that; it belongs essentially to an historical frame of reference, because it depends directly upon the coming of the Lord—it is what we must do when, as now, the Lord is coming. Christianity is not only an ethical or ascetic system, but unchangeably a relationship of men to the living God, to him that cometh on our behalf to achieve wonders beyond compare.

The coming of Jehovah is something that concerns the whole creation, heaven and earth, as the Angel said to the shepherds, emphasizing the universal import of Christ's nativity:

'Glory to God in high heaven, and peace on earth.'[3]

The point is even more plainly evident in the astonishing description, in Habacuc's Prayer, of the Lord's progress through the visible world of nature. Land and water, heaven and hell, the very elements of creation are thrown into disarray at his approach, showing the limitless consequences

[1]Isa. 40: 3–5.　[2]John 1: 23.　[3]Luke 2: 14.

of the Creator's action when he is pleased to intervene in
the work of his hands.

> 'Melted were the everlasting mountains,
> bowed were the ancient hills'—

thus, in the first place, it is the earth that quakes. 'The
everlasting mountains', a symbol of stability, abiding
through all the passing generations, are themselves up-
rooted from their place. Next comes the element of water:

> 'Is it the rivers, Lord, that have awaked thy anger? . . .
> has the sea earned thy vengeance?'

The fury of the waves bears the mark of God's wrath, which
yet is not exhausted, for now the bottomless pit is opened:

> 'Earth is torn into ravines . . .
> the depths beneath us roar aloud'—

that deep which is the abode of the powers of darkness, and
the place of the dead. And the wrath of Jehovah, compassing
the limits of creation, penetrates not only the infinite abyss
but the heights of heaven too:

> 'Sun and moon linger in their dwelling-place: so bright
> thy arrows volley.'

The powers above are stayed in their courses and stand
transfixed with dread.

In another place, in the Song of the Three Holy Children,
the Scriptures set before us the whole creation, sun and
moon, fish, flesh and fowl, singing together a hymn of
praise to Jehovah. The prayer of Habacuc is such another
cosmic liturgy, but penitential: its theme is not creation,
but destruction. Jehovah, the creator and ruler of all things,
now comes to exercise his unchallengeable sovereignty by
destroying them. The elements are his to dispose of as he
will. The occasions of his intervention are various, revealing

various aspects of his nature. From his creative activity we may know his power and wisdom; from his covenants we learn his faithfulness and loving-kindness; from his judgements we come to the knowledge of his righteousness and his wrath. In the last case as in the first, the whole universe is involved, whether to be established or abolished. Destruction as well as creation exceeds all human understanding. The Lord God is omnipresent, whether his faithfulness is manifest in the order of nature, or whether the disruption of the natural order reveals his anger.

Other passages of Scripture attest the wholesale recasting of the elements of creation as a mark of Jehovah's judgements. In the Hellenistic book of Wisdom, earth, water, air and fire are shown to be all dislocated in turn by the power of the Lord at the time of the plagues of Egypt: 'All the elements may be transposed among themselves, keeping up the same answering rhythm, like the notes of a harp altering their mood . . . Land-beasts turned to water-beasts, and the firm ground was trodden by creatures born to swim. Fire surpassed its own nature, when water forgot to quench it.'[1] And yet the ten plagues of Egypt were only a figure of the universal cataclysm foretold by Habacuc, and again by St John in the Apocalypse, where he writes of the angels pouring out the seven vials, the first upon the earth, the second upon the sea, the third upon the rivers, the fourth upon the sun, the fifth upon the beast's throne. . . .[2]

The passage of Jehovah through the universe of his creation is thus likened to a storm of such ferocity as to confound the very elements themselves. But he goes through human history too, like a victorious army overturning empires: 'There stood he, and scanned the earth; at his look, the nations were adread; . . . I saw the Ethiop quail in his tent, the dwellings of Madian astir with terror.' Jehovah is the Lord of history, as he is the Lord of creation. In Deuteronomy, we are told that he 'divided the nations apart';[3]

[1]Wis. 19: 17–19. [2]Apoc. 16: 2–10. [3]Deut. 32: 8.

that he made them the instruments of his purpose, to punish his own people for their sins;[1] and that he afterwards broke and discarded them: 'Should the victors boast it was their own power, not mine, that had won the day?'[2] The Prayer of Habacuc exhibits the execution of this verdict upon the nations. There is no other chosen race but the people of God, the new Israel; all the nations are guilty. So God's judgement upon the nations is not by way of punishing one and rewarding another: all nations alike are subject to his judgement, and must acknowledge their nothingness and their incompetence to plead against him.

The disasters and afflictions that accompany Jehovah's visitation give effect to his judgement, as it were a sentence: 'pestilence his outrider, the wasting sickness in his train.' We cannot fail to be reminded of that triumphal riding of the Word of God throughout all the earth, with the horses of death, pestilence, and famine. 'And when he broke the second seal, I heard the second figure say, Come and look; and a second horse came out, fiery-red, whose rider was empowered to take away all peace from the world, bidding men slay one another; and a great sword was given to him.' This is war. 'And when he broke the third seal, I heard the third figure say, Come and look; so I looked, and saw there a black horse, whose rider carried in his hand a pair of scales; I thought, too, I heard a voice that came from where the living figures were. A silver piece, it said, for a quart of wheat, a silver piece for three quarts of barley; but do the wine and the oil no hurt.' That is famine: and the last is pestilence: 'when he broke the fourth seal, I heard the voice of the fourth living figure say, Come and look. So I looked, and saw there a cream-white horse; its rider was called Death, and Hell went at his bridle-rein; he was allowed to have his way with all the four quarters of the world, killing men by the sword, by famine, by plague, and through wild beasts that roam the earth.'[3]

[1]Deut. 32: 21.   [2]ibid. 27.   [3]Apoc. 6: 3–8.

The mystery of the divine dispensations becomes even more inexorable as the wrath of God is more plainly realized, taking now the form of a direct infliction upon the human race of actual historical disasters, war, disease, dearth. It is altogether too much for modern susceptibilities: belief in the goodness of Almighty God seems incompatible with a world where innocent children are killed by atomic bombs and famine decimates the poverty-stricken masses of India. Such a world is admittedly unjust by human standards, and Albert Camus was perfectly right, on his own assumptions, to bring in a verdict of guilty when trying the case of God by the principles of purely human justice. Any system of apologetics which attempts to justify the ways of God to men by the criteria of man's righteousness is a monstrous absurdity, and obviously doomed to utter failure.

For crime and punishment are out of all proportion. It is nonsense to talk of an immanent justice of retribution, as though every trial were the consequence of a particular offence: all such theories were exploded in Job's day. When it is plain beyond the possibility of dispute that the innocent suffer in this world as much as the guilty, what conceivable excuse is left for a mechanical view of the historical process as providential? How can the great disasters of history be interpreted as chastisements, when it is the faithful peoples that are oppressed by the victorious infidels? The Bible never recognized the triumphs of Egypt or Babylon as evidence of God's favour; rather it was always those whom the Lord loved that were defeated. It is the worst kind of pharisaical self-righteousness to regard national success as a mark of God's blessing.

But if historical afflictions are not to be regarded as the punishment due to sin, how are they to be explained? Must it follow that we are the chance victims of tyrannical caprice? The question is fraught with anguish for too many sorrowful hearts to be lightly put off: we must get to the bottom of it. We must accept all the evidence, admit that

L.H.—M

the ills of this world are distributed at haphazard, without rhyme or reason: we must acknowledge that suffering humanity is engaged in a meaningless farce, and that an attitude of revolt is the most fitting response a man can make to such a situation. We must allow all this to be a fair presentation of the case according to the principles of human justice. But if the world is subject to another and a better jurisdiction, that will be a different story.

Great catastrophes, whether in the order of nature or of history, have just this very purport—a fierce call to order, because men are prone to self-sufficiency, and unmindful of their creaturely estate. Historical disasters are a visitation of the Almighty, to strip mankind of vanity and utterly confound his self-possession, like the coming of Habacuc's army on the march, bringing pestilence and death. 'Such was the tale that set my whole frame trembling; at the rumour of it my lips quivered with fear; there was a faintness overcame my whole being, my steps faltered as I went.'[1]

When these things happen, the world is struck dumb. Men retire within themselves, silently, for there is a religious quality in the terror that is inspired by such immense catastrophes as the downfall of a mighty empire. They are as it were cracks in the protective covering of our little private world; light shines in from outside. They are like an open wound in the heart of our human existence. The self-sufficiency of man is rudely shaken, and himself violently thrown back upon the stark tragedy of real life— which he is always trying to forget; always taking any excuse not to think about, though it is all that really matters to him; always finding ways not to see, though this overhanging shadow of death contains his only hope of escape out of captivity. God comes then to awake mankind out of sleep, like the warning bell ringing for judgement. The disasters of human history are a call to repent while there is yet time.

[1] Hab. 3: 16.

So that which earth-bound man can only call wrath, as it utterly confounds all his ideas and way of life, is really a manifestation of the mystery of divine love. Apart from the attitude of revolt, there is one other possible response for mankind, faced with an apparently irrational world, namely faith, which is trust in love. By faith we acknowledge that God is working out a mysterious plan of salvation, albeit in ways incomprehensible to us. Death and hell accompany his footsteps, but we know from the Song of Songs that love is strong as death, and cruel as the grave.[1] There is love hidden in the wrath described in Habacuc's prayer. We have said that the wrath of God was a kind of secret kernel of the divine transcendence, but within that hidden nucleus the quintessence of the mystery, the innermost secret of the Holy of Holies, is love. Love is the answer to the questions of suffering mankind— transcendent love, whose ways pass our understanding.

From this point we may return to the text of Habacuc. In the first verse, we read:

'We have earned thy anger, bethink thee of mercy—'

not 'instead of anger have mercy'. The petition does not seek to mitigate the fury of the visitation by concessions: but in the midst of his wrath, in the full activity of his supereminent being with all that this implies and requires, God is implored to reveal his love, as the supreme fulfilment of one and the same intense divine reality. Paradoxically, the terms 'anger' and 'love' are brought together, as simultaneously indicating two equally essential aspects of the Godhead. They are indeed irreconcilable at the level of human understanding: 'If God is good, how can he be so stern and angry?' The theological answer is that the two qualities are really one and the same in God himself, though we can only conceive them as distinct: we are here faced with the essential mystery of God's being, wherein we know

[1] 8: 6.

that the two things co-exist; that there is in him this wrath, this perfect incompatibility with sin, this all-surpassing holiness—and also this mercy, this infinite love of sinners, which brings the Son of God to offer up his life for them, the same divine Word, whose unappeasable wrath ceases not to mark the nature and extent of his claims upon us.

In the light of these considerations we can the better appreciate the prayer of Habacuc. This terrible, over-whelming mystery of love and wrath is unfolded for us by the Church on Good Friday: Golgotha exhibits wrath and love together in their fullest intensity.

> 'The depths roar aloud . . .
> Sun and moon linger in their dwelling-place':

it is impossible for us to hear of these supernatural portents of the coming of Jehovah without thinking of the circum-stances of Calvary, when St Luke tells us that 'it was about the sixth hour, and there was darkness over all the earth until the ninth hour. The sun was darkened';[1] and St Matthew tells us of the dead who arose, the deep lifting up his hands to restore what belonged there.[2] At this moment of Christ's death, nature is thrown into confusion: an event to all appearances absurdly insignificant, a routine hanging by the gate of a small town in the Levant, proves to be a turning-point in heaven and earth. The Passion of Christ is the fulfilment of Habacuc's prophecy, the coming of Jehovah.

Jehovah being compared in the text with the sun, the sun's rays flashing through the clouds are naturally taken as arrows from the hand of the Lord of Hosts. But Christian eyes, from medieval times onwards, have seen in these 'rays that stream from his hand' the streams which flowed from the pierced hands of Jesus on the Cross. In the midmost point of the vision of divine glory stands the figure of the Crucified, who is in truth the source of light and

[1] 23: 44–45. [2] 27: 51–53.

healing for all creation. The work of omnipotence is effected in the Cross of Christ. This is the solution of the paradox of wrath and love; what seemed an act of wrath proves a work of love. The same God whose wrath alone had been apparent, is now revealed as a God of love, whose almighty power fulfils itself through a supreme act of love on the cross of salvation.

Another parallel inevitably comes to mind, from a passage in the Apocalypse: a moment of high tragedy, when the Book has been 'sealed with seven seals'—the circle of history is closed; there is no escape. A cry goes up for one to break the seals. 'I was all in tears, that none should be found worthy to open the scroll or have sight of it; until one of the elders said to me, No need for tears; here is one who has gained the right to open the book, by breaking its seven seals, the Lion that comes from the tribe of Juda, from the stock of David. Then I saw, in the midst, where the throne was, amid the four figures and the elders, a Lamb standing upright, yet slain (as I thought) in sacrifice. He had seven horns, and seven eyes, which are the seven spirits of God, that go out to do his bidding everywhere on earth.'[1] He that should break the seals was announced as a lion, and comes as a lamb: and from his wounds goes forth a mystic power to cure the wounds of men.

For just as wrath turns out to be love, so love is found to be mighty. Habacuc tells us explicitly: 'it is to rescue thy own people, rescue thy own anointed servant, that thou goest out to battle. Down fall the turrets in yonder castle of godlessness, down sink the foundations to their very base.'[2] Salvation with the anointed, that is, in Christ, is here plainly described. Jehovah comes to rescue his anointed by destroying the foundations of the castle of godlessness, where the anointed was held captive; he was a prisoner of death, in the power of death and hell, but the Lord destroyed the house of captivity from top to bottom, and his anointed

[1] Apoc. 5: 4–6. [2] 3: 13.

came forth victorious, together with those he had himself set free. This is the essence of the Paschal mystery, wherein Jesus Christ, death's prisoner, breaks down the gates of Hell on Easter morning to save captive humanity from every kind of thraldom and bring men forth into the joy of his rising.

'Lights thy ban on its princes, on the heads of its warriors, whose blustering rage would overthrow me, confident now as some petty tyrant who oppresses the poor in secret. Over the sea, over the ooze beneath its waves, thou hast made a path for thy horses to tread.'[1]

There is a last paradox to come: the prophecy ends with a picture of desolation, which yet evokes a strange atmosphere of peace and tranquillity: 'What though the fig-tree never bud, the vine yield no fruit, the olive fail.'[2] The world is desolate indeed, creation mourns the death of Christ; but after the stormy violence of the earlier descriptions, after all those cataclysmic upheavals, it is a homely figure: the countryside is ravaged, but familiar. As on Easter Eve, after the death and burial of the Saviour, the world is paralysed, inert, dumb, as it were with the silence that was before the creation: but from this annihilation there will arise a new creature. Christ's death is a plenary satisfaction of wrath: Christ's death is a plenary satisfaction of love.

We have here confined our attention to a single text, but the theme demands a reading of the whole Bible. The Scriptures tell us of a mystery, a hidden content of the historical process. The prophets learnt it from that Spirit who is at once the maker and interpreter of history. It is the mystery of the works of God, creation, judgement, and redemption: these are the reality, the inwardness of temporal events, concealed behind the outward seeming. Here, then, is the source of all Christian theology of history. Yet that which God accomplishes on man's behalf is not accom-

[1]Hab. 3: 14–15.   [2]ibid. 3: 17.

plished apart from man. The chronicle of the *magnalia Dei* tells only half the story: the other half consists of the response of mankind, and this, too, is described in the Bible.

CHAPTER TWO

THE SONG OF THE VINE

ONE of the three canticles which are still in use in the new liturgy of the Vigil of Easter is the song of the Vine, taken from the prophet Isaias (5: 1–2); and there is a sermon of St Zeno[1] which shows that this text occupied a similar place already in the fourth century. Apart from this evidence, it is clear from constant allusions to the theme of the Vine in the earliest Christian writings that the passage was regarded as particularly significant. There are explicit references in the New Testament, for instance the parable of the wicked husbandmen in the Lord's vineyard,[2] and St John's contrast between the true vine and the vine of Israel. Again, the oldest Christian liturgical text, the *Didache*, mentions the vine of David, which is the Church, spreading over the plains and the hills. It is another of the basic themes of Scripture, running through the whole history of salvation.

We have now to examine the import and bearings of this theme.[3] In the last chapter we were considering the scriptural chronicle of the wonderful works of God, with special reference to the work of judgement; it would have been equally appropriate to have directed our attention to the work of creation, or of redemption: for all these events constitute what might be called the cycle of Jehovah's faithfulness. With the Vine, we come upon another cycle, concerning the works of men, the unfaithfulness of Jehovah's

---

[1]PL. 11: 471–2. [2]Matt. 21: 33 et sqq.

[3]See J. Guillet, *Thèmes bibliques*. The present chapter, which was inspired by this admirable book, contains much that was borrowed from it.

people. The prophetic books of the Old Testament belong almost entirely to this cycle, for it is their essential concern to contrast the unfaithful people with their faithful Lord, and to give warning of the penalty so incurred. In the canticle of the Vine, which we are now about to analyse, these fundamental topics are as it were recapitulated in epitome.

A song, now, in honour of one that is my good friend; a song about a near kinsman of mine, and the vineyard that he had. This friend, that I love well, had a vineyard in a corner of his ground, all fruitfulness. He fenced it in, and cleared it of stones, and planted a choice vine there; built a tower, too, in the middle, and set up a winepress in it. Then he waited for grapes to grow on it, and it bore wild grapes instead. And now citizens of Jerusalem, and all you men of Juda, I call upon you to give award between my vineyard and me. What more could I have done for it? What say you of the wild grapes it bore, instead of the grapes I looked for? Let me tell you, then, what I mean to do to this vineyard of mine. I mean to rob it of its hedge, so that all can plunder it, to break down its wall, so that it will be trodden under foot. I mean to make waste-land of it; no more pruning and digging; only briars and thorns will grow there, and I will forbid the clouds to water it.[1]

As with the Palestinian countryman and his vine, so it is with the Lord and his chosen race, the Hebrews: 'it is the house of Israel that the Lord called his vineyard; the men of Juda are the plot he loved so'.[2] God has done everything for them. They are his dearest possession. All his hopes are wrapped up in them. The long account of his kindness to this people is recalled in the song of the Vine—'this friend, that I love well, had a vineyard in a corner of his ground, all fruitfulness': just as the grower selects a sheltered slope with the right exposure before he plants his vines, even so Jehovah had bespoken Palestine to be his people's home-land. 'He fenced it in, and cleared it of stones': thus the

[1]Is. 5: 1–6. [2]ibid. 5: 7.

whole of world-history before Moses is interpreted as a
providential preparation for the people of Israel.

At length, when the ground has been thoroughly cultivated, God plants it with a choice vine. Osee has the
same image: 'When I kept tryst with Israel long ago, rare
the encounter, as of grapes out in the desert.'[1] Thenceforward he lives in hopes of the harvest that shall repay
his efforts; like the husbandman, he examines his vine
every day, anxiously protects it from anything that might
interfere with its progress, scrutinizes the earliest shoots: in
anticipation of his crop, he 'built a tower in the middle,
and set up a winepress'. The entire history of Israel is
summed up in these verses, with all the favours God
bestowed upon his people: the exodus from Egypt, and
the forty years' preservation in the wilderness, the covenant, the tabernacle, and the Law; then the conquest of the
promised land, the victories of the Judges, the kingdom of
David and the empire of Solomon.

In the seventy-ninth Psalm, the same development is described in the same imagery:

> Give audience, thou that art the guide of Israel, that leadest
> Joseph with a shepherd's care. Thou who art enthroned above
> the Cherubim, reveal thyself . . . Long ago, thou didst bring
> a vine out of Egypt, rooting out the heathen to plant it here;
> thou didst prepare the way for its spreading, and it took root
> where thou hadst planted it, filled the whole land. How it
> overshadowed the hills, how the cedars, divinely tall, were
> overtopped by its branches! It spread out its tendrils to the
> sea, its shoots as far as the great river.[2]

Thus, from the time of Moses to the time of Solomon, the
vine of Israel grew until it spread from the Lebanon to
Egypt, and from the Jordan to the sea.

That is how God honoured his promises. His hopes were
all set upon this vine, that it should bear his grapes. This is

[1]Os. 9: 10. [2]Ps. 79: 2, 9–12.

the key-signature of the Song of the Vine, for its theme turns wholly upon the hopes that God has of man, the mystery of the divine expectations. Primarily, it is the response of Israel that was expected, for Israel was the vine of the Lord's planting, from which he looked to have grapes. But apart from the Hebrews, all mankind is involved in these transactions. The vine of Israel is a type or figure of each one among us. The whole drama of sacred history is in this contrast of man's unbelief and God's fidelity: and the Song of the Vine recounts this drama.

God is the husbandman, expecting, hoping, desiring such great things from us. He prepared the soil in which our souls were to grow up and flourish; he ceases not to nourish, protect and encourage their growth, all our lives long. Every circumstance of our environment is an instance of God's care for us. The soul of the least little African negro, however unconsidered and forgotten, or of the poorest Blackfellow's child in Australia, or of the wretchedest Chinaman's, is a costly vine of Jehovah's planting, which he expects to bear luscious fruit.

The point of the Song of the Vine is that it reveals how much store God sets by the spiritual profit of our lives, and how much he depends for this upon our help. 'Spiritual profit' is of course quite a different thing from temporal success. Successful lives, in the temporal order, may be spiritually disastrous: brilliant lives in the world's estimate, with riches, happiness, and fame, but in spiritual currency a total, ruinous failure. And there are lives that seem wasted, intellectually null, baulked of affection, economically valueless, which may still yield a glorious return in terms of spiritual achievement.

Some things are beyond our control, and temporal success is one of these; other things are at all times within our control, such as the spiritual response we make to the situations in which the Lord is pleased to put us, or the determination to find God in all the circumstances of our life, be they joys or crosses. If we do this, everything that happens to us is nourishment for the sap of that spiritual vine, namely our eternal soul, everything co-operates in its growth to perfection.

This is not only true for individuals but also for nations. If we were to reckon the measure of God's favour by the level of national prosperity, we should be in the thick of pharisaical delusions. It is true that Bossuet incurred this kind of condemnation when he accepted the fact of Louis XIV's successes as a divine endorsement of his political principles and practice; but the Old Testament should have been enough to shatter all such dreams. When Israel prospered, it betrayed its sacred trust, the custody of eternal values. But from Israel in adversity came forth some of the most astounding language in all human utterance, a message which has not yet lost its revolutionary power. This is the kind of achievement God looks for, from his own people —simply that they should be faithful to him.

It is just what the chosen people, loaded with his benefits, refused to their Lord. The Song of the Vine, after telling of God's hopes, goes on to describe his disappointment: he

> waited for grapes to grow on it, and it bore wild grapes instead. And now, citizens of Jerusalem, and all you men of Juda, I call upon you to give award between my vineyard and me. What more could I have done for it? What say you of the wild grapes it bore, instead of the grapes I looked for?

This is primarily the history of Israel. They were the first to disappoint God's hopes, and how bitterly! As we have seen, they were 'a choice vine', the treasure of Jehovah's vineyard, upon which he had lavished all his fondest care, until it spread from Lebanon to Egypt: and now this vine, in the fullness of its growth, proceeds as it were to destroy itself. So far from bearing fruits of holiness, it yields only sour grapes of impiety and unrighteousness.

Woe upon you, that must ever be acquiring house after house, field after neighbouring field, till all the world goes wanting! . . . Woe upon you, the men who must be up betimes to go a-drinking, and sit late into the evening, till you are heated with wine! Still you must have zither and harp, tambour and flute, and wine for your entertainment; you give no thought to God's dealings, to the world his hands have made . . . Woe upon you, the men who call evil good, and good evil; whose darkness is light, whose light darkness; who take bitter for sweet, and sweet for bitter! Woe upon you, that think yourselves wise, and boast of your own foresight! . . . that take bribes to acquit the guilty, and rob the innocent of his rights.[1]

That is what the vine of Israel came to, with social injustice on every hand, and hedonism and falsehood, and, worst of all, the sin of those who 'call evil good, and good evil', that is, such as will not even admit their own guilt, but seek to justify their conduct, thinking themselves wise, and boasting of their foresight.

And all this which was true of Israel is equally applicable to our own world and to each one of us. We know how God cares for his Church, the love and all the graces he has lavished upon it, with the blessed Eucharist perpetually at work in the world, the body and blood of Christ constantly nourishing us, as the living sap gives life to the branches of the vine, so that God continually bestows his own life upon the souls of men. Yet the vast world of men seems blind to all this, and deaf, and dumb, so that God seems to be wasting his time and his pains on them to no purpose; and among the rest, so many seem failures, more or less—not, indeed, a total loss, but partial failures, mediocrities. Seeing all this, and seeing the boundless expectations of Jehovah, it is impossible not to feel profoundly sad to think how we can disappoint him so much. It is no wonder that some people, namely the Saints, should want to mitigate this disappointment, and try to fall a little less short of God's

[1] Is. 5: 8, 11–12, 20–21, 23.

hopes by offering him a vine that he can sometimes bear to look at, consoling him with the knowledge that not all his labour is utterly in vain.

But if the vineyard is thus really profitless, if nothing comes of it, what shall Jehovah do? 'I call upon you to give award between my vineyard and me.' You have judges among you who are competent in human causes: how would you decide in such a case as this? What is to be done in such a situation? Clearly the useless, unprofitable investment is not worth keeping.

Let me tell you, then, what I mean to do to this vineyard of mine. I mean to rob it of its hedge, so that all can plunder it, to break down its wall, so that it will be trodden under foot. I mean to make waste-land of it; no more pruning and digging; only briars and thorns will grow there, and I will forbid the clouds to water it.

Well; but the husbandman must be heartbroken at finding himself obliged to ravage his own vineyard. There is nothing so sad for a craftsman as having to destroy his own tools; the worst thing that can happen to a sailor is to have to scuttle his own ship: when all one's heart and hopes are set upon a thing, there is no sorrow to equal the sorrow of having to throw it away because it is no good. That is what God has to bear because of the utter and irremediable worthlessness of his people, when it is just this people that he loved. We ourselves may have experienced the same thing from someone we loved and had great hopes of. We waited and waited, until there came a time when we felt it was all over. The spark we had hoped to see kindle in that heart was not there after all; we had thought that person capable of devotion, of spiritual achievement, but we saw him now sink deeper into his mediocrity, his moral or intellectual aberrations.

Such bitter disappointment, culminating in the knowledge that 'nothing can be done about it any more', was what the people of Israel did to God: and why he laid the vineyard waste. There was nothing for it but to let the land lie fallow under a grim crop of thorns and bramble. God gave it up; it might grow as it would: he left it to itself. 'Farewell, my home; I have done with my chosen people; the life that was so dear to me I have handed over to its enemies.'[1] These are the saddest words in the Bible, with all the poignant associations of that description, 'that was so dear to me.'

> My people grown strange to me, as lion snarling in its forest lair; what marvel if I am weary of it? My people grown strange to me as carrion-bird, its mottled plumage all bathed in blood! Gather here, beasts that roam the earth, eager for your prey. Drovers a many have laid waste my vineyard, trampled down my lands; the land I loved so, turned into a lonely wilderness! Desolate they have made it, and desolate it mourns for me now; a very picture of desolation, and all for the want of men with heeding hearts.[2]

If that were the end of the story, it would be a picture of everlasting despair; but it is not so, because through all the worst excesses of his faithless people, the heart of Jehovah was never finally turned against his vine. He allowed weeds to invade it, to take possession of the vineyard and altogether overgrow it, but he could never forget that it was his own vine; the memory of the love he bore it never died in him. He loved it too much for that, with a love too absolute, too irrevocable for him ever to be able not to love, in spite of the vilest degradation of the beloved; just as a man whose wife has utterly disgraced herself will never see her again, of course, and reckons her for lost, as though she were dead, yet she is still his wife, he cannot marry another. The Scriptural images that describe the bond between Jehovah and Israel mean all that. Whatever the infidelities of his people, Jehovah remains ever faithful to them. And so from

[1] Jer. 12: 7. [2] Jer. 12: 8–11.

the very depths of its abandonment, and in full consciousness of how it has belied all his hopes, the vine still
dares appeal to Jehovah, and ask him once more to take pity
on it.

This is the sense of the seventy-ninth Psalm, which is a
kind of sequel to the canticle in Isaiah, showing how the
chosen people never lost hope, for all their faithlessness.
After all they had done in God's sight, they were still not
afraid to remind him of his covenant, and tell him he had
no right to cast them off.

> Give audience, thou that art the guide of Israel . . . Lord God
> of hosts, wilt thou always turn away in anger from thy ser-
> vants' prayer? . . . Long ago, thou didst bring a vine out of
> Egypt, rooting out the heathen to plant it here; thou didst
> prepare the way for its spreading, and it took root where thou
> hadst planted it, filled the whole land. How it overshadowed
> the hills, how the cedars, divinely tall, were overtopped by its
> branches! It spread out its tendrils to the sea, its shoots as far
> as the great river. Why is it that in these days thou hast levelled
> its wall, for every passer-by to rob it of its fruit? See how the
> wild boar ravages it, how it gives pasture to every beast that
> roams! God of hosts, relent, look down from heaven, look to
> this vine that needs thy care. Revive the stock which thy
> own hand has planted, branches that by thee throve, and
> throve for thee.[1]

There is something sublime about the assurance, not to
say the impudence, of this reproachful attitude—'after all
it is your vine'! And the conclusion is splendid, too: 'Henceforth we will never forsake thee; grant us life, and we will
live only to invoke thy name.'[2] It is the old delusion of
turning over a new leaf: but all the same it still has this
much of real worth in it, that it springs from a right intention—less fruitful in subsequent performance, maybe, than
could have been expected, but real enough while it lasts to
be an opening for God's work in a man's heart.

[1] Ps. 79: 2, 5, 9–16.   [2] ibid. 79: 19

Just how far the chosen people would go in their ingratitude is shown by St Matthew in the parable of the wicked husbandman: and what is especially interesting about this passage is the quotation from the fifth chapter of Isaiah with which it begins, relating the parable directly to the Song of the Vine.

> Listen to another parable. There was a rich man who planted a vineyard; he walled it in, and dug a wine-press and built a tower in it, and then let it out to some vine-dressers, while he went on his travels. When vintage-time drew near, he sent his own servants on an errand to the vine-dressers, to claim his revenues. Whereupon, the vine-dressers laid hands upon his servants; one they beat, one they killed outright, one they stoned. And he sent other servants on a second errand, more than he had sent at first, but they were used no better. After that, he sent his own son to them; They will have reverence, he said, for my son. But when the vine-dressers found his son coming to them, they said among themselves, This is the heir; come, let us kill, and seize upon the inheritance. And they laid hands on him, thrust him out from the vineyard, and killed him. And now, what will the owner of the vineyard do to those vine-dressers when he returns? They said, he will bring those wretches to a wretched end, and will let out the vineyard to other vine-dressers, who will pay him his due when the season comes.[1]

To appreciate the full force of this Gospel parable, one must read it after the Song of the Vine, for it shows how the story ended. After waiting patiently for two thousand years, God at length sent his Son in person, to save his vine at all hazards, thinking: 'At least they will respect him.' But now, after all God's disappointments throughout the Old Testament, we see the crowning disappointment of all; for where the Prophets had failed, Christ himself was to fail. This is the last extremity and uttermost depth of defeat. Where the Son of God failed, who could have succeeded? Surely this

[1]Matt. 21: 33–41.

L.H.–N

must seem final, irreparable disaster. God's patience has been strained to its farthest limit in this tragedy of Christ, the Lord of the Vineyard's own son, rejected by the husbandmen, crucified, treated by his own people as a stranger and an outcast.

But from these lowest depths arises a sudden hope, the point of view is completely reversed: 'He will bring those wretches to a wretched end, and will let out the vineyard to other vine-dressers, who will pay him his due when the season comes.' Christ's failure with the people of Israel, the tragedy of Good Friday, when Israel rejected him that was sent, becomes in God's plan the means whereby the vine planted in Israel was to break out in a new and vigorous growth. In fact, it was to bring forth for the first time the fruit expected of it. Hitherto there had been nothing but wild grapes: the whole of the Old Testament, so far as concerns the chosen people, is nothing but wild grapes, with here and there at most a few single fruit a little less sour— but no produce from the vine of mankind that God could really appreciate; the whole thing was a failure. Now, through the Passion and Resurrection of Christ, stems the true and faithful vine. At this moment of time the Divine plan is modified and enlarged: God plants another vine beyond the boundaries of Israel, the vine of the Catholic Church grafted upon the stock of Jesus Christ, the vine that shall at last bring forth from the souls of men the quality of fruit that God had looked for.

> I am the true vine, and it is my Father who tends it. The branch that yields no fruit in me, he cuts away; the branch that does yield fruit, he trims clean, so that it may yield more fruit. You, through the message I have preached to you, are clean already; you have only to live on in me, and I will live on in you. The branch that does not live on in the vine can yield no fruit of itself; no more can you, if you do not live on in me. I am the vine, you are its branches; if a man lives on in me, and I in him, then he will yield abundant fruit; separated from me,

you can have no power to do anything. If a man does not live on in me, he can only be like the branch that is cast off and withers away; such a branch is picked up and thrown into the fire, to burn there. As long as you live on in me, and my words live on in you, you will be able to make what request you will, and have it granted. My Father's name has been glorified, if you yield abundant fruit.[1]

Here is the whole story in a few words: it is quite simple after all, and easily explained. 'Separated from me, you have no power to do anything'—there is the history of Israel; no wonder Israel was a failure: 'separated from me, you have no power to do anything'. The whole burden of the story of the chosen people was that man is powerless to achieve for himself the result that God expects of him; the purpose of the story was to deepen man's desire and longing for the true vine. Then the true vine appeared, in the person of Jesus Christ: and as he is the true vine, God's perfect masterpiece, it is only through our share in his life that we too may become the true vine.

In the first place, Christ, the true vine, the absolute perfection of the divine working, crowns with final success the labour of God's hands ever since the world began. So we may fairly say that everything else was only preparing the ground: up to this point, God was still removing the stones from the earth, and tilling the soil. Not until now was it possible for the true vine to grow. Thus Israel was not the true vine. Jesus Christ alone represents the fulfilment of God's purpose. All the trouble God had taken was justified, by this complete and perfect success in Jesus Christ. The grace of God bears its plenitude of fruit in him; God can rest for ever from his labours, now that human nature brings forth this incomparable harvest of holiness. The response which the people of Israel had never been able to give is now given in perfection by God himself in the manhood of Jesus Christ, of the seed of Israel. All God's pleasure

[1] John 15: 1–8.

is in Jesus Christ, his everlasting vine, the eternal source of satisfaction without end: 'This is my beloved Son, in whom I am well pleased.'[1]

Then we too may take our pleasure in him for ever: this is a second aspect of the mystery. Jesus Christ is there for us to rest in, and when we see our own failures, he is there to be relied upon in his unfailing perfection: when we have nothing to give, his priestly action is there for us to offer, glorifying God perfectly and for ever. And, what is more, he is the stock upon which we are grafted; he is the beginning and the head, the vital principle of the true vine, not only in his personal humanity, but in the whole Church, spreading from the cedars of Lebanon, as the seventy-ninth Psalm says, to the great river, and from the sea to the rising of the sun, covering the whole world with its shadow, in which all men may come and rest.

This puts the whole problem in a new perspective: it is only a matter of being engrafted upon Christ. That is what baptism does for us. Hence the relevance of that commentary of St Zeno upon the Song of the Vine, delivered in the presence of the catechumens whom he was about to baptize in the course of the Easter Vigil:

Dearly beloved brethren, this parable of the Vine would require much time for a full interpretation; but the hour of the sacraments is upon us, so that I cannot develop the theme as it deserves. Here, then, is a foretaste of what it means, and no more, lest we should delay the solemnities to come. The Lord's vine was first of all the Synagogue . . . which produced thorns instead of fruit, or wild grapes instead of sweet. Then the Lord was angry with it, and laid it waste, and planted another according to his will, our holy Mother the Church. He tilled it with the labours of his priests: . . . he fixed it to the blessed wood of the Cross and taught it to bear an abundant crop. Even so the new branches among you to-day have been brought up to the Cross, and shall fill the Lord's cellar with single-hearted rejoicing.[2]

[1]Matt. 3: 17.　[2]*Tractatus* II: 28. P.L. 11: 471–2.

There could hardly be a more compendious account of the whole theology of that Vine, which was formerly the Synagogue and is now the Church. It grows throughout the centuries, as new branches are grafted upon the one stock, until it fills the whole earth. Each of the great nations of the world shall bear its bunch of saints. There will be no Second Coming until all the great systems of civilization have been evangelized and have fulfilled themselves in Christianity. We are only at the sixth hour of the day: there are labourers standing in the market-place, whose contract of service, or covenant, will not begin until the ninth, or the eleventh hour. To every one the same wages of grace are offered, but not to all at once. This method of management is part of the mystery of God's redemptive plan, a jealously-guarded secret: 'am I not free to use my money as I will?'[1] Who will be the labourers of the ninth hour? What new bunch will ripen next on the vine of the Church? We can only watch, and wonder at the miracle of God's plan as it mysteriously unfolds. Will it be China that shall reveal a new age of Christendom in the world, and bear new fruits of sainthood? Or perhaps it will be the cultures of the black races, whose profoundly religious instinct shall renew within the Church the sense of mystery, and the liturgical spirit, and the heart of a little child. Economic crises may come and go, and empires cease to struggle for the mastery of the world, but the Church will still be engaged in her unalterable task of building up to its full stature the incorruptible Body of Christ.

As with the salvation of mankind, so in the life of each one of us the solution of the problem is the same. There is no question of achieving perfection for ourselves: all that matters is to have within us the strength of Jesus Christ, and then he will achieve in us the results we never can produce by our own efforts. We have used the word 'success': it would be dangerously misleading if it were associ-

[1] Matt. 20: 15.

ated with any idea of self-confidence; but now it is clear that success is quite unattainable except through Jesus Christ, who alone can achieve it in us, causing our own life to flower in a radiant life of love; and then our soul will really be a fertile and a fruitful vine, answering God's expectation.

Thus it is that the true romance of the vine, which began with the eager hopes of first love and betrothal in the bright days of the Patriarchs, and which then turned to stark tragedy in the failure of God, concludes with fresh triumphs in Jesus Christ, whose incomparable achievement surpasses all the earlier promise.

CHAPTER THREE

CHRISTOLOGY AND HISTORY

I<small>N</small> working out the two themes with which we have been engaged, the history of salvation can be traced through the Old Testament along two lines: on the one hand, it appears as a series of divine interventions, a narrative of the *gesta Dei*; on the other, as the story of successive human responses. The human aspect of this reciprocity has been shown as rather negative; though strictly there is another side to the picture; there is progress in the Old Testament as well, as will appear later. But just as it was not our aim, when speaking of the wrath of God, to exhaust the tale of his visitations, so here we were concerned only to give instances.

It remains true to say that throughout the Old Testament the two lines of our exposition belong to two separate fields of thought and experience. At the end of each inquiry it was found that this dual history could only be fully apprehended, and only reached its own fulfilment, in the person of the incarnate Word. Here is the end of the chapter of the works of God, itself the most wonderful of all: here, too, the culmination of the progress of the people of God through the ascending scale of types. In this point of view, Christ is seen to be at once the key, and the central point, of history. The dogmatic definition of the two natures in Christ by the Council of Chalcedon illuminates the whole theology of history.

The Protestant theologian Jean-Louis Leuba, in a recent book (*L'institution et l'évènement*), has compared the

New Testament doctrine of Christ with the Christological
definitions of Chalcedon, criticizing the latter for having
'suppressed one dimension of the gospel message, namely,
time'. He goes on to say:

> The Council's formula shows the full development into Chris-
> tological speculation of the theological doctrine of the Logos; it
> is instinct with the same notions of substance as characterize
> the whole philosophical movement from which it springs. The
> concepts employed are entirely static—essence, nature, person.
> In the New Testament, the unity of Christ exists and appears
> only in the unfolding story of the conception and birth of
> Jesus, his death, resurrection, ascension, kingdom and second
> coming . . . This is not to say that the definitions of Chal-
> cedon are false, but that they bear the same relation to New
> Testament Christology as the trace of a movement bears to the
> movement itself.

According to this account, the distinguishing mark of the
doctrine of Chalcedon is anti-historicism. It is perhaps an
over-simplification to say that the theologians of the fifth
century no longer concerned themselves with the time-
process: Jacques Liebaert, in his book on the Christological
doctrine of St Cyril of Alexandria, shows how important it
was for him at least. But the period was, admittedly, one of
recession in regard to those historical preoccupations which
dominated much of the thinking of the earlier centuries,
from Irenaeus to Augustine. The shift of emphasis can be
traced in the evolution of Augustine's own work. It corresponds to a change in the situation of Christianity, which had
at first to vindicate its own historical emergence upon the
pagan and Jewish scene, but was now itself a part of history.
A certain fading of eschatological prepossessions occurs even
in the text of the Creed, where the words 'in these last
days', qualifying the article of the Incarnation—which was
part of the primitive Kerygma, and is still found in the
fourth century[1]—finally disappears. Consequently, the de-

[1] Gal. 4: 4; 1 Pet. 1: 20; *Const. Apost.* VII: 41 (Funk, I: 444).

finition of the Council of Chalcedon is indeed designed rather to establish the intrinsic principles of Christology than to situate the person of Christ in the history of salvation.

But the definition is by no means irrelevant to the theology of history. On the contrary. This very preoccupation, at the time of Chalcedon, with the substantive principles of the Incarnation, means that the fundamental problems of eschatology were, in the last analysis, to be resolved along these lines. It is because of the union of the two natures that Christ can be understood as the fulfilment of the Old Testament, and as the end ($\tau\acute{\epsilon}\lambda o\varsigma$) of the whole plan of salvation; it is in the same way, finally, that his second coming can be shown to represent the consummation of this plan. The dogma of Chalcedon thus provides a basis for the theology of history, which, otherwise, is liable either to founder in a doctrine of endless Becoming, or to evaporate in a timeless Ideal. These aberrations are actually found in the first ages of Christianity, as Ebionism on the one hand and Gnosticism on the other; the last traces of them persist among Nestorians and Monophysites. The same errors reappear even now when thinkers disregard the precise terms of Chalcedon, and consequently abandon all real eschatology: for it is just this definition that gives a structure to time, and turns it into history.

I

As far as it concerns the theology of history, the essential contribution of the New Testament is the affirmation of Christ as the present reality of the prophetic predictions of the Old. It is not the purpose of the New Testament to proclaim the existence of a paradise to come—the Old Testament is full of that message, but in the New, paradise is here and now, with Christ: 'This day thou shalt be with me in Paradise.'[1] It is not the purpose of the New Testament to declare that a servant of God shall be sacrificed for the sins of the world, but that Christ is this lamb that was slain: 'Look, this is the Lamb of God; look, this is he who takes away the sin of the world';[2] and that the immolation of this victim fulfils the destiny of mankind.[3] The New Testament is precisely the record of this present reality, this *Dasein*. The operative words are *hodie, ecce*. This is what makes the Gospel 'news', as St Irenaeus rightly saw: it 'introduced an altogether new thing, bringing forth now him that had been foretold'.[4]

With the coming of Christ, 'the last days' of which the Old Testament speaks have arrived. The New Testament declares it in many passages. 'In old days, God spoke to our fathers in many ways and by many means, through the prophets; now at last in these times he has spoken to us with a Son to speak for him.'[5] These 'last times' refer to the Incarnation: '. . . till the appointed time came. Then God sent out his Son.'[6] Again, the reference is to the Passion and Resurrection: 'he has been revealed once for all, at the moment when history reached its fulfilment, annulling our sin by his sacrifice'[7]; 'it was his loving design, centred in Christ, to give history its fulfilment by resuming everything in him'.[8]

These are the 'last days' spoken of by the prophets of the Old Testament: and it appears on examination that the eschatological prophecies belong to two quite distinct traditions. In one, the Old Testament declares that Jehovah will perform such wonders at the end of time as shall put into the shade all the mighty works he has accomplished for Israel in the past. These prophecies directly concern God himself, whose coming is thus foretold by Isaiah: 'Make way for the Lord's coming; a straight road for our

[1]Luke 23: 43.   [2]John 1: 29.   [3]Apoc. 5: 6–7; 1 Pet. 1: 19–20.
[4]*Adv. haer* IV: 34.1.   [5]Heb. 1: 1–2.   [6]Gal. 4: 4.   [7]Heb. 9: 26.
[8]Eph. 1: 9–10.

God through the desert.'[1] It is Jehovah that will 'create new
heavens and a new earth',[2] and dwell in the new Zion,[3] and
sit in judgement on the nations.[4] The Scriptures as a whole
are a chronicle of the *gesta Dei*, revealing God, not in his
eternal being, but in his actions in the world of time. The
God of the Bible is always a living God, breaking in upon
history, drawing near to men. This immediate presence of
God, which is the mark of the Old Testament, is to be
incomparably accentuated in the last days.

There is also a second, altogether different tone of prophetic tradition in the Old Testament, the prediction of a
Messiah to come, the instrument of God's purpose in the
fullness of times. Just as God at first made man and put him
in Paradise, so a new man shall be created in the last days,
and brought into the Paradise to be.[5] Abraham receives the
promise of a seed in whom 'all the races of the world shall
find a blessing'.[6] Jehovah declares to Moses that he will raise
up from the midst of his brethren a greater prophet than
himself.[7] David learns from Nathan that God 'will grant
thee for successor a son of thy own body, established firmly
on his throne . . . dynasty and royalty both shall endure;
thy throne shall remain for ever unshaken'.[8] This is the
typological relationship of Israel to Christ, not strictly a
matter of theology: the reference here is not to God himself,
coming again to complete the series of the divine interventions in the history of his chosen people, but to a human
being, a representative of that same people prefigured,
albeit dimly, by its kings and prophets. This is the authentic
Messianic tradition.

The two streams of prophecy remain radically distinct
throughout the Old Testament: the coming of Jehovah in
the last days to judge the world from his eternal habitation,
and the coming of Messiah to set Israel free from her

[1]Is. 40: 3.   [2]ibid. 65: 17.   [3]ibid. 4: 5.   [4]ibid. 2: 4.
[5]Daniélou, *Sacramentum futuri*, pp. 6–7.   [6]Gen. 12: 3.
[7]Deut. 18: 15.   [8]2 Kings 7: 12, 16.

enemies and to inaugurate a new people, are envisaged in reality as two separate events, and give rise to two divergent literary traditions. From the first comes the idiom of transcendental eschatology, culminating in the apocalyptic books; from the second, temporal messianism, represented in the main by the prophetic books. In later Judaism, some efforts were made to harmonize these points of view, but for the most part only through introducing an order of succession between two phases: the earthly kingdom of Messiah, to be followed by the coming of Jehovah in the end of the world.

The essential doctrine of the New Testament is that these two things come together in Jesus. The evangelists attribute to him the fulfilment at once of the prophecies that foretold the coming of Jehovah, and those concerning the Messiah. They quote of him the words of Isaias about the preparations for Jehovah in the desert,[1] and identify in him the new Moses leading the chosen people out into the desert in a new Exodus.[2] He is that new Israel, whose faithfulness is contrasted with the infidelity of the old;[3] he is also that God who sets up his dwelling in the midst of the new Israel.[4] He is at once God, giving the New Law from the Mountain,[5] and the Prophet foretold by Moses, making known to the people what is the will of God. His name is κύριος, Lord, the scriptural designation of divine sovereignty—and χρίστος, the messianic king.

Two kinds of history terminate in the one person of Christ. He appears within the historical framework of mankind, which he brings to its fulfilment—that is the significance of the genealogies of Christ at the beginning of Matthew and Luke. St Leo, using this argument against Eutyches, as proving the reality of human nature in Christ, brings out the force of the two-fold genealogy: 'The evangelist Matthew, following the sequence of generations, shows how the promise made to Abraham was fulfilled in Christ,

[1]Matt. 3: 3. [2]Mk. 9: 4. [3]Matt. 4: 4. [4]John 1: 14. [5]Matt. 5: 21.

in whom all families of the earth shall be blessed. The evangelist Luke, starting from the birth of the Saviour, traces back the series of his ancestors, to show that the ages before the Flood are included in this mystery, so that all generations from the beginning culminate in him that is the salvation of all men.'[1] And in another sermon, St Leo emphasizes Christ's kinship in the seed of David.[2] Thus the three filiations of Christ, from David, from Abraham, and from Adam, are successively brought out into prominence.

But on the other hand, part of Christ's activity visibly continues the record of Jehovah's action in the Old Testament—the creation, the dwelling in a tabernacle made with hands, the making of a covenant, the destruction of death. These are works of God, in line with the wonders chronicled in the former narrative of divine interventions. Together with the genealogical continuity, linking Christ with the sons of Adam, we find a theological continuity: his work belongs to the historical framework of the *mirabilia Dei*, of which it is the last and supreme instance. How these two successions come together in one was the critical problem of primitive Christology. Christ himself indicated the terms of it when he asked the Pharisees: 'David calls Christ his Master; how can he be also his son?'[3]

There was no doubt of the fact that Christ fulfils both types of prophecy: the question was as to the manner of this fusion of two things in one person. Some of the Biblical formulae were open to several interpretations. By attending too exclusively to the human filiation of Christ, and his prefiguration in the heroes of the Old Testament story, it was possible to fall into an adoptionist solution, in which the Saviour is regarded simply as a man full of the presence of God. The Antiochene theologians ran this risk; Nestorius succumbed to it. Alternatively, when soteriology alone was taken into consideration, as by the school of Alexandria,

[1]*Serm.* X *in Nat.* P.L. 54, 234. [2]*Serm.* IV *in Nat.* P.L. 54, 204.
[3]Matt. 22: 45.

and the Incarnation was seen as nothing else but the saving work of God, there might be a tendency to minimize the humanity of Christ, and the significance of his human genealogy for the seed of Abraham which he assumed and brings to perfection.

The dogma of Chalcedon, however, furnishes an unambiguous answer to the eschatological problem of Christianity. If Christ is 'the last Adam' the mystery of his personality contains the truth about 'the last things'. Christological definition opens the way to a right judgement of the theological meaning of history. The formula for the union of the two natures in the incarnate Word, saving the perfect integrity of each and the unity of the person, was the key for interpreting much evidence that was otherwise indecisive. In the words of Dom Jean Leclercq epitomizing the thought of St Leo: 'Among the prophetic witnesses to the Messiah, some foretold him as God, others as man. The hypostatic union harmonizes the testimony.'

II

Granted that the person of Christ is the point of intersection of the two Old Testament themes, there is a further stage to make good, namely to grasp that this is not simply a point among others, a term of reference for a continuous line, but an absolute termination, in the sense that there can be nothing beyond: the possibilities of development are exhausted. Here we face a characteristic paradox of Christianity. Although the time-process continues, and the last day, or chronological end of the world, is in the future, yet the ultimate reality is already present, in the person of the incarnate Word; there is not, because there cannot be, anything beyond this.

This note of finality is clearly marked in the New Testament—especially in the Epistle to the Hebrews, where the twofold conception of definitive achievement, and eternal validity, is strongly emphasized: '. . . . to enter, once for

all, into the sanctuary; the ransom he has won lasts for
ever . . . Thus, through his intervention, a new covenant
has been bequeathed to us . . . and then the destined
heirs were to obtain, for ever, their promised inheritance
. . . He has been revealed once for all (ἅπαξ), at the
moment when history reached its fulfilment . . . By a
single offering he has completed his work, for all time, in
those whom he sanctifies.'[1] These passages deploy a whole
series of terms to indicate the absolute finality of Christ's
work—accomplished once for all, obtained eternally, perfected for ever. This last expression covers both senses, the
attainment of the goal, and also total perfection. In the
Incarnation of Christ, then, we have a beginning, compris-
ing all futurity: perhaps the most paradoxical feature of the
Christian idea of time.

It is the whole creative work of God that is brought to its
conclusion in the incarnation. E. Stauffer summarizes, on
this point, the content of New Testament theology: 'Thus
the λόγος of the first day, the Creator's *fiat*, himself takes
on historical form and becomes subject to successive development, completing in himself the entire work of the
creation in its substantive historical reality.' The Fathers
make use of similar language, as for example in this passage
of St Hilary, recorded in the patristic collections of Theodoretus: 'The only son of God is born a man of the Virgin
Mary, to achieve in his own person the elevation (προκοπή)
of man to God in the fulness of time.'[2] It is of particular
interest to find in this single text the three main themes of
our present study assembled together: the human birth of
Christ, the fulness of time, and the deification of man.

But if the incarnation of the eternal Word is in fact the
ultimate, unsurpassable fulfilment of things, there remains
the metaphysical question why this must be so: and here
again the answer is to be found in the definitions of Chalcedon. The incarnation is the τέλος precisely because it

[1] Heb. 9: 12, 15, 26; 10: 14.   [2] P.G. 83: 205 D.

admits of nothing further. In the person of the Incarnate
Word, the union between the two natures, man and God,
is such that no better identification is conceivable, for the
humanity taken by the Word becomes the personal nature of
the son of God himself. The hypostatic union defined by the
Council expresses that perfection of unity which is τέλος because τελείωσις, not just the end but the total fulfilment of man.

By this union, the purpose of mankind's existence is completely achieved. In the first place, mankind enters upon
the life of God. The grace of the hypostatic union, belonging as of right to the Son in person, is the source of deification for all who belong to him. So, for St Paul, and for
the Fathers of the fourth and fifth centuries who borrowed
his language, Christ is the 'firstfruits' of sanctified humanity. Gregory of Nyssa, in particular, developed this line of
thought, against Apollinaris. 'In the last days, the Word of
God, uniting himself to the lowliness of our human nature,
is made flesh for the love of man, and being made one with
mankind has taken the whole of human nature into himself, so that mankind should be deified in him through this
union with the Godhead, the whole mass being sanctified
through these firstfruits'.[1] This deification of mankind is
the destiny for which the race was providentially intended.

Here, once more, the definition of Chalcedon is closely
relevant, for it is an intrinsic element of the broad patristic
tradition (though particularly evident in the Cappadocian
Fathers) that 'nothing is deified but what is assumed': so
that only the complete integrity of human nature in Christ
guarantees its deification. Thus Gregory of Nyssa argued
against Apollinaris, from the fact that free-will is essential
to man, that if Christ had not human freedom, the deification of man would be illusory. Theodoretus makes the same
point against Eutyches: 'Christ did not simply weave a vesture for the Godhead, as heretical impostures would have it;
he achieved the firstfruits of victory for all his kind, through

[1]P.G. 45: 1152 C.

his assumption of human nature in its entirety.'[1] In another expression, Theodoretus echoes the unanimity of tradition: 'He took upon him the whole of sinful human nature in order to heal it wholly.'[2]

Inasmuch, then, as the final purpose of creation requires the union of the Lords of creation with their Maker, this is fulfilled in the hypostatic union: but the same is true of the larger conception of the end of creatures, namely 'to glorify God'. To give glory to God is the priestly work *par excellence*, and is accomplished in perfection by Christ, whose eternal priesthood flows from the incarnation itself.[3] He is not priest by reason of his divine nature antecedently of the Incarnation, as some of the Fathers maintained; nor does his priesthood begin with his baptism, or with the Passion or the Ascension, as others have held. It flows from the hypostatic union, and dates from the first instant of his incarnate existence, according to the received doctrine, finally worked out by St Thomas Aquinas.[4] The priestly work of Christ glorifies God in the most perfect manner possible; it is the ultimate act of worship, putting an end to all other sacrifices: Christ's sacrifice is for ever the public liturgy, or common prayer, of the whole creation. Through him all creatures attain to their last end, which is to glorify God.

And again we are back at Chalcedon, since it is as man that Christ is priest, through the hypostatic union in which humanity freely offers to God the homage of a perfect worship—for which alone it was created. If this worship were not the act of Christ's human nature, then it would not be mankind that glorified God in him: but Christ as man is priest as well as victim. This was not always clearly understood before the Council of Chalcedon. A number of the Fathers, as has been said, derived Christ's priesthood from the divine nature of the eternal Word, which may be regarded as an aftermath of subordinationist theories; and

---

[1]*Adv. haer.* V: 11. (P.G. 83: 492.)   [2]ibid. P.G. 83: 489 D.
[3]Heb. 5: 5–6.   [4]*S. Th.* III: xxii.

Cyril of Alexandria emphasized the personal agency of the Word in offering the perfect sacrifice, in such a way as to obscure the instrumentality of his human nature in the performance of this act. Theodoretus on the other hand is perfectly clear: 'The proper work of a priest is to offer gifts: Christ was anointed priest in his human nature, and offered no other sacrifice than that of his own body.'[1]

In defining the absolute perfection of the union of natures in the person of the incarnate Word, the Council of Chalcedon defined also the eschatological quality and significance of this hypostatic union. For, as we have seen, this quality consists simply in the fact that the uniting of human nature with the divine was effected in Christ for ever: which follows from the eternal inseparability of the two kinds, each maintaining its perfect identity. Christ is truly mediator because he is both perfect God, and perfect man, without confusion of natures. So the Epistle to the Hebrews links the idea of Christ's mediation with the notion of irrevocability: what was 'once for all' accomplished in him will not be undone 'for ever'. This is how the incarnation belongs to eschatology.

Hence the special danger of the doctrine of Eutyches, which obscured the permanent distinction of the two kinds, each perfect in itself, and could imply some measure of absorption of the human nature into the nature of God. It was the eschatological aspect of the theology of the incarnation that was, we may say, undermined by Eutyches. His system seemed to imply that the glorification of human nature in its union with the Word of God transposed this nature into the Godhead, so that there was a difference in kind between the humanity assumed in the Incarnation and the humanity glorified in the resurrection, the latter having lost its distinctive properties by a sort of amalgamation with the divinity of Christ.

Against this tendency towards confusion, the Council of

[1] P.G. 83: 57 D.

Chalcedon reacted by declaring that the humanity of Christ preserves its own proper quality for ever, albeit transfigured: thus affirming that the Incarnation, the union of the two distinct natures without confusion, belongs with 'the last things', to eschatology, being the goal and conclusion of God's plan, subsisting for ever in its own unique reality. This Christian idea is quite incompatible with any pantheistic theory of the eventual absorption of creatures into the essential oneness of God. For us, creation keeps for ever the ultimate form it once attained in the personal union of mankind with the divine nature: history, having reached an end in this reality, loses nothing of its real structure. Christian eschatology requires for its right understanding a knowledge of the truly human origin of Christ's humanity, and of the persistence of this humanity to the end: the definitions of Chalcedon safeguard both alike.

III

Jesus Christ, God and man in the unity of one person, represents the last end, the $\tau\acute{\epsilon}\lambda o\varsigma$ of history, but not indeed the finish, $\pi\acute{\epsilon}\rho\alpha\varsigma$. After this there is a period of waiting, while the work done by Christ is promulgated and takes effect throughout the human race. He is the culmination of the Old Testament, but also the First-born of the new creature: not only $\dot{\alpha}\rho\chi\acute{\eta}$ and $\tau\acute{\epsilon}\lambda o\varsigma$, alpha and omega, but also, from another point of view, the $\tau\acute{\epsilon}\lambda o\varsigma$-$\dot{\alpha}\rho\chi\acute{\eta}$, the end of one world and beginning of another, the turning-point of history. This pattern is another of the distinguishing marks of the Christian theology of history. It is prefigured in the story of Noah, who represents both the judgement and destruction of the old world and the inauguration of a new.[1] It is finally worked out in the mystery of the passion and resurrection of Jesus Christ, when the old world came to an end and the new creation was brought into being, both alike in the one divine person. What is now awaited is

[1]Daniélou, *Sacr. fut.*, p. 61.

the completion of the new creature in the gradual building up of the body of Christ.

The word eschatology is, in any case, normally used only in connexion with events which have yet to come about. It refers to 'the last things', *novissima*, that is, the events which determine the conclusion of this world as we know it: the Second Coming, judgement and general resurrection. True, the New Testament declares that these last things are substantially fulfilled in Christ himself. Christ is called He that was to come; with him, judgement is given: 'Sentence is now being passed on this world.'[1] He is 'the resurrection and life'.[2] But Christ is still He that cometh: the Apocalypse ends with the ancient Jewish-Christian prayer *Maranatha*, 'Come, Lord'.[3] The prince of this world is already cast out, but not yet powerless; it is only in the end of time that the last enemy shall be dispossessed, death.[4] This victory is to be established in the general resurrection, when Christ's personal conquest, already effective in the souls of mankind, shall be extended over the whole physical world.

How are we to understand this period of waiting, which constitutes 'time' for the universal Church militant? The questions involved here were tentatively approached, but only partially answered, in the first part of this book. Are we to think of 'waiting' for the end of a process of development? What sort of development—that of the Church, growing to its full stature? What sort of growth—numerical extension (as the early Fathers believed) until the number of the elect is made up? or the dissemination of the Gospel in all the civilizations of mankind, a world-wide extension of Christianity? Then, again, are we to suppose a direct relation between our time of waiting and the development of secular history? Is mankind itself progressing towards some kind of maturity or full growth that will one day be attained? If so, is there any connexion between the secular achievements of men—the progress of civilization—and the

[1]John 12:31.　[2]John 11: 25.　[3]Apoc. 22: 20.　[4]1 Cor. 15: 26.

second coming of the Lord? Or, contrariwise, is the Lord's coming connected rather with the mystery of iniquity, a sort of persistent degeneration of the world until the measure of wickedness is full?

These contrasting points of view, which are by no means equally valid, are not exhaustive. It can be held that the second coming of Christ is in no way determined by any extraneous circumstances, but depends solely on the sovereign freedom of God's will. So understood, the present situation of mankind is an unconditional awaiting—a looking forward to something, without any possibility of human preparation, something which is essentially unpredictable. In this point of view, the whole duty of man is to be in suspense, and the Church's mission is simply to preach repentance before the coming doom. The growth of the Church on earth is entirely irrelevant to this issue—there can be no question of measuring the stages or accelerating the progress of the last judgement. Still less is it possible to imagine any relationship between the approach of the last day and the unfolding of human history. History has no common measure with the expectation of the Second Coming, and is therefore quite devoid of any eschatological significance. In a word, there is no more history after Christ.

Here, then, are two irreconcilable conceptions: but arguments in favour of either can be drawn from the New Testament.

On one hand there are outlines of a theology of history, and a distinction of successive times. Christ himself enumerated, among the signs foretelling his second coming, this, that 'this gospel of the kingdom must first be preached all over the world, so that all nations may hear the truth; only after that will the end come'.[1] This looks as if evangelistic progress were a pre-condition of his coming again. St Paul, again, in the Epistle to the Romans, says that the conversion of the Gentiles will be followed by the re-uniting of

[1] Matt. 24: 14.

Israel, which suggests one more in a series of stages.[1] In the
Second Epistle of Peter, against those who wonder at the
Lord's delaying his return, it is said that 'the Lord is not
being dilatory over his promise . . . he is only giving you
more time, because his will is . . . not that some should be
lost':[2] a clear indication, it would seem, that the world-wide
extension of Christian preaching was required before the
Second Coming could take place. It is, of course, in each case,
not the advance of civilization, but the growth of the
Church, that is under discussion.

Yet on the other hand, there are even more texts that
can be adduced in favour of the contrary opinion. The very
next words in the passage just quoted from the Second
Epistle of Peter, about the prolongation of the penitential
time, are one example: 'But the day of the Lord is coming,
and when it comes, it will be upon you like a thief.'[3] The
same theme is of frequent occurrence in Christ's own
preaching: 'if the master of the house had known at what
time of night the thief was coming, he would have kept
watch . . . And you too must stand ready; the Son of
Man will come at an hour when you are not expecting
him.'[4] The end of the world is presented as proceeding from
an act of the Divine will, utterly free and wholly un-
conditioned. It will be in God's good time: as with all other
καιροί, in Cullmann's words, 'regarded from the historical
standpoint as man sees it, the choice of the *kairoi* that constitute the redemptive history is arbitrary. The New
Testament, therefore, gives as the principle of this divine
"selection" of the *kairoi* only the "sovereign divine power".
. . . To men, even to the disciples, it is not granted to
know the date of the still future *kairoi*.'[5]

Both conceptions are represented in the writings of the
Fathers on the subject of the moment of Christ's first coming. In some of these there may be found traces of an

[1]Rom. 11: 15.   [2]2 Pet. 3: 9.   [3]2 Pet. 3: 10.   [4]Matt. 24: 43–44.
[5]*Christ and Time* (trs. Filson, 1951), p. 40.

attempt to define circumstances characteristic of 'the last days' in which it was fitting that this event should occur. Irenaeus already saw the history of mankind as a progression leading up to its proper term in the birth of Christ. Such views were still represented in the fourth century. Gregory of Nyssa describes the continuous process of education through which God prepared mankind for the coming of the Son: monotheism must first take deep root in men's minds before they could receive the revelation of the Holy Trinity;[1] God dwelt in the Temple to prepare us for that closer indwelling represented by the Incarnation.[2] All such teaching concludes or presupposes that 'the last days' (whether of the first or the second advent) come at the end of a process of human development. This process is not always presented as progress. The 'last days' are sometimes related to the limit of a course of degeneration. St Gregory of Nyssa, in particular, elaborates this theme: 'The invisible God, by a merciful dispensation, in the end and consummation of the world when sin has done its worst, unites himself to our human nature.'[3] The reasoning here (derived from Origen) is that every symptom of evil had to be actualized before the remedy could be adequate to the disease: 'In the last days of mankind, our sin having done its worst, so that no disease should be left without remedy, the Word consented to share the lowliness of our nature.'[4] Thus the unfolding of history is conceived both as progress and as decadence.

But on the other hand there is the point of view from which it is not by any means obvious that the moment of Christ's first advent really was that in which mankind achieved its fullest stature, or the sins of men came to a climax. St Leo represents this opposite conception, when he refers to 'the fulness of time, determined in the inscrutable

[1]P.G. 46: 697 A. [2]P.G. 44: 532 C–D. [3]P.G. 45: 1180 B–C.
[4]P.G. 45: 1252 B. Cf. Cyril of Alexandria, P.G. 76: 1121 A–1125 D; Leo, *Serm.* III *in Epiph.*, P.L. 54: 241.

decrees of divine wisdom'.[1] The timing of the Incarnation is reckoned among the darkest secrets of providence. It cannot be tied to any human preconditions whatever. There is no question of a progress leading up to this as to its goal, or yet of a degeneration requiring this in its ultimate phase. There could be no formula for prognosticating the moment of Christ's coming.

What the Fathers had to say of the first advent is equally applicable to the Second Coming. The eschatological attitude essentially involves this duality.

Among those who conceive a direct relation between human history and the second coming of our Lord, various Fathers of the first three centuries, and Hippolytus in particular, devoted much effort to speculations upon the 'weeks of years' in the book of Daniel, or upon the seven millennia, with a view to dating the end of the world. Others worked out a system based on the succession of empires. Eusebius founded the theology of history upon the providential coincidence of Christian monotheism and Constantinian monarchy. People are always elaborating such projects—Bossuet made the framework of his *Discours sur l'histoire universelle* to this pattern, and in our own generation, the idea of successive civilizations, as Toynbee, for instance, exhibits it, springs from the same source.

As early as the third century, however, the particular hypothesis of Hippolytus was already challenged by Origen, who declared for the radical independence of the Church's growth from the course of human history. After him, Augustine inclined for a while towards the chiliastic doctrines prevalent among the Latin Doctors of the West, but eventually came round to the idea of a distinction and discontinuity between the history of the *civitas Dei* and the history of human empires. The point is well taken by Karl Löwith: 'It is true that Augustine failed to relate the first cause, that is, God's providential plan, to the "secondary

[1] *Serm.* I *in Nat.*, P.L. 54: 191.

causes" operative in the process as such. But it is precisely the absence of a detailed correlation between secular and sacred events which distinguishes Augustine's Christian apology from Bossuet's more elaborate theology of political history.'[1] Reinhold Niebuhr's contemporary eliminating of any ideological notions of progress from the history of salvation is evidence of a similar reaction.

But neither of these two contrasting points of view can finally be held to the exclusion of the other: which brings us back once more to the definitions of Chalcedon, showing how the two theological positions involved are strictly complementary. Just as the dogma of the hypostatic union, illuminating the course of past history, enabled us to reconcile the two opposing tendencies of the Old Testament, reaching their single culmination in Christ, so the same doctrine, illuminating time to come, provides the definitive interpretation of world history in the period of waiting before the second advent.

On the one hand, the history of this time consists of the mighty works of God, the Sacramental activity of the Church, foreshadowing and preparing the eschatological events to come in the end of the world. In this aspect, the history of salvation, from the creation to the last day, concerns one everlasting presence of God among men; its supreme moment is in Christ's Incarnation, as its termination will be in his Second Coming. This history has no other laws than the sovereign wisdom and liberty of God himself.

But it is also true to say of this period that it consists in a development of the Incarnation. The Word of God took flesh in the unbroken succession of human generations to ensure the completion of the series; and it is in the generations of men that he continues to bring about, by his grace, the deification of mankind, sharers in his Resurrection. This work is not solely a salvation of individual souls, for 'the whole of nature, as we know, groans'[2]; 'creation is full

[1]*Meaning in History*, p. 172.   [2]Rom. 8 : 22.

of expectancy . . . waiting for the sons of God to be made known.'[1] This long-awaited liberation is indeed an effect of the power of God alone, but all humanity is included in its scope. History thus takes on a new significance, as consisting of that which is to be set free. And mankind shares in the achievement, as well as in the gift, of this saving freedom: every one of Christ's members co-operates, 'each limb receiving the active power it needs', so that the whole body 'organized and unified by each contact with the source which supplies it, . . . achieves its natural growth, building itself up through charity';[2] and it depends on man to hasten the coming of the Lord's day.[3] Thus then, the union of the two natures in the person of Christ, the Head of the mystical body, is as it were projected in the life of that body, the Church. Every misconception about the theology of church history arises from some neglect of either the divine or the human element therein. To consider this history as a series of divine operations outside any context of institutional fact, as K. Barth does, is to ignore the human element, where the humanity of Christ lives on in the perfection of unity with God that continues from the hypostatic union. But equally, to regard the Second Coming as belonging to the evolution of mankind, and as marking the final achievement of human progress, is to ignore the divine element, the work of the creator himself in the history of his creation. The truth is that Christ will come again at the end of the world, and that the end of the world will be the coming again of Christ.

[1]Rom. 8: 19.   [2]Eph. 4: 16.   [3]2 Pet. 3: 12.

CHAPTER FOUR

'LET MY PEOPLE GO'

SYNERGISM is one primary characteristic of the Christian theology of history. We have traced the reciprocal development of a dual series, the *mirabilia Dei* and the gradual advancement of mankind, through the Old Testament up to the focal point of intersection in Jesus Christ, whence the line is produced through the life of the Church until the Second Coming. Another aspect of the theology of history is, as we have seen, the analogical relationship between successive stages, whereby each of these is a figure or 'type' of the rest. This phenomenon of correspondence is our next topic. We need not now spend time on the proof of it, having done so already in Part I: our concern is only to describe how it works, for which purpose we may select two concrete examples to start from—first, the work of liberation, focused upon the sacrament of Baptism; and secondly the action of the common meal, in relation to the Eucharist.

One reason for taking the Sacraments as the co-ordinates of our point of view is the need to show the place they occupy in the history of salvation, being the continuation, into the ecclesiastical era, of the *mirabilia Dei* recorded in the Old and New Testaments. Another reason is the need to emphasize the importance of this current period of history. In this way, we may arrive at a comprehensive view of the whole course of the history of salvation; having shown the preparatory stages in the Old Testament, and the moments of fulfilment in the New, we now observe the full deployment of the historical process in the Church, the Sacraments being the decisive events of this period. And it is the more necessary to pay particular attention to this present phase, inasmuch as it is commonly neglected. We must not overlook the glorious mystery which is enumerated in the Creed between the Ascension and the Second Coming, namely the sitting at the right hand of God, where the glorified Christ, the Head of the mystical Body, continually accomplishes miracles of conversion and sanctification within that body by means of his holy sacraments.

'Rescue them from the power of the Egyptians.'[1] The Old Testament shows us the design of God's mighty works; the New Testament shows us their definitive execution; the Church exhibits their repercussions. Of all these works, the Exodus is one of the most important. It is specifically a work of liberation, and as such, it is only a single aspect of the complex Paschal mystery, which includes the whole significance of Christian life, expiation and purification as well as liberation. The Song of Moses[2] celebrates one of these themes by itself, God's people set free from the bondage of the powers of evil. The mystery of God's redemption of captives recurs at every stage of the history of salvation, like the swelling reverberations of a single note. On the shores of the Red Sea, Israel is set free from the horsemen of Egypt in hot pursuit; beside the deep waters of death, Jesus is set free from the prison of the Prince of this world; from the baptismal font, the pagan comes forth free of heathenism and idolatry—this is the inwardness of the Mission, the growth of a mystical Body of Christ through the reception of souls into the church; and at last beside the sea of glass mingled with fire described in the Apocalypse, the elect are set free in the last day from the captivity of the Beast, Death.[3] The same song of triumph is intoned on each occasion by the redeemed upon the farther bank, after their miraculous escape from the enemy's pursuit.

Thus, the people of Israel following the pillar of a cloud, fled from the tyranny of Egypt. Pharaoh and his chariots

[1]Exod. 3: 8.　　[2]Exod. 15.　　[3]Apoc. 15: 2-3.

set out in pursuit of them. Then the people came to the sea-shore, and found their way cut off before them; they faced the alternatives of annihilation or a return into captivity. They were like an army driven back upon the coast, due to be cut to pieces or taken prisoner. The desperate situation of the people of Israel must be emphasized, for it explains the full significance of what followed. It was just when they were finally incapable of saving themselves that the power of Almighty God brought to pass that which was humanly impossible:

> Moses stretched out his hand over the sea, and the Lord cleared it away from their path. All night a fierce sirocco blew . . . So the Israelites went through the midst of these dry-shod, with its waters towering up like a wall to right and left. And the Egyptians, still in pursuit, pressed on after them . . . through the midst of the sea . . . And when Moses stretched out his hand towards the sea, . . . back came the water, overwhelming all the chariots and horsemen of Pharaoh's army; . . . not a man escaped.[1]

This divine intervention to save his people from a desperate situation was always the most precious memory in Israel's history: 'what other power dried up the sea, with its deep rolling waters, made the sea's caverns a highway, for a ransomed people to cross?'[2]

So it was that Moses and the children of Israel made up their canticle, the Song of Moses, when they saw in the morning the bodies of the Egyptians cast up by the waves upon the shore, after that tragic night of miracle: 'A psalm for the Lord, so great he is and so glorious; horse and rider hurled into the sea! Who but the Lord is my protector, the pride of my song; who but the Lord has brought me deliverance?'[3] Miriam, or Mary, 'the prophetess, Aaron's sister, went out with a tambour in her hand, and all the women-folk followed her, with tambour and with dances.'[4]

[1] Exod. 14: 21–23, 27–28. [2] Is. 51: 10. [3] Exod. 15: 1–2. [4] Exod. 15: 20.

This Mary answered antiphonally to the children of Israel: 'A psalm for the Lord, so great he is and so glorious; horse and rider hurled into the sea!'[1]

It was a first institution of the Paschal liturgy upon the shores of the Red Sea. Dom Winzen fairly claims this moment as 'the Birth of the Divine Office'; for the action was strictly liturgical, with one choir, of women, singing a response in alternation with the men singing the verses. It was the very same canticle as we still sing at the Easter Vigil. Throughout the history of salvation, at every Pasch, the song of Mary-Miriam is heard for ever. There is something altogether extraordinary about this textual continuity: liturgy is here the mistress of theology, in teaching the lesson of God's faithfulness as the Saviour of his people.

For while the crossing of the Red Sea was by itself a great miracle, the Old Testament gives notice that God will afterwards perform an even more wonderful work of liberation. The announcement of these coming events is indeed the especial function of the Old Testament books, which are essentially prophetic; their only concern with the past is to establish a foundation of hope for the future—and not to afflict us with a despairing nostalgia for what is either irretrievably lost, or only recoverable by retrogression. Herein the sacred book of the Hebrews differs fundamentally from those of the nature-worshippers: for the latter are invariably concerned with a primordial myth, perpetually enacted in an ideal or archetypal time-circle; mankind's participation in this mythical action, which is a kind of escape from the mortal effluxion of the temporal process, consists in a ritual renewal of the life-force through recourse to the primal sources of creation.

The Passover was the anniversary of the crossing of the Red Sea, celebrating the memory of a great miracle: but that other foretold escape, which was to be effected in the last days, is so much more wonderful that in practice our

[1]Exod. 15: 21.

Easter recalls nothing but the resurrection of Christ. No doubt we are right, in a way, not to think about the former covenant any more; as St Basil said, there is no need of lamps once the sun is up. But there is still something to be gained from the contemplation of the Old Law, of those first drafts which can sometimes help us to a fuller understanding of the more perfect enactment of the New Law. Besides, the excellence of the latter is all the better appreciated in contrast with the former.

Such is the sense of Isaias's prophecy of the new Exodus, made in the very midst of the Old Testament: 'A message to you from that same Lord, who could once lead you through the sea, make a passage for you through the foaming waters . . . Do not remember those old things, he says, as if you had eyes for nothing but what happened long ago; I mean to perform new wonders.'[1]

Of course the crossing of the Red Sea was miraculous; but the new thing that God should do would be such as to blot out all recollection of the other. Just as Isaias had foretold how the new creation would dim the glories of the former heaven and earth, so he prophesied in the same words concerning the new Exodus. It was on the anniversary of the night when God saved his people from the Egyptians, that the new and definitive freedom was won for us by the resurrection of Christ. The New Testament is not especially concerned to inculcate the doctrine that there is a salvation more glorious than the Exodus itself; the Old Testament had done that already: but it is the purport of the New Testament to inform us that this ultimate salvation has now been achieved in fact. The keyword of the New Testament is *hodie*—'This day thou shalt be with me in Paradise'.[2] The Gospel message is to this effect, that the prophetic eschatology, the salvation to come, is now a present reality. The life of Christ in the Gospels is related step by step to the symbols

[1] Isa. 43: 16, 18–19. [2] Luke 23: 43.

of the Exodus—the brazen serpent,[1] the rock of living water,[2] the manna from heaven,[3] the pillar of fire.[4]

Yet the scope of the new freedom was out of all proportion to the scale of the former escape. Then, only the Jews in a heathen captivity were affected, but now it was all mankind, the prisoners of evil, of what we call original sin. Just as the Israelites were in desperate straits, so the entire human race was without hope in the world. Man's plight was beyond human remedy; he could not work out his own salvation: wanting the grace of God in his soul and the life of God in his body, man was the helpless prey of death. Evil is a problem that mankind has no way of tackling. There is a mystery in it, as it were a taproot of infection perpetually throwing up poisonous growths in the world, and still defying all human efforts to get at it.

One man alone has arrived at this heart of the matter, and effected a radical cure, namely he that went down into the kingdom of death in the blackness of the first Good Friday, there to break the power of death and set free those whom death imprisoned. When Christ died on the cross that afternoon, it seemed as though night was falling on the world for ever, as though all hope was lost, for death had overcome his last enemy. But in the dark prison of death, Christ shattered its bolts and bars, and came out from hell victorious on Easter morning; he had finally broken the power of death, both in himself and for all us men.

The *gaudium paschale* is expressed in the words of the song: 'A psalm for the Lord, so great he is and so glorious; horse and rider hurled into the sea.' But now it is not only the Israelites' song, celebrating the blessing of freedom from the pursuit of the Egyptians by the shores of the Red Sea; it is the song of humanity, saved from the deep waters of death, hailing the miraculous triumph of the Word of God. The canticle of the Exodus has become a hymn of

[1] John 3: 14.   [2] John 4: 10; cf. 1 Cor. 10: 4.
[3] John 6: 58.   [4] John 8: 12.

redemption for all those who had been overwhelmed by death, and being now set free, and seeing the powers of evil, their ancient captors, now impotent in defeat, rehearse the tale of their salvation in the words of Moses.

The freedom of mankind, once secured for all in the resurrection of Christ, has still to be personally conferred upon individual men. This private manumission is effected through baptism, as provided in the Easter Vigil: it is the specifically missionary aspect of the Exodus mystery, and the aspect which characterizes our current epoch, namely, the interval between the Ascension and the Second Coming —the missionary age. Throughout this period, the life of the Church prolongs that miraculous work of salvation which was prefigured in the crossing of the Red Sea and accomplished in the Resurrection of Christ. The sacrament of baptism is part of this continuation of the wonderful works of God; it is our contemporary equivalent of the scriptural miracles, something historically more important than any scientific discovery, or than the fate of empires.

The idea of Paschal continuity was plainly marked in the oldest baptismal rites. Thus the candidate, at the outset of his preparation for baptism, was marked upon his brow on the first Sunday in Lent, with the seal of Christ, just as the houses of the Israelites had been anointed with the blood of the Lamb: for he was exempted in Christ's blood from the punishment due to his sins. This was a beginning of Christ's taking possession of his soul. It was followed by forty days of Lenten preparation, which can only be understood by reference to both Testaments: Jesus was tempted by Satan for forty days, and his faithfulness under temptation was the counterpart of Israel's falling away.

The catechumen's forty days of Lent are a time of trial, a time of serious conflict while Satan and his angels strive to keep possession of his soul. This is no figure of speech, but must be understood in literal reality: for a pagan is not merely ignorant of the Christian revelation, he is subject to

the active domination of the powers of darkness, and needs
to be wrested out of captivity. Every conversion thus involves a measure of dramatic conflict, and all missionary
activity partakes of the nature of this mystery. It is not just
the presentation of the gospel message in a form suitable
to each of the various non-Christian cultures, but an engagement of hostilities with the powers of evil: and the operations of this war take place in the supernatural field; they
belong to the mystery of sainthood; it is through prayer and
penance that devils are cast out. If this aspect of the matter
is ignored, there is no understanding the essence of missionary work. Even after Christ's victory, the human nature
of those who are not his remains imprisoned: he crushed the
serpent's head, but its coils are writhing yet to ensnare the
peoples of the earth. Satan, seeing his prey about to escape,
redoubles his efforts against the catechumen; but during
the forty days, Christ's hold is strengthened too. The real
meaning of the liturgical 'scrutinies' appointed for this time
depends on an understanding of the spiritual campaign that
is now engaged. These scrutinies consist partly of exorcisms,
to drive back the power of the enemy step by step and set
the catechumen free from his gripe; partly of blessings,
which indicate how the grace of Christ more and more
hallows the soul, gradually consolidating possession of it:
but the devil keeps up his pressure all the while until the
very moment of the Easter Vigil and the very edge of the
font.

Then, and only then, the impossible thing comes to pass;
the sea is divided; the impassable barrier, against which the
soul was beating in vain, crumbles away and opens a practic-
able breach. There is a way of escape, after all, and a means
of salvation, but only by a miracle in the strictest sense of
the word, that is, by an exercise of omnipotence to bring
about in reality something that was really impossible. The
Song of Moses celebrates this mighty wonder, the unpredictable, unthinkable intervention of God whereby he opens

a way of escape from perdition, offers salvation to the lost, reveals a hope of the world's redemption.

As the waters were opened for the Israelites, and the gates of death were opened for the Lord Jesus, even so the catechumen goes down into the water of baptism, makes his crossing, leaves behind him Pharaoh and his host, the devil and his angels, and comes out on the other side. He is saved. Saved, that is, quite literally, like a shipwrecked survivor brought to land.

> The pertinacious wickedness of the devil hath power up to the saving water, but . . . in Baptism he loses all the poison of his wickedness. An example whereof we see in King Pharoah, who having long struggled and lingered on in his perfidy, could hold out and prevail until he came to the water . . . At this day also, when the devil is scourged and scolded . . . by the exorcists . . . he often says that he is going out . . . yet in what he saith he deceiveth . . . When however they come to the saving water . . . of Baptism . . . the devil is there overcome, and the man dedicated to God is by the Divine mercy set free.[1]

This dramatic theme was a favourite in patristic literature —the picture of man, beset on all hands, humanly speaking without hope, looking to the power of God alone for his salvation, finding his way of escape marked out through the pathless, overwhelming sea itself, Dostoievsky's 'wall of the impossible.' So, for example, in Origen: 'Know that the Egyptians pursue thee, and would bring thee back into bondage: these are the powers of this world and the evil spirits thou wast wont to serve. They make haste to pursue thee, but thou goest down into the water and thou art saved. Thou dost arise a new man, cleansed from all stain of sin, ready to sing the new song.'[2] This 'new song' is the canticle of Exodus. Once more, after Moses, seeing the bodies of the Egyptians washed up on the shore of the Red Sea, after Jesus, rising again on earth out of the bitter waters of death,

[1]Ep. LXIX: 15 (trs. Carey, 1844).   [2]*Hom. Ex.* V: 5.

the catechumen in the renewal of his manhood, wearing the white garment of his regeneration, born again into new life, he too may now sing on his own account the song of the redeemed:

'A psalm for the Lord, so great he is and so glorious; horse and rider hurled into the sea.'

It was necessary to explore all these aspects of the case in order to understand the full significance of the Song of Moses in the Easter Vigil. The canticle exactly describes the work of the liberation enacted within that rite, the release of souls from captivity in our midst—a real divine intervention, comparable at all points with the crossing of the Red Sea and the Resurrection. The salvation of the heathen, which is the ultimate meaning of all missionary work, is nothing less than that. So the Church, welcoming the nations, is like Mary, the sister of Aaron: she led the responses to the men's choir on the shore of the Red Sea, and St Zeno spoke of the Churches joining in the psalmody of all the redeemed peoples, to sing, each in his turn, the Song of Moses: 'Mary-Miriam, with her timbrel is a figure of the Church, singing a hymn with all her daughter-churches as she leads the Christian people forward, not into the wilderness, but into Heaven.'[1]

All this is not so say that our freedom is now absolute. It is true that the multitude of the baptized belong absolutely to Christ, and in him, have made good their escape; but the devil prowls about them still, seeking a weakness in their armour of liberty whereby he may once more overcome them. We are still tossed in the waves of this world's turmoil, and though we have nothing to fear in the deep waters of death, we have still to make our way across them. Life is still a time of trial: the Enemy is already defeated, but has not yet laid down his arms. So our Exodus is past but not yet over. All our life on earth is one long exodus.

But one day—it will be our last—we shall cross the sea

[1] *Tract.* II: 54. P.L. 11: 510.

again. That is when the last enemy, which is Death, shall be overcome. In that day the conquerors of the beast, standing on the bank of the river of fire, will take into their hands —not timbrels now, made of dried pelts, but—celestial harps; and they shall sing for ever the Song of Moses: 'I saw, too, what might have been a sea of glass, tinged with fire. And by this sea of glass the victors were standing, safe now from the beast, and his image, and the mark of his name, with harps of God's fashioning. Theirs is the song of God's servant Moses, theirs is the song of the Lamb.'[1] From the shores of the Red Sea onwards throughout the history of salvation, the Song of Moses echoes and re-echoes into eternity.

[1] Apoc. 15: 2-3.

CHAPTER FIVE

THE BANQUET OF THE POOR

TYPOLOGY is the study of correspondences between the Old and the New Testaments. One special difficulty arises from the fact that the New Testament itself is a complex document, containing records and interpretations which correspond to different strata of historical reality. It is concerned with Christ in his earthly life, with Christ living on in the Church, with the life of Christ in each Christian soul, and with the second coming of Christian glory. Consequently the typological or figurative interpretation of a given passage will vary with the various aspects of the literature; there will be a Christological sense, an ecclesiastical sense, mystical and eschatological senses. This poses a question of method: in what order should these different interpretations be examined? The chronological order, corresponding to the form in which we have stated the case, involves a measure of artificiality in handling the texts themselves; for the historical emergence of the four types of interpretation was in quite a different sequence, so that a chronological method would mean discussing late texts first, and the oldest texts later.

Thus the better method seems to be to follow the order of genesis, corresponding to the actual sequence in which the several figurative senses were invented. On this scale, the earliest of the typological correspondences proves to be the eschatological. This sort of interpretation is evidenced already in the Old Testament: for the aim of the prophetic predictions, which are the nucleus around which that document was formed, is to recall to the mind of the people in their adversity the mighty works, the *mirabilia*, which God performed for their benefit in the past, in order to sustain their hope of similar benefits to be conferred upon them in the future. So, for instance, the historic Exodus will be matched by a new and greater Exodus,[1] and the old Jesusalem by a new Jerusalem.[2] The New Testament shows how the coming of Christ into the world is a first fulfilment of these eschatological figures. Next comes the Christological interpretation, showing in the person and in the actions of Jesus the fulfilment of that which the Old Law typified. Then, as the life of the Church is a continuation of Christ's life, the distinguishing features of the Christian community—especially the sacraments—are recognized as a second fulfilment of the ancient figures. And last of all in the evolution of the Christian consciousness of spiritual reality, the typical themes of the Old Testament come to be applied to the life of each individual soul, as *alter Christus*: so Origen represents the wanderings in the wilderness as a prefiguration of the spiritual itinerary of the soul towards God—this is the interpretation we have called 'mystical'.[3]

I

It is in the light of these considerations that we have decided to open the present inquiry with a study of the Old Testament evidence, notwithstanding that our main concern is with the Fathers: for the whole conception of typology is rooted in the prophetic books of the Bible. There is no need to labour the obvious point that the Old Testament accords a potentially religious significance to the act of sharing a meal; this act is recorded in Deuteronomy as an intrinsic element of the Temple liturgy at Jerusalem: 'the Lord your God will choose out one tribe among you, and one place in that tribe, to be the sanctuary of his name, the shrine of his presence . . . There, in the presence of the Lord your God, you and your households shall eat, glad at

[1]Isa. 43: 18–21.   [2]ibid. 2: 2.   [3]Daniélou, *Sacr. fut.*, pp. 257–8.

heart, what your own hands have reaped with his blessing to aid them'.[1] Here is the common meal as a liturgical action, taking place in Jehovah's habitation, consisting explicitly in the enjoyment of Jehovah's blessings. The theme of the sacred banquet, as an Old Testament commonplace, always implies an intimacy with God, the social union of the people, and the enjoyment of heavenly gifts.

But our particular concern at the moment is with the typological treatment of this theme, as a figure of eschatological blessings, which begins to appear in the prophetic books. Thus, in the Deutero-Isaias, Jehovah calls his people to the joys of the messianic revelation as to a feast: 'So many athirst . . . so many destitute . . . Do but listen, here you shall find content; here are dainties shall ravish your hearts.'[2] Exactly the same figure reappears in a passage of Proverbs (whose literary connexions with Isaias have been demonstrated), the famous Banquet of Wisdom: 'See, where wisdom has built herself a house, carved out for herself those seven pillars of hers! And now, her sacrificial victims slain, her wine mingled, her banquet spread . . .'[3] And the Psalms, too, celebrate the messianic feast to be given by the Shepherd: 'Envious my foes watch, while thou dost spread a banquet for me; richly thou dost anoint my head with oil, well filled my cup.'[4]

This special interpretation seems to belong most properly to the apocalyptic tradition: it is clearly brought out in a noteworthy passage of the apocalypse of Isaias[5]: 'the Lord of hosts will prepare a banquet on this mountain of ours; no meat so tender, no wine so mellow, meat that drips with fat, wine well strained.'[6]

The same theme of the Messianic feast recurs throughout the later apocalyptic books, where it is regularly represented as something miraculous: this is in keeping with the whole

[1]Deut. 12: 5, 7. [2]Isa. 55: 1, 2. [3]Prov. 9: 1–2. [4]Ps. 22: 5.
[5]Viz. Chapters XXIV–XXVIII; so-called because of their particular literary character. [6]Isa. 25: 6.

tradition of supernatural abundance as characterizing the conditions of life in the new world to come. It is evinced in the fantastic descriptions taken from the book of Enoch by Papias, and from him by St Irenaeus. According to another tradition, which is evidenced as early as 4 Esdras, the mythical monsters Leviathan and Behemoth, symbolizing the powers of evil, are there 'to be devoured of whom thou [God] wilt, and when'.[1]

Another striking feature of the description in the Apocalypse of Isaias is that the feast will be given in the Mountain, which, together with the Temple, represents the habitation of God. The apocalyptic writings recognize this habitation in four mountains, that of the North, that of Eden,[2] Sinai, and Mount Sion. In Exodus there had been mention of a meal shared by the seventy elders who went up into Mount Sinai with Moses and Aaron: 'they saw God, and ate and drank.'[3] So the verse quoted from Isaiah gives notice of another feast on the analogy of this one, but to be given in the mountain of the new Jerusalem, and for the benefit not merely of seventy elders but of 'all people'— 'seventy' being, in the apocalyptic tradition, the symbolic number of the nations. This is, then, a clear instance of the figurative use of Exodus by an apocalyptic writer. In other examples, the eschatological banquet is not situated in the Mountain, but in the City of God, or in God's house— alternative expressions for the ineffable Presence: thus, in the passage quoted from Proverbs, the house that Wisdom built symbolizes the Temple; and in 4 Esdras the banquet is associated with the building of the new Jerusalem— 'plenteousness is made ready, a city is builded'.[4] It is a typological development of the theme noticed in Deuteronomy: the liturgical meal was to be eaten in 'the place which the Lord your God will choose', that is, in the Temple of Jerusalem, which now becomes a figure of the eschatological Temple.

[1] 4 Esdr. 6: 52; cf. Ezek. 39: 17.   [2] Ezek. 28: 13–14.   [3] Exod. 24: 11.
[4] 4 Esdr. 8: 52.

This complex of ideas and images, a liturgical feast in God's habitation regarded as typifying the eschatological banquet of the Kingdom to come, was destined to be still further elaborated and enriched with new associations in the sapiential, apocalyptic and rabbinical books before we come to the New Testament. In the first place, there was a reciprocal influence between this theme and the wedding-symbolism belonging to the theology of the Covenant, which plays so large a part in the prophetic books and was perfected in the Song of Songs. Hence follows the representation of the future Kingdom as a wedding-feast—a conception which was to have its place in the New Testament. The first example of this conflation occurs in the Song of Songs, where the bridegroom asks his friends to take part in his wedding-feast with the Bride: his invitation was dated from the garden of Paradise, the locality appropriated before all others to the presence of God: 'The garden gained, my bride, my heart's love . . . Eat your fill, lovers; drink, sweethearts, and drink deep.'[1] Here is to be noted not only the nuptial character of the feast, but particularly the *venue* in Paradise, which, like the Temple and the Mountain, means the place where God is: for the banquet-image is common to the cycle of Genesis as well as the cycle of Exodus.

A second development at this stage was to establish an analogical relationship between the eschatological banquet and one, in particular, of the sacred meals of the Old Testament, and that one of the highest importance, namely the Passover. This liturgical meal was essentially a commemoration, recalling—or, rather, renewing, through the active participation of the recipients—Jehovah's saving of the first-born. But in the rabbinical books we find this Paschal meal taking on an eschatological meaning; it becomes a figure of the new freedom to come for the people in captivity. F. J. Leenhardt rightly emphasized this aspect of the case when he wrote:

[1]Song, 5: 1.

The thought of the passover meal was governed by the
memory of a redemption once obtained, and by the expectation of another in which all the potentialities of the former
would be realized once for all and for ever. . . . The chalices,
closely connected in the ritual to their particular blessings,
which referred directly to the messianic fulfilments, were themselves an earnest to the faithful of the glory to come in the final,
endless redemption.

One more theme, in conclusion, that came into contact
and interaction with that of the eschatological banquet, was
that of the Son of Man. This was peculiar to the apocalyptic
tradition, where the feast is not merely held in the presence
of Jehovah, but in company with the Messiah: whence a
more distinctively Messianic quality in the eschatological
banquet itself, as appears particularly in a verse from the
apocalypse of Enoch: 'The Lord of spirits will abide over
them, and with that Son of Man shall they eat and lie down
and rise up for ever and ever.'[1]

This background, of a progressive enrichment of the idea
of an eschatological feast, by the accretion of new associations, throughout the development of Jewish theology, is
important for any consideration of the theme in the New
Testament, where all the traditional elements are still current, but orientated towards a new significance.

II

The eschatological significance of meals in the New Testament is sometimes no further developed than it was in the
Old Testament and in the traditions of Judaism. The three
directions of this development, which have been analysed in
the foregoing pages, are all exactly represented—the theme
of the wedding-feast, that of Messiah's feast, and that of the
Passover feast. The former two belong directly to the
Jewish apocalyptic literary tradition, whose great importance for New Testament studies is beginning to be

[1] Enoch LXII: 14 (Charles, *Apocr. and Pseudep.*).

recognized. For example, the wedding-feast appears in the Apocalypse of St John, not only with eschatological, but also —which is especially noteworthy—with Paschal associations: the Kingdom to come is represented as the wedding-feast of the Lamb. "And now the angel said to me, Write thus: Blessed are those who are bidden to the Lamb's wedding-feast.'[1] This succinct formula includes all three similitudes of the world to come—the feast, the wedding, and the sacrifice: and thus preserves in the New Testament the whole range of typological meal-symbolism elaborated in the Jewish apocalyptic literature.

One instance of the second line of development, the theme of the messianic banquet, is even more characteristic. As we have seen, the book of Enoch represents the world to come as a feast which the righteous shall share with the Son of Man for ever and ever. The New Testament uses the same language to describe the future life that Christ has prepared for his own: thus, in St Luke's gospel we find: 'as my Father has allotted a kingdom to me, so I allot to you a place to eat and drink at my table in my kingdom'[2]—the parallel with the text of Enoch is here remarkably close. An analogous expression is to be found in another place, namely in the Apocalypse of St John (thus confirming the impression that this particular development belongs to the apocalyptic literary tradition): 'if anyone listens to my voice and opens the door, I will come in to visit him, and take my supper with him, and he shall sup with me'.[3] Once again, a meal shared with Christ symbolizes the kingdom to come.

The third development, as we have seen, was the attribution, in the Rabbinical tradition of the Jews, of an eschatological significance to the Passover meal. This is plainly evident in the words uttered by Christ in the course of the last Passover meal just before his death: for before the institution of the Eucharist, he began by showing how the Passover meal itself was a figure of the kingdom to come, and

[1]Apoc. 19: 9.   [2]Luke 22: 29–30.   [3]Apoc. 3: 20.

this both in respect of the food and of the cup. 'I have longed and longed to share this paschal meal with you . . . I shall not eat it again, till it finds its fulfilment in the kingdom of God . . . I shall not drink of the fruit of the vine again, till the kingdom of God has come.'[1] As we saw earlier, it was especially the Passover cup that had been endowed with eschatological meaning by the Rabbis.

In these three points the New Testament simply follows out the indications of the Old: but the distinctive characteristic of New Testament typology is to represent as already fulfilled, in Jesus Christ, those 'last things' which are always foreseen in the Old Testament as yet to come. This characteristic is clearly discernible in connexion with the theme now under discussion: the meals of Jesus, as described in the gospels, have a religious significance; and moreover they are represented as fulfilling in reality that which was prefigured by the Old Testament meals which we have been discussing. Thus, in the first place, the fact of Christ's presence at festival banquets is interpreted in the Messianic context, as an expression of the rejoicings foretold in the prophetic books: after the feast given for Christ by Matthew, we learn that the disciples of John were scandalized thereat—'How is it that thy disciples do not fast, when we and the Pharisees fast so often? To them Jesus said, Can you expect the men of the bridegroom's company to go mourning, while the bridegroom is still with them?'[2] The act of feasting is seen as an expression of the Messianic joy, arising from the presence of Christ.[3] The days of John, which were the period of waiting, are superseded by the

---

[1] Luke 22: 15–16, 18.   [2] Matt. 9: 14–15.

[3] This particular question and answer is immediately followed, in the other two synoptic Gospels, by the episode of the disciples plucking ears of corn on a Sabbath day: and H. Riesenfeld (*Jésus transfiguré*, p. 326) observes that this passage (Mark 2: 23 et sqq.) 'refers to the eschatological banquet, and may even be said to represent the Eucharist'. The same author (p. 322) points out the connexion, in this same passage, between the eschatological feast and the eschatological Sabbath.

day of Jesus, which is the period of presence and fulfilment. The same contrast is pointed out in another passage: 'When John came, he would neither eat nor drink, and you say, He is possessed. When the Son of Man came, he ate and drank with you, and of him you say, Here is a glutton; he loves wine; he is a friend of publicans and sinners.'[1]

This particular quotation exhibits a second characteristic of the meals of Jesus, which struck the attention of those who saw him, and incurred the disapproval of the Pharisees, namely that he was ready to eat with 'publicans and sinners'. It is noticeable that the very next following verses of St Luke's gospel describe the meal in the house of Simon the Pharisee, where Jesus allowed the woman who was a sinner to touch him. The Pharisees raised the same objections when they saw the feast that Matthew the publican gave him, as described just before the above-mentioned discussion on fasting: 'How comes it that your Master eats with publicans and sinners?'[2] Jesus answered: 'I have come to call sinners, not the just.'[3] It is a clear indication of the meaning and purport of that meal; in Fr de Montcheuil's accurate analysis: 'By accepting this intimacy of a common life with sinners, Jesus shows that he has come to break down the barrier that separates sinful men from God. . . . It is properly a religious action, revealing the essence of Christ's mission.'

Another feature of the messianic banquet, in the apocalyptic tradition, was its miraculous abundance, corresponding to the conditions of the earthly paradise before the earth was cursed,[4] when the soil bore wonderful crops without any labour of tillage. Just such a miraculous meal was recorded in Exodus, where the Hebrews in the wilderness found manna, as well as living water, without working for it, and in such quantity that 'each gathered according to the number of mouths that must be filled'.[5] The feeding of the

---

[1]Luke 7: 33-34.   [2]Matt. 9: 11.   [3]Matt. 9: 13.   [4]Gen. 3: 17-19.
[5]Exod. 16: 18.

five thousand came as a renewal of this miracle, to signalize the new Exodus with its own appropriate signs and wonders: 'all ate and had enough'.[1] In St John's gospel, the parallel between the two episodes is explicit and direct, as is also the eschatological interpretation which the Jews had come to read into the gift of manna; so that the feeding of the five thousand figures as one of the signs of the messianic age.[2] The passage should be studied in connexion with St John's accounts of other miracles performed by Jesus at meals—at Cana,[3] and at the sea of Tiberias.[4]

So much for the ways in which the meals of Christ reproduce in reality the characteristic features predicted of the eschatological banquet in the apocalyptic books. We have shown elsewhere how the theme of the banquet came to be interconnected in the Old Testament with the theme of marriage, producing the theme of the wedding-feast: the same thing can be traced in the New Testament. It was, as we have seen, in connexion with a feast that Jesus said there could be no mourning while the bridegroom is still present. The meals which Christ shared with his apostles were thus a true fulfilment of that feast to which the bridegroom invited his friends in the Song of Solomon. In St Matthew's gospel, the same theme of the marriage feast reappears when Christ likens the kingdom, which he has come to establish, to a royal wedding: 'there was once a king, who held a marriage-feast for his son, and sent out his servants with a summons to all those whom he had invited to the wedding . . . bidding them tell those who had been invited, By this, I have prepared my feast, the oxen have been killed, and the fatlings, all is ready now; come to the wedding.'[5] The fact that the corresponding passage in St Luke's gospel[6] mentions no marriage, but only 'a great supper', shows that the idea of a wedding is an association, or harmonic, of the banquet theme, but not an essential part of

[1]Matt. 14: 20.   [2]John 6: 26, 31, etc.   [3]2: 1–11.   [4]21: 1–14.
[5]Matt. 22: 2–4.   [6]14: 16 et sqq.

it, which directly confirms the evidence of the Old Testament.

With all this accumulation of convergent details, we can now proceed to the interpretation of the gospel meals in the light of one last aspect of the traditional figures of eschatology, namely the meal shared with the Son of Man. We have seen that this figure is sometimes used in the New Testament to represent the world to come: but the world here and now, with the future Kingdom already present by anticipation, itself contains a fulfilment of the former expectations. This aspect of the matter is particularly marked in the case of one group of meals, characterized by a special emphasis on the eschatological quality of the action—those of the risen Christ: such as the breaking of bread at Emmaus, in St Luke;[1] or the meal on the lake shore, in St John.[2] The theological significance of these meals is made clear in the Acts, where also one of their distinctive features is singled out for emphasis, namely the fact that they were shared only by chosen witnesses: 'on the third day God raised him up again, and granted the clear sight of him, not to the people at large, but to us, the witnesses whom God had appointed beforehand; we ate and drank in his company after his rising from the dead.'[3] This group of meals was in a class apart. But all the meals of Christ in the gospels were a fulfilment of the eschatological vision of a feast in the presence of the Son of Man: the Good News was not only the preaching of a Kingdom to come, but the present reality of that Kingdom—a reality which yet, however, left room for further extension and growth. Other aspects of the typology of meals and feasts, which remain to be examined, refer to this last-mentioned development.

III

The synoptic gospels, especially St Matthew's, are concerned to exhibit historical events in the life of Christ as fulfilling the eschatological figures of the Old Testament—this

[1] 24: 30 et sqq.   [2] 21: 12 et sqq.   [3] 10: 40–41.

kind of typology is consequently called Matthaean. In later times it fell largely into desuetude, surviving chiefly in the West, with Hippolytus of Rome and Gregory of Elvira, but also in the tradition of Jerusalem. In St John's gospel there is a new tendency to pay more attention to the sacramental aspect. Not, indeed, that the events of Christ's life were no longer recognized as fulfilling the Old Testament figures: we have seen, for example, how the miracle of Cana fulfilled the conditions of the eschatological banquet. But these events come to be seen as themselves figures, in their turn, of sacramental realities—the point has been well brought out by Cullmann. The Old Testament banquets, and also the meals of Christ which were a first realization of the figurative significance of those banquets, both now appear as types, or figures, of the eucharistic meal. This 'Johannine' kind of typology, unlike the Matthaean, was intensely cultivated in the earliest catechetical tradition.

Strictly speaking it is not altogether absent even from the synoptic gospels. In a striking passage of St Luke, Jesus tells the Jews, who can say 'we have eaten and drunk in thy presence'[1] during Christ's life on earth, that this by itself does not amount to the final enactment of the Promise. On the contrary, 'Weeping shall be there, and gnashing of teeth, when you see Abraham and Isaac and Jacob and all the prophets within God's kingdom, while you yourselves are cast out. Others will come from the east and the west, the north and the south, to take their ease in the kingdom of God.'[2] This last sentence echoes, from the prophetic descriptions of the eschatological banquet, the essential point that it was to include all peoples; on the other hand the words contained a clear allusion to the reception of Gentiles within the Church. So the eschatological feast appears in the Synoptic tradition with a twofold typological reference, both to the meals of Jesus in his earthly life, and also to the sacramental life of the Church.

[1] 13: 26.   [2] 13: 28–29.

Furthermore, there is synoptic warrant for the idea that the meals of Jesus, besides fulfilling the messianic prophecies, were themselves a prefiguration of the common life that Christ was to share with his Church. By his recorded words, Jesus emphasized this particular signification of his own actions, as a figure of that free entry of all nations into the intimacy of friendship with God, which belongs to the period of the Church. This is the exact point of the parable of the great supper, in St Luke, which was given as a commentary upon a meal when Jesus was the guest of 'one of the chief Pharisees'.[1] One of the company said: 'Blessed is the man who shall feast in the kingdom of God'[2] (which shows that the symbol of feasting was normal in contemporary Jewish eschatology); and Christ answered: 'There was a man that gave a great supper, and sent out many invitations. And when the time came for his supper, he sent one of his own servants telling the invited guests to come, for all was now ready. And all of them, with one accord, began making excuses . . . Whereupon the host fell into a rage, and said to his servant, Quick, go out into the streets and lanes of the city; bring in the poor, the cripples, the blind and the lame.'[3] And it was only just before this that Christ had been telling the Jews: 'Others will come from the east and the west, the north and the south, to take their ease in the kingdom of God.'[4]

A first observation to be made upon the parable of the great supper is that it reproduces, among the Old Testament themes we have discussed, particularly the banquet of Wisdom.[5] Just as Wisdom dispatched her maidens to invite all the passers-by to come to the feast that stood ready in her house, so here the master of the house sent his servant out to fetch in all and sundry to his supper, 'that so my house may be filled'.[6] The Church, then, is the house of Wisdom,

---

[1]Luke 14: 1.   [2]14: 15.   [3]14: 16–18, 21.   [4]13: 29.
[5]Prov. 9: 1–5. The parallel was drawn by Origen (*Com. Cant.* III; P.G. 13: 154–5).   [6]Luke 14: 23.

whose bread and wine are given to the guests in a sacrament of divine reality, and no longer only in a figure: the liturgical appropriation of this passage to the Eucharist is perfectly just. But the particular interest of the case, for our immediate purpose, is the teaching of Jesus himself, which here suggests, beyond the direct signification of the meals he shared with men, a prefiguration of his fellowship with the Church.[1] This is the transition from the 'Christological' sense to the 'ecclesiastical' and sacramental sense.

As we have said, the whole tendency of Johannine typology is to concentrate on the latter class of figures: Cullmann's book *Early Christian Worship* furnishes enough examples to show the importance of this feature of the fourth gospel. Thus, while the miracle of Cana is certainly presented as a fulfilment of the idea of the marriage-feast in the prophetic books, it is also (and much more) a prefiguration of the eucharistic banquet, through the symbolism of the water and the wine. The feeding of the five thousand[2] is an even more striking instance of the same thing: for whereas the Synoptic writers saw in it only a fulfilment of the messianic feast of prophecy, St John explicitly relates it to the discourse concerning the bread of life, and thus brings out its eucharistic significance: the three levels of figure and reality—the manna, the multiplication of the loaves and fishes, and the Eucharist—are plainly set out. In the Passover discourse before the Passion,[3] it may be, as Cullmann suggests in a delicate piece of analysis, that the washing of the feet, which can be done over and over again, represents the Eucharist, by contrast with baptism, which is once for all. It would be highly characteristic of the Johannine method to teach the institution of the Eucharist through the symbolic circumstances of the meal, instead of narrating it, as is done in the Synoptic gospels.

[1]Similarly, the forgiveness of Mary Magdalen was regarded by the Fathers as a figure of the conversion of the Gentiles.
[2]John 6.   [3]John 13: esp. 8–10.

The gospel of St John, then, put forward the eucharistic interpretation of the banquet-figure, noting two Old Testament themes in particular as susceptible of this kind of typological reference, the marriage-feast and the manna: both had already an eschatological significance in the Old Testament itself. Following these indications, the Christian catechetical writers proceeded to take up and apply to the Eucharist a number of the Old Testament texts which we have recognized as prefiguring the eschatological feast. As we saw, this kind of typology occurs, before the apocalyptic literature, in the Prophets and in the Psalms; the twenty-second Psalm is a notable instance of it. Now, the twenty-second Psalm played a leading part in the primitive catechism relating to the sacraments. It is known that in some churches, this Psalm, like the Creed itself, was inculcated in a formal *traditio* during the catechumenate: and Dom de Bruyne considers that it was partly responsible for the use of the Shepherd figure in the liturgical ornamentation of baptisteries. It was certainly sung during the ritual of Christian initiation at the Easter Vigil. The patristic commentaries show that it was accepted by the Fathers as typifying the successive phases in this ritual.

The description of the eschatological banquet in this Psalm is as follows: 'Thou dost spread a banquet for me; richly dost thou anoint my head with oil, well filled my cup.'[1]

Christian tradition unanimously applied this verse to the Eucharist. So St Ambrose wrote of the newly-baptized convert, that 'when he has put off the rags of his former errors, . . . he makes haste towards the heavenly banquet, and seeing the most holy altar made ready, he cries: "thou preparest a table before me".'[2] So Eusebius of Caesarea, after explaining that the eucharistic interpretation of the text formed part of the preparations for baptism, concluded: 'In these words, "Thou preparest a table before me" etc.,

[1] Ps. 22: 5. [2] P.L. 16: 403 B; cf. 14: 876 A.

the Word plainly shews forth . . . the holy sacrifices of Christ's table.'[1] While the 'table' means Christ's body, the 'cup' means his blood: 'You see that in this psalm that cup is spoken of, whereon Christ said, after he had given thanks, "This is my blood".'[2]

It was this latter point, showing in the 'well-filled cup' of the twenty-second Psalm a figure of the blood of the Lord in the Eucharist, that was most extensively developed in patristic times. St Cyprian comments at length upon it:

> The same figure is used by the Holy Spirit in the Psalms, making mention of the Lord's cup, and saying: *calix tuus inebrians quam praeclarus est* . . . But because the inebriation of the Lord's cup is not such as the inebriation of this world's wine, when the Holy Spirit speaks in the psalm of the inebriating cup, he adds how excellent it is: for the Lord's cup so inebriates them that drink it, as to make them sober; it brings back their minds to spiritual wisdom. Through this cup a man loses his taste for earthly things and comes to savour the things of God. And as ordinary wine gives wings to the mind, enlarges the heart and dispels sadness, so the precious blood and chalice of the Lord effaces the memory of the old man, affords forgetfulness of earthly cares; the sad and mournful breast, which before was oppressed with the choking sense of sins, is set free by the joy of Divine forgiveness.[3]

This passage, and a number of other patristic texts like it,[4] show how the twenty-second Psalm was brought into connexion with the eucharistic liturgy—a connexion so intimate that the *calix . . . praeclarus* of the Vulgate appears also in the Canon of the Roman Mass: *accipiens et hunc praeclarum calicem*. On the other hand, the same passage exhibits a whole new range of eucharistic symbolism,

[1] *Dem. Ev.* I: 10. P.G. 22: 89–92.
[2] Cyril of Jerusalem, P.G. 33: 1104 A.
[3] Ep. LXIII: 8 (trs. Carey, 1844, adapted).
[4] e.g. Gregory of Nyssa, P.G. 46: 692 A–B.

depending on the *species* of wine: the *sanguis Domini* is represented as inebriating. This means, substantially, that it takes us out of the world of sin, and lets us into the world of grace. Like wine, it produces oblivion; and like wine, it rejoices the heart, for the blood of Christ is the source of spiritual joy. This symbolism is both sacramental and 'mystical', because the transformation which is effected by the sacrament affords the soul a personal experience of divine things.

St Cyprian links up the twenty-second Psalm with the Banquet of Wisdom[1] in the prefiguration of the Eucharist:

> Moreover by Solomon, the Holy Spirit, shewing beforehand a figure of the Lord's sacrifice, making mention of the immolation of the victim, and bread, and wine, and the altar . . . : 'Wisdom' saith he 'hath built herself a house, she hath carved out her seven pillars: she hath slain her victims; she hath mingled her wine' with water; 'she hath also furnished her table'. Then she sent forth her servants, crying . . . 'Come, eat of my bread, and drink of the wine which I have mingled for you.' He says 'mingled wine', prophesying the Lord's cup of mingled wine and water.[2]

It will be observed that St Cyprian not only sees in this reference to bread and wine a figure of the Eucharist, but regards the altar of sacrifice as corresponding in reality to the table in the house of Wisdom. So the ancient theme of the consecrated place for holding the feast is now applied to the Christian Church, just as in the parable of the great supper.

An equally important element in the eucharistic catechism was the application to this sacrament of the text in the Song of Songs,[3] where the bridegroom invites his friends to the marriage-feast. This, as we have seen, was another eschatological prophecy; so that its application to the Eucharist can be recognized as an example of the strictest sort of typology, as soon as it is established that the 'last

¹Prov. 9: 1-5. ²Ep. LXIII: 4. ³5: 1.

things' are already present in the Kingdom of God, mystically realized in the sacramental actions here and now. The commentary of St Ambrose on the holy communion, in *De Mysteriis*, shows it as a fulfilment of this prophecy: ' "I have eaten my bread with my honey." You see that there is no bitterness in this bread, but it is all sweetness. "I have drunk my wine with my milk. . . ." As often as you drink, you receive forgiveness of your sins, and you are inebriated by the Spirit. . . . He that is drunk with wine, staggers; but he that is inebriated by the Spirit stands fast in Christ— a wonderful inebriation which sobers the soul.'[1] The close of this passage alludes to the words 'drink deep,' used by the bridegroom in the Song: it is in the direct line of messianic feast-symbolism. We shall have more to say later about the idea of 'sober drunkenness' which makes its appearance in this place.

There is an even more explicit passage in St Gregory of Nyssa, bringing together the invitation by the bridegroom, in the Song of Solomon, to join in the messianic marriage-feast, and the invitation by Christ at the Last Supper to drink of his blood: ' "Eat your fill, lovers; drink, sweethearts, and drink deep." For such as understand the hidden sense of the Scriptures, there is no difference between these words and the words of institution of the Sacrament, addressed to the Apostles. In both places it is written "Eat" and "Drink".'[2] The objection might be raised, as St Gregory observes, that there is no invitation by Christ to 'drink deep', no mention of inebriation: the reason is that what the Song means by inebriation is something which Christ actually gives: 'For if drunkenness is to be beside oneself, then this heavenly food and drink effects it indeed and continues to effect it, changing the worse into the better.'[3] Inebriation is here taken as a description of the positive operation of the Sacrament, exalting a man out of his common existence and taking him up into the life of

[1] P.L. 16: 449 B.   [2] P.G. 44: 989 B.   [3] 989 C.

God. It is then a dogmatic rather than a mystical interpretation, though the mystical ecstasy, the being 'beside oneself', appears in St Gregory as an extension of the sacramental ecstasy proper to the Eucharist.

IV

The close connexion between the sacramental actions and the mystical life, which appears in the text last quoted, is a regular characteristic of the typological method of interpretation, corresponding to the dual character of the Christian life, at once ecclesiastical and interior, public and private. It is therefore in no way surprising to find a mystical sense juxtaposed to a sacramental interpretation of one of the figurative banquets. While the latter exegesis shows how the Eucharist fulfils certain prophetic themes of the Old Testament, these same themes appear from the former point of view as realized in the union of the human soul with God. This mystical typology was first intensively developed in the school of Alexandria and by Origen, with SS Gregory of Nyssa and Ambrose: it stems partly from Philo, and partly from the normal Christian tradition. For our immediate purpose, it is only necessary to consider this development as applying to three of the texts already discussed; they were closely connected in this tradition: they are the twenty-second Psalm, the Song of Songs, and the book of Proverbs. A number of the predominantly sacramental interpretations examined earlier in this chapter foreshadowed the mystical typology; we shall now consider certain passages in which the mystical sense is more directly emphasized.

Here, Origen is the obvious starting-point. In his Commentary on the Song of Songs, he describes the mystical marriage-feast, in such a way as to show its intimate connexion both with the invitation of Wisdom, and with the twenty-second Psalm:

The bride asks the bridegroom's friends to bring her into the
abode of joy, where there is wine to drink and a feast made
ready. She has seen the king's chambers; now she would partake of the royal banquet and drink of the wine of bliss. The
friends of the bridegroom are the prophets, and servants of the
word: even so it is to these that the bride, faithful to God's
word, goes for admission into the banqueting house, where
wisdom hath mingled her wine, and hath sent forth her
maidens to invite the simple, saying, Come, eat of my bread,
and drink of the wine which I have mingled. This is the banqueting house whither many shall come from the east and west,
and shall sit down with Abraham, and Isaac and Jacob in the
kingdom of God. . . . And David, marvelling at the wine of
this feast, said, My cup runneth over. The Church, and every
soul, being made perfect, longs to come into his banqueting
house, to enjoy the teachings of wisdom and the mysteries of
all knowledge, as it were the sweets of a banquet and the
pleasures of wine.[1]

Origen here collects together several of the texts we have
been discussing; especially noteworthy is his correlation of
Old Testament eschatological pieces, e.g., from Proverbs
and Psalms, with the particular Matthaean verse[2] which
shows the fulfilment of them. This excellent example of
strict typology is applied, as always in the Commentary on
the Song of Songs, primarily to the Catholic Church. So far,
Origen is exactly in line with the New Testament teaching,
which regularly shows how the ancient scriptural figures
pointed forward to their fulfilment in the mystery of the
Church. But Origen proceeds further to apply his typology
to the individual Christian soul. This is the point of insertion of the strictly mystical, interior interpretation—here,
as always, entirely dependent on the ecclesiastical sense.
The same mystical symbolism of the Psalmist's 'well-filled
cup' reappears frequently in Origen.[3]

The mystical sense of the banquet-figure is given still

[1]*Comm. in Cant.* III (P.G. 13: 154–5). [2]8: 11.
[3]*Com. Ser. Mtth.* LXXXV (P.G. 13: 1734); *Hom. Lev.* VII: 1.

more prominence in Gregory of Nyssa. On the twenty-second Psalm, for instance, he writes: 'Christ, bringing the wine that maketh glad the hearts of men, produces in the soul that condition of sober drunkenness whereby it is transported from transitory to eternal things. He that is thus inebriated exchanges what lasts but a day for that which is for ever.'[1] The sacramental exegesis which underlies the whole passage is here developed in a spiritual sense. A more frequent source of inspiration in Gregory's writings is the Banquet of Wisdom:[2] 'Through wine, the hearts of the more perfect are rejoiced, for they are no longer concerned about childish things, but can slake their thirst from the cup of Wisdom';[3] and again, with an even more explicit allusion to the Banquet, 'the vine in flower foretells that wine which will one day fill the cup of Wisdom, drawn forth for the guests so that they may drink their fill of the heavenly Revelation, being inebriated with that sober drunkenness which lifts men up from earthly to divine things'.[4]

Up to this point, however, there is no evidence of a mystical interpretation of the text in the Song of Songs where the bridegroom invites his friends to the marriage-feast: Gregory of Nyssa explains it in terms of sacrament. In St Ambrose, this text is associated both with the twenty-second Psalm and with the Banquet of Wisdom: and his insistence upon the theme of *sobria ebrietas* is well known. From among many passages, one may here be quoted which links the various themes together:

You would eat, and drink: come to the feast of Wisdom, who calls all men from on high, saying 'Come, eat of my bread, and drink of the wine which I have mingled.' . . . Hearken to the Church, exhorting you not only in her own songs, but in the Song of Songs: 'Eat, O friends; drink, yea drink deep, beloved.' But this abundance is to sobriety, this inebriation causes the joy of grace, not of madness. . . . 'Wisdom hath

[1] P.G. 46: 692 B.   [2] Prov. 9: 5.   [3] P.G. 44: 956 D.
[4] P.G. 44: 873 B; see also 477 B, 661 A, 845 B.

built herself a house, she hath carved out her seven pillars.'
The Lord Jesus tells us himself that in his Father's house are
many mansions. Thus in this house you shall feast upon food
for the soul and upon spiritual drink, so that you shall never
hunger or thirst any more.[1]

V

So far, in studying the Patristic evidence, we have not
considered the most important of all the ritual meals in the
Old Testament, namely the Passover. There can be no question of examining here the typology of the Passover as a
whole, which would be a vast topic to undertake: our concern will be with certain developments arising out of the
essential ingredients of the meal itself, the symbolism of the
lamb, the unleavened bread, and the bitter herbs, together
with the preparation of the lamb, and certain circumstances
of the meal. As we have seen, there was already an eschatological interpretation of the Passover meal within Judaism
itself, since the meal was regarded as a figure of the banquet
in God's Kingdom: and this same typology recurs in St
Luke.[2] The tradition is continued in the Patristic literature.[3]
But, as we have seen already in connexion with other meals,
the tendency of the Christian witness is to exhibit the actual
fulfilment of the Old Testament figure in Christ and in his
Church. Consequently we shall find the same stratification
of figurative interpretations of the Passover meal as we
found in respect of the others.

Starting once more from the New Testament, we shall
find, as before, that the subsequent patristic developments
are all in a direct line of continuation therefrom: with this
notable difference, that the typological interpretations of
the Passover meal in the New Testament are uniformly of

[1]*Cain et Abel*, I: 19. P.L. 14: 326–7. In *De bono mortis* (20–22; P.L.
14: 550–1), St Ambrose brings together the bridegroom's invitation and
the parable of the great supper, interpreting both in the mystical sense.
[2]22: 16–18.   [3]e.g. Origen, *Hom. Num.* XI: 1.

the kind we have called 'mystical', exhibiting the fulfilment of the scriptural figures in the qualities or dispositions of the individual Christian soul. Of the two fundamental texts, the first is as follows: 'Rid yourselves of the leaven which remains over, so that you may be a new mixture, still uncontaminated as you are. Has not Christ been sacrificed for us, our paschal victim? Let us keep the feast, then, not with the leaven of yesterday, that was all vice and mischief, but with unleavened bread, with purity and honesty of intent.'[1]

The unleavened bread of the Passover meal is thus a figure of the Christian state of mind after the enactment of the second and supreme Passover. This state of mind is properly a complete renewal of the whole personality of each individual member of the new creation, which sprang from Christ's resurrection in the juvenescence of the year. The Christian soul must be entirely free, like unleavened bread, from anything left over from before; it must be pure and sincere.

The second of our cardinal passages in the New Testament is at the beginning of the First Epistle of Peter. Here the whole of the Passover ritual is really represented as typifying the Christian character; but it is possible to select the points which refer to the meal itself.

> Gird up the loins of your mind, keep full mastery of your senses, and set your hopes on the gracious gift that is offered you when Jesus Christ appears . . . What was the ransom that freed you from the vain observances of ancestral tradition? You know well enough that it was not paid in earthly currency, silver or gold; it was paid in the precious blood of Christ; no lamb was ever so pure, so spotless a victim. Before the beginning of the world, God had foreknown him, but it was only in these last days that he was revealed, for your sakes.[2]

The last part of this passage does not directly concern the present inquiry, and accordingly need not be discussed at length here. The 'spotless' lamb refers back to Exodus

[1] 1 Cor. 5: 7–8.   [2] 1 Pet. 1: 13, 18–20.

(12: 5); the 'fore-knowing before the beginning of the
world' and the 'revelation in these last days' certainly seem
to be a symbolic interpretation of the rules whereby the
lamb was chosen on the tenth day and killed 'on the
evening' of the fourteenth.[1] For our immediate purpose,
however, it is the beginning of the passage that is important: and this is obviously a typological interpretation of
the Passover meal. 'Gird up the loins of your mind' is a
symbolic rendering of the instruction in Exodus (12: 11):
'Your loins must be girt'. The next words are an allusion to
the austerity of the Passover meal itself. The steadfast hope
supporting the soul throughout the time of waiting may
well symbolize the 'staff in his hand'.[2]

In the subsequent Christian tradition, the hints given in
the New Testament were followed up, and extended by
application to other circumstances of the ritual. Thus Origen
developed a complete allegory of the Passover: the flesh of
the lamb stands for the word of God, as the soul's spiritual
food: 'If we speak perfect things to you, we bring you the
flesh of the son of God to eat.'[3] The wild herbs represent
the godly sorrow of repentance for sin.[4] The meat of the
lamb is not to be eaten raw ('as the slaves of the letter do'),
or boiled in water ('as those do who dilute the sense of
scripture by explaining it away'), but roast over the fire;
'fervour of spirit, and the burning words of God, shall cook
for us the flesh of the Lamb, so that those which eat thereof
shall say that their heart burned within them by the way

[1]Exod. 12: 3, 6. (See Pseudo-Chrysostom, *Hom. Pasch*, VI; P.G. 59:
724, 735.)
[2]Exod. 12: 11; cf. *Greg. Nyss.* P.G. 44: 357 B. It may here be observed
that the Passover meal was already subject to symbolic commentary in
the ancient Jewish literary tradition. In the *Mishna*, the unleavened
bread and the wild herbs represent the haste of the exodus, and the
hardships of captivity. Philo explains unleavened bread in the same
manner as in 1 Corinthians and in 1 Peter (*Spec. leg.* II: xxviii: 159
161)—as well as in other ways.
[3]*Hom. Num.* XIII: 6. P.G. 12: 752 A.
[4]*Comm. in Joh.* X. P.G. 14: 336 C.

as he explained to them the Scriptures.' The 'head' of the
lamb represents the doctrine of heavenly things, and the
'feet' the doctrine of hell. The 'entrails' refers to mystical
and esoteric teaching.

Here then we find that the most traditional exegesis is the
spiritual type, exemplified in the New Testament: but
there are also instances, albeit on a small scale, of the
Matthean typology, and also of the sacramental interpretation, applied to the Passover as to other meals. The Matthean approach leads to a recognition of the circumstances
of the Passover as prefiguring the events of Christ's passion;
this is favoured rather by the Western Fathers: Tertullian
reads the wild herbs as meaning, not the sorrows of the
Christian soul, but rather the bitterness of the Passion of
Christ.[1] Melito of Sardis works out this symbolism more
fully in his *Homily on the Passion*: 'You killed him on the
Great Feast. Therefore your feast of unleavened bread is
bitter unto you, as it is written that with "unleavened
bread, and with bitter herbs they shall eat it". For bitter
are the nails you pierced him with, bitter the wounding
words you gave him, bitter the gall for his thirst, bitter the
thorns of his crown.'[2]

The same kind of typology was applied to other details of
the Passover rites in the *Paschal Homily* of the Pseudo-
Chrysostom. Here, the period of four days between the
taking and the killing of the lamb, which in 1 Peter represented the distance between the eternal pre-existence of the
incarnate Word in the divine ordinance, and his coming in
the last days, is now taken as a figure of the time between
the capture of Jesus in the garden and his crucifixion—a
very characteristically Matthean interpretation. This may
be compared with the passage in the Fourth Gospel,[3] where
the fact that the legs of Jesus on the cross were not broken
is related to the injunction not to break the bones of the

[1]P.L. 2: 630 B.   [2]93–94, ed. Campbell Bonner (1940), pp. 153–5.
[3]John 19: 33, 36.

Paschal Lamb:[1] another characteristically 'anecdotal' interpretation of a detail of the Passover ritual. Then the meat
'roasted over the fire' represents the divine nature of Christ;
the head, the feet and the entrails mean 'the height, the
depth and the breadth' of the love of the crucified, who
draws all men unto him. These particular indications are
indeed more theological than the former, but still relate to
the historical circumstances of Calvary.

On the other hand, the strictly sacramental, eucharistic
interpretation of the Passover texts is found particularly in
a group of Paschal homilies closely associated with those we
have discussed, but certainly, as it appears, from another
hand. The author first relates the action of marking with
blood the lintels of the Hebrews' houses to the operation of
holy baptism, and proceeds thus to relate the eating of the
lamb to the holy communion: 'After the anointing comes
the eating, whereby the divine body is received within ourselves and is mingled with our being to make us one.'[2] From
this point of view, the circumstances of the Passover meal
represent the preparation for holy communion: the prohibition against eating the lamb raw emphasizes the need
for a right predisposition; the unleavened bread and the
wild herbs are still the traditional symbols of simplicity
and penance, but with special reference to these spiritual
attitudes as preparatory to a worthy reception of the Eucharist. 'The Law shows us how to approach communion, and
how to live after we have partaken of it.'[3] The same interpretation is found in St Cyril of Alexandria;[4] but admittedly
there is no evidence for it in the earlier tradition.

It may be found surprising that the one recorded meal of
Christ that has not been discussed so far should be the most
important of all, namely the last meal of his life on earth
among his own people, the last supper. But any treatment
of this meal would have been premature until our examina-

[1]Exod. 12: 46.   [2]P.G. 59: 727.   [3]729.   [4]P.G. 68: 1073 C.

tion had covered the whole typology of meals in Scripture; because the Last Supper is affected by each one of the considerations under which we have looked at this question, and reappears at each level of our discussions. This may even be the answer to one of the conundrums of modern New Testament theology; for it is a well-known point of controversy among scholars, and particularly among Protestant scholars, to decide what kind of meal the Last Supper was—a Passover meal, or an ordinary common meal among the many shared by Christ with his apostles? A meal with sacramental significance? or eschatological? Arguments can be adduced in support of any of these views—which shows that none of them is unanswerable.

The explanation is surely this, that the Last Supper of the Lord incorporated all that wealth of manifold significance which we have found in the whole typology of spiritual meals. First of all, it was a meal which Christ shared with his friends; from this point of view it fulfilled the prophecies of the messianic banquet, where all men are invited to the table of the Son of Man, thus answering to the figurative meaning of Old Testament feasts. But it was also itself a figure of the eschatological banquet, where Christ in his Kingdom shall drink of the fruit of his vine and entertain his people in his own house. It was a Passover meal; and in this respect, too, it was both a fulfilment of the promises figured in the sacrifice of the Paschal lamb, and itself a prophecy of the sacrifice of the true Lamb of God. And, more than all this, it was not merely a prefiguring but the actual institution of the sacrament of the Eucharist. From this point of view, it was altogether *sui generis*, belonging equally to the earthly life of Christ and to the sacramental life which it inaugurated. Thus it unified in the reality of one historical event all the various planes of our previous discussion: it is, as it were, the central mystery around which the whole biblical significance of the Meal is developed.

CHAPTER SIX

THE DEVELOPMENT OF HISTORY

T HE second distinctive characteristic of history, as understood in the light of Christian conceptions, is the organic interconnexion of its successive stages, which we have seen exemplified in the scriptural typology. It is the business of theology to seek out the intrinsic principles and laws of this systematic coherence, which represents the working out of the divine plan itself. As we have already seen,[1] St Irenaeus, faced with the gnostic theory of a radical discontinuity between the Old and the New Testaments, was the first to demonstrate that both alike are the work of one and the same God, and that both belong to a single dispensation. This conception of sacred history as one process of growth was worked out, in patristic times, especially by the Eastern writers, and received its definitive formulation in the work of St Gregory of Nyssa. God's plan, and the sum of history in its widest acceptation, is here seen as an ἀκολουθία, an orderly progression towards the 'fulfilment of history' when God shall 'resume everything in Christ'.[2]

Gregory took the term ἀκολουθία from the language of Greek philosophy, especially from Aristotle, who uses it in connexion with the laws governing physical change and motion: Gregory applied it to the gradual unfolding of God's plan through all its phases. The material creation itself exhibits this orderly succession: 'If we look at the wonderful works of nature, we know that the fruit cannot ripen except there be first a seedling and then shoots and so on; it is the

[1] v. supra pp. 5–6. [2] Eph. 1: 10.

result of a skilfully ordered succession of events (ἀκολουθία)'.[1]
Natural laws are not the expression of blind fate, but of
Providence, guiding all things towards their last end, which
is union with God. 'It is unreasonable to grieve and to mur-
mur about the inevitable and necessary succession of events,
for all that is arranged (οἰκωνούμενα) in the whole universe
tends towards an end: everything, through a regular progression (τάξει καί ἀκολουθίᾳ) according to the careful art of
him that rules it, must come to partake of divine nature.'[2] This
passage really includes the whole notion of ἀκολουθία, which
mankind experiences as the ineluctable law of consequence,
but which is in reality an ordered progress towards a goal,
the goal of assimilation to God: ἀκολουθία is a process of
deification.

So understood, the term helped Gregory to formulate one
of his fundamental theses, namely that all things were
created entire from the beginning of time, and come forth
by a progressive development through the working of their
own innate dynamism.

When it is said that the world was created 'in the beginning'
(*in principio:* ἐν ἀρχῇ), this means that God established in one
and the same instant, all at once, the principles, the potentialities, and the causes of all things, which were thus brought
into existence from the first act of his creative will. . . . But
the power and the wisdom bestowed upon them were elicited
through a chain of eventuation, so that each constituent part of
the whole should be brought to its perfection in one order. . . .
Things came forth in their turn, each one as a necessary consequence of the former, according to the laws of nature's work-
manship, throughout the whole chain of succession (ἀκολουθία).[3]

One particular case of this evolution of reality according
to its intrinsic laws of development is of special interest and
importance: the human soul and the human body follow
parallel lines of development from the seed, where both
exist in principle.

[1]P.G. 46: 517 D.   [2]46: 105 A.   [3]44: 72 B–C.

We hold that mankind is progressively developed and made manifest by a physical evolution (ἀκολουθία) towards the full growth of manhood, without the accession of any extraneous element for its completion, but through its own regular advance to perfection. . . . So the form of the man that is to be is potentially in the seed, but cannot yet be detected there, because its manifestation is necessarily gradual and successive.[1]

Whether in the case of living creatures or of the whole universe, the ἀκολουθία is ultimately always linked to the reality of time; and this is the real importance of the principle. Gregory was obsessed by the mystery of time, more than by any other problem. From his position at the meeting-point of Greek and Christian thought, he was conditioned to feel all the tragedy of time and its inexorable law; he knew the impatience that comes of waiting and the anxieties that attend the recurrence of things. But his response to this situation was not the platonic flight from time; it was the Christian affirmation of a true sense of time, giving it positive value as the stage and scene of a divine action. Certain points of detail in the passages we have quoted already indicate something of this conception; it becomes clearer in larger generalizations.

Thus on one hand, ἀκολουθία, the law of successiveness, is presented as the universal condition of the creation as such, the basic criterion of creatureliness as distinguished from the creator. This is Gregory's philosophical starting-point.

Creation is extended in space; the regular succession of phenomena in time is contained within the aeons: but that Nature which is from beyond the aeons suffers no distinction of before and after. . . . So the whole creation, as we have said, evolving by an orderly system of consequence (ἀκολουθία τάξεως) is measured by the extent of the aeons. And if a man should lift up his mind through the entire succession of the aeons to the first principle of begotten things, his enquiry would still be limited by the law of the aeons. . . . But that Nature which

[1]44: 236 B, C.

is above creation, being apart from the categories of mensuration, suffers no temporal succession (χρονικὴ ἀκολουθία) knows neither progress nor interruption, has no beginning, no end and no change, is subject to no order.[1]

The whole of this passage depends on the idea of ἀκολουθία, succession, the order of before and after, which characterizes created reality. Creation can never escape this law of successiveness, which is the very definition of created being, the intrinsic condition of everything in space and time. For Gregory, it is not only the physical and material world that is subject to this law, but every creature without exception; this may well be due to the influence of Poseidonius. In any case, the analysis of ἀκολουθία is here carried through to its metaphysical foundation, the common essence of all its forms and manifestations. Nothing whatsoever, neither mental not vital nor material, but is subject to the condition of development in temporal succession.

Gregory recapitulates his position as follows: 'The divine nature is not in time, but time originates from it. Creation follows out its course, from a clearly-defined principle towards its proper end, through spaces of time; so that there can be, as Solomon says, "certain knowledge of . . . the beginning, ending, and midst of the times";[2] his enumeration of the divisions of time in this passage stands for the successive evolution of "the things that are".'[3] But 'he by whom all things were made (the Word) is above all beginning of creation, and all categories of time, and all order of succession (τάξεως ἀκολουθία)'.[4]

Thus far we have been concerned with ἀκολουθία as a philosophical concept for the law of successiveness which governs all temporal reality. One aspect of this law is the inexorable necessity of the regular, but implacable cycle of birth and death. Another aspect of the same law would be the orientation of reality towards an end; but on the

[1]45: 364 C, 365 A–B; see also 813 D.   [2]Wis. 7: 17–18.
[3]45: 365 B.   [4]369 B; see also 433 D and 436 A.

philosophical level, this teleological implication of the word in Gregory's thought remains vague. Christ alone both reveals and fulfils ἀκολουθία, which thus becomes the expression of God's design for the deification of mankind.

But at this point there emerges, between the plan of creation and the plan of redemption, a special field of activity in which ἀκολουθία plays a significant part, namely the world of sin. If we consider the present condition of man in the knowledge of how he was created, we are faced with a new problem: 'We must not leave unexamined anything that concerns mankind. At first sight there appear to be contradictions in man; the conditions of his natural existence today seem to have no continuity (ἀκολουθία) with those of his origin. This is something that we have to put right, through the record of Scripture and through the exercise of reason, discovering the organic arrangement and connexion between the apparent contradictions.'[1]

This passage is full of interest. There are links missing between man as he was created and man as he is now, an ἀκολουθία that has to be reconstructed; for which purpose the contents of the Scriptures are at our disposal, but we should make use of reason to try to understand them. It would be true to say that a great part of Gregory's writings are devoted to the quest of this ἀκολουθία—to the search for a coherent explanation of the way in which mankind passed from the first state to the present state; an inquiry conducted on the basis of biblical data subject to interpretation. This is Gregory's typical method, which essentially consists in the co-ordination of scriptural materials with an explanation of the connexions between them—theology being defined as just this use of human understanding in order to arrive at the object of faith, *intellectus quaerens fidem*.

Whereas, then, Gregory had spoken of the ἀκολουθία of creation as a regular progression of values, he was now to exhibit a contrasting process of dissolution. This breaking-up

[1] 44: 128 A–B.

was traced in the genealogy of sin and death, beginning
with the sin of Adam, The word, ἀκολουθία, again proves its
importance in Gregory's theology, for it served to indicate
the transmission of original sin. In his system as a whole,
one of the distinctive features is this possibility of a dual
interpretation of the historical process, both in terms of
growth and in terms of dissolution.

The consequences of sin are plainly set out: 'The whole of
God's creation is good, there is nothing in it to be con-
temned. But when once the life of man was corrupt, when
once it was engaged in the train (ἀκολουθία) of sin, which
from small beginnings grew up in man out of all measure,
then the godlike beauty of the soul no longer wore the likeness of its prototype.'[1] The central idea is evident: from the
moment of mankind's first sin, the inevitable succession
(ἀκολουθία) of the consequences of sin began to unfold itself
in mankind. The development was twofold: first, that of the
penal effects of sin, inflicted upon the human creature; and
secondly, the transmission and continuity of sin throughout
the human race.

In the former of these two contexts, ἀκολουθία means the
order in which the consequences of the first sin were successively manifested: 'The successive stages, whereby we
were driven out of Paradise into exile with our first father,
are the same as we may now retrace in the contrary direction to come back into the former bliss. What, then, was
this succession of events (ἀκολουθία)? The pleasure of a lie
was the beginning of the fall. Shame and dread followed
upon the passion of pleasure, when they no longer dared
appear in the Creator's sight, but "hid themselves . . .
amongst the trees of the garden". And after that they were
banished into that unwholesome and dangerous situation,
where marriage was allowed them as a compensation for the
penalty of death.'[2]

It will be observed that death is here reckoned among the

[1] 46: 372 B.   [2] 46: 373 D–376 A.

consequences of sin. Gregory is even more explicit in a subsequent passage. After showing that our aim must be to find a way of life which no longer involves the consequential necessity of death, and after showing that this way is the life of virginity, he continues: 'It is thus that we may halt that continuous propagation (ἀκολουθία) of death and corruption which has persisted in mankind from the first man until the life of him who keeps his virginity: for death could not be stayed so long as men were engendered through the act of marriage.'[1] Death, then, which earlier had appeared as a consequence of nature, is here represented in a new light as a consequence of sin.

The second aspect of ἀκολουθία in connexion with sin is the diffusion of Adam's sin throughout the human race, by the transmission of original sin. 'The first man having been brought down to earth in consequence of sin, and being therefore called "earthy", carried along with him (ἀκόλουθον) all his issue, which were born earthy and mortal in like manner.'[2] Adam's sin was thus the principle of a 'propagation of sin (ἀκολουθία τῶν κακῶν).'[3]

Besides the transmission of sinfulness through all mankind, there is a kind of progression of sin in each individual man. Baptism halts this development, 'interrupting the continuity (ἀκολουθία) of sins'[4]: but sin is not only a continuum, nor even only a progressive condition; sins propagate themselves in a regular series. 'Within its own pattern and by an evil rule of development (ἀκολουθία), sin methodically makes headway in the soul, from wickedness to wickedness.'[5] If concupiscence is overcome, pride ensues, 'as the devil directs this perverse system of succession (ἀκολουθία) in sins'.[6]

In this last instance, ἀκολουθία describes how the devil may

[1] 377 A, D.
[2] 44: 1312 A. Cf. 45: 892 B, on the propagation (ἀκολουθία) of sin from Eve.
[3] 44: 477 A.　[4] 44: 364 B.　[5] 44: 416 B.　[6] 416 C.

be driven back, step by step; but there is also the opposite series, in order of successive depravity.

> As when a chain is pulled at one end, each link is necessarily set in motion right up to the last, the movement being transmitted in a continuous succession (ἀκολουθία) from the first through all the intermediate links, even so the passions of man are all interconnected. If this chain of wickedness is to be enumerated, pleasure leads man on to vainglory, vainglory excites desire, desire pride, pride jealousy, jealousy brings with it (ἀκολούθον) hypocrisy which produces cruelty, and the end of all is hell. See how the chain of vices all depends on one vice, namely pleasure. If once the series (ἀκολουθία) of passions is begun in a man's life, he has but one way to escape from it, which is to abandon that life into which this succession of evils has entered.[1]

In a further passage, Gregory goes on to explain roundly that 'it is nature itself, obeying the law of its being, that necessarily brings down upon all those who walk in its ways this accumulation of pains'.[2] So 'he that would occupy himself in the contemplation of invisible things must withdraw from the train (ἀκολουθία) of human occupations';[3] otherwise he will be caught up 'in the procession (ἀκολουθία) of the vanities of this life'.[4] This account of the ἀκολουθία of human life is obviously more pessimistic than the conceptions previously discussed, for it implies a natural inevitability of sin, to be escaped only through flight. Most of these texts, however, come from Gregory's earliest work, the *de Virginitate*, written in praise of the monastic life; which may account for some exaggeration in this statement of the case.

Over against this order of sin, Gregory described the contrasting order of grace. Immediately after the passage quoted above concerning the transmission of original sin, he went on to observe that 'God established of necessity a second ἀκολουθία in opposition (to the ἀκολουθία of sin),

[1] 46: 344 B; see also 44: 560 A, where the image is of a snake.
[2] 46: 345 A–B. [3] 349 B. [4] 44: 560 A.

whereby mankind is restored from death to immortality, as
St Paul declared in another way when he says that "one
man makes amends, and it brings to all justification",[1] just
as "one man commits a fault, and it brings condemnation
upon all" through the succeeding generations.'[2] Gregory
thus uses the same word, ἀκολουθία, for the Pauline doctrine
of the transmission of sin from Adam and for the diffusion
of grace in Christ.

In the order of grace, ἀκολουθία primarily means the re-
percussion throughout the human race of the new creation
that was brought about in the resurrection of Christ. 'In the
passion of his human nature, Christ fulfilled the dispensation (οἰκονομία) of our redemption; he parted for a time his
soul from his body, but was never parted himself from
either of these which were united to his person; then once
again he brought together that which had been parted, to
inaugurate the resurrection from the dead, which should
follow (ἀκολουθία) to all mankind.'[3] The juxtaposition here of
οἰκονομία and ἀκολουθία is worth notice. Gregory tends to
substitute the latter term for the former, which was characteristic of the more archaic vocabulary of Irenaeus.[4]

In a curious passage, he describes the diffusion of the
grace of Christ as covering first the holiest souls, and thence
extending progressively until it reaches the greatest sinners:
'The destruction of sin and the annihilation of death began
in Christ, being thereafter accorded to the generations of
men in a regular succession (τάξις καί ἀκολουθία).'[5] Grace
comes first to such as Paul, then to such as Timothy, 'and
so on, until the succession (ἀκολουθία) comes to include all the
followers, even those whose share of merit is less than their
share of evil.'[6]

This process of propagation is continued 'proportionally.

[1] Rom. 5: 18.   [2] 44: 1312 B.   [3] 45: 548 B–C. Cf. 52 C.
[4] Clearly, for instance, in the expression ἡ ἀκολουθία τοῦ μυστηρίου (45: 65 A, and *passim*).
[5] 44: 1313 B.   [6] 1313 D.

Starting with those whose share of sin is the least, the series (ἀκολουθία) of such as are recovered for righteousness is extended by regular progression to the most sinful; until the development of grace reaches the furthest confines of sin by destroying it.'[1] The history of salvation is represented as a forward march of grace to reduce the range and power of evil.[2]

For our purposes, the importance of this account lies in the statement that the restoration of mankind in Christ is successive. If this is true, as we have seen, of the race as a whole, since grace takes possession of it only by degrees, it is no less true of each individual soul. Here, then, is a great difference between the new creation and the first, in which mankind was created perfect. Gregory emphasizes the distinction in a noteworthy passage: 'This is the doctrine: it was not according to the same arrangement (ἀκολουθία) that beings were first created, and then re-created.'[3]

The difference is this. 'When, in the beginning, created nature came into existence through the power of God, every creature was immediately constituted from the first in its full stature. Now one of these creatures was mankind, which, like the rest, knew no progress towards perfection, but was made perfect from the beginning of existence. . . . But since men, being partakers of mortality through the inclination towards sin, have fallen from their place among the good, mankind's return to perfection is not all at once, as it was in the beginning, but by a gradual process of improvement, the evil tendencies being counteracted step by step in regular succession (τάξις καὶ ἀκολουθία).'[4]

So the mystery of time is finally explained, and its religious content becomes apparent. The purpose of it, as Origen had recognized, is to allow of the return of free wills to God,

---

[1]44: 1313 D–1316 A.

[2]Gregory observes that for the followers of him that inaugurated the new life, there are two stages: baptism and resurrection (45: 89A).

[3]44: 1109 A.   [4]44: 1109 A–C; cf. 256 A.

which cannot but be gradual.[1] Once again, it is the stage and scene of the unfolding action of deification: 'everything, through a regular progression (τάξις καί ἀκολουθία), according to the careful art of him that rules it, must come to partake of the divine nature.'[2] In another place, Gregory expresses the same thought thus: 'It is by successive stages (ὁδῷ καί ἀκολουθίᾳ) that human nature comes to participate in the divine. There was first the illumination of prophecy and the law, and afterwards the full glory of the Light'.[3] So ἀκολουθία defines that structural law of the history of salvation, which is the succession of covenants.

Not only so: for the rule of progress towards union with God applies also to each individual soul. 'As the first age, that of nurslings, requires breast milk for its nurture, while another sort of food comes next, suitable to the child and appropriate for its digestion, until it comes to full growth, so I believe the soul also partakes of life after its own kind, proportionably, and receives in a regular order of progress (τάξει καί ἀκολουθίᾳ) those good things which are put before it in beatitude according to its measure.'[4] Once again the term ἀκολουθία serves to indicate another characteristic theme in Gregory's works, the idea of constant progress in the spiritual life by a process of organic growth.[5]

Gregory's teaching represents one of the most determined attempts that have been made to enucleate the structural principles of development of the history of salvation on the full scale, that is, as embracing the totality of history. St Augustine's comparable work in the *City of God*, to which we have referred, is quite unlike it. If one had to compare the two, one could say that Augustine is the more concerned with the divine initiative, Gregory with the free

---

[1]See 46: 525 B–C, with the expression περιοδική ἀκολουθία.
[2]46: 105 A.   [3]44: 864 C–D.
[4]46: 180 A. There is a series (ἀκολουθία) of virtues, opposed to that of the vices (44: 1253 B).
[5]There is even an ἀκολουθία of liturgy, in the 'regular succession' of festivals (46: 701 C). See also 46: 788 C, 789 A, 813 A.

human response. These attitudes reflect the general trends of Western and Eastern theology; from the point of view of that theandric synergism which we have recognized as part of the inwardness of history, they represent complementary systems, each emphasizing one of the two inseparable aspects of the case.

CHAPTER SEVEN

LENT AND EASTERTIDE

IT is time to consider the last of the three characteristics of sacred history, namely its eschatological aspect. Sacred history does not consist in a simple homogeneous development, but involves an opposition between this world and the world to come; for the whole trend of the historical process is teleologically ordained towards a consummation, and towards the coming of the new Jerusalem. There is, in the Christian view of things, an end of history: which means that the world is neither everlasting and static, nor evolutionary *ad infinitum*. We have alluded to this question often enough already, and now come to the last mention of it. Our discussion starts, as heretofore, from the Biblical typology. The figure of the two contrasting aeons is variously represented—for instance, in the distinction between the cosmic week and the eighth day: a subject which we have studied in another place, showing how it degenerated into millenarism.

Another figure appears in the distinction between the forty days of Lent, representing the time of this world, and the fifty days of Pentecost, representing the world to come. We shall be concerned with this Biblical and liturgical theme on each plane of its symbolic significance in the history of salvation; for it is intimately connected with the theology and eschatology of history. Our first point will be to elucidate the origins of this connexion by a study of the symbolic significance of the forty days in Scripture. Then we shall see how it affects the concept of history as a whole, being one long preparation for eternity. The particular interest of such an inquiry derives from the fact of its Biblical and liturgical basis: for it serves thus to show how the common Christian practice of the present day implies, in Lent and Eastertide, the Christian intuition of history as a preparation and a waiting for the world to come.

The normal rule of Biblical typology is that the events recorded in the Old Testament prefigure first of all the mystery of Christ, and are fulfilled in him. In the former of the two examples now under discussion, the forty days' fast and temptation of Christ in the wilderness are thus obviously central to the argument. This period is visibly related to the forty years' wanderings and trials of Israel in the desert, and also to the forty-day fasts of Moses and of Elijah. The relationship with the forty days of Lent is equally indubitable. Thus we are introduced at once to the three planes of the history of salvation—the Old Testament, Christ, and the Church. Again, just as the sacraments of the Church are themselves a figure of eschatological reality, so Lent is a liturgical symbol of that particular aspect of the present age which is indicated in the word 'preparation'.

In the writings of the Fathers, the consideration of the symbolic number forty normally arises in connexion with the forty days which Christ spent in the wilderness. Thus St Hilary declared that 'the devil knew how the waters of the Flood increased throughout forty days, and how it took the same time to explore the promised land, and for God to indite the Law of Moses, and how it was for forty years that the people lived upon the food of Angels in the wilderness'.[1] And St Ambrose wrote, upon the same occasion: 'Forty days —you recognize the sacred (*mysticum*) number. You recall that this was the period during which the Flood spread, and during which the prophet sanctified himself by fasting . . .; the holy Moses was found worthy to receive the Law in this same space of time, and for the same number of years the fathers ate the bread of angels in the desert.'[2]

[1] P.L. 9: 928 A–B.   [2] *Expos. in Luc.* IV: 2. P.L. 15: 1617.

There is no need to multiply instances of such catalogues. One fact is immediately apparent: some references are peculiar to individual writers, while others are commonplace. It is the latter that concern us here, because they represent an ecclesiastical tradition, and thus carry a certain guarantee of genuine antiquity. These universal references are twofold: one to the forty years of temptation in the wilderness; the other to the forty-day fasts of Moses and Elijah. All the rest are only secondary and derivative. Our task is therefore to elicit the substantial significance of these two main themes; for the particular numeral '40' is nothing but a sign: our concern is with the reality signified. It is not a matter of abstract number-symbolism, founded on arithmetical properties, but of the exact overtones and undertones of meaning belonging to a particular number, in the Jewish and Christian tradition, on account of the historical events associated with that number.

The first of these events which we have to consider is the wanderings of the Hebrews in the wilderness. This period of forty years is represented in the Book of Numbers as the time of God's anger against the generation which came out of Egypt, and was not to be allowed into the promised land: 'For forty days you surveyed the land, and for each day you shall have a year of penance for your sins, and feel my vengeance'[1]; and again: 'Still angry, he led us this way and that through the desert, till the generation that had offended him died out.'[2] This appears to be the older interpretation of the facts. The same symbolism of 'forty' as a measure of punishment recurs in connexion with the Flood, and in the prophet Ezekiel.

In Deuteronomy, however, we find a different way of looking at the forty years, which are now seen as a period of probation imposed by God upon the people; he is with them all the time: 'the Lord has . . . watched over your journey through this wild wilderness, secured you from

[1]Num. 14: 34.   [2]ibid. 32: 13.

want by forty years of his companionship'.[1] The years in the wilderness were years of grace, when God worked great wonders for his people.[2] The decisive statement of the case is as follows: 'Do not forget the long journeying by which, for forty years, the Lord thy God led thee through the desert, testing thee by hard discipline, to know the dispositions of thy heart, whether thou wouldst keep his commandments, or not. He disciplined thee with hunger, and then sent down manna . . . he would teach thee that man cannot live by bread only, there is life for him in all the words that proceed from the mouth of God.'[3]

This latter interpretation was adopted in the rest of the Old Testament literature. The forty years were a time of grace,[4] when God was very near to his people, and fulfilled all their needs: but it was a time, too, of trial and probation, when he would have them learn to trust him only; it was the age of faith. And what the trial proved, in the event, was just the hardness of the people's heart, as appears in the ninety-fourth Psalm:

> Would you but listen to his voice today! Do not harden your hearts, as they were hardened once at Meriba, at Massa in the wilderness. Your fathers put me to the test, challenged me, as if they lacked proof of my power, for forty years together; from that generation I turned away in loathing; These, I said, are ever wayward hearts, these have never learnt to obey me. And I took an oath in anger, They shall never attain my rest.[5]

The New Testament took over from the Jewish tradition this familiar interpretation of the forty years' wandering in the wilderness. The author of the Acts of the Apostles seems to have attributed an exceptional importance to the number forty: dividing the life of Moses into three periods of forty

---

[1]Deut. 2: 7.   [2]Exod. 15: 25.   [3]Deut. 8: 2–4; cf. 29: 4–5.
[4]Amos, 2: 10; Nehemiah 9: 21; Judith 5: 14–15.
[5]Ps. 94: 8–11.

years each,[1] allotting forty years to the reign of Saul,[2] mentioning (alone among New Testament writers) that it was forty days after the Resurrection that Christ ascended into heaven.[3] . . . His two references to the forty years in the wilderness are consequently of special interest: 'He it was who led them out, performing wonders and signs in Egypt, and at the Red Sea, and in the wilderness, over a space of forty years';[4] and later: 'stretching out his arm to deliver them from it (*sc.* Egypt), for forty years he bore with their hard hearts in the wilderness.'[5]

What is of still more consequence for our present purpose is the way in which the New Testament, recognizing that the trial of the forty years ended in failure, shows that it was thus no more than the prefiguration of another trial. On this point, the decisive text is in the Epistle to the Hebrews, where the ninety-fourth Psalm is quoted: 'If you hear his voice speaking to you this day, do not harden your hearts, as they were hardened once when you provoked me, and put me to the test in the wilderness. Your fathers put me to the test, made trial of me, and saw what I could do, all those forty years. So I became the enemy of that generation . . . and I took an oath in my anger, they shall never attain my rest.'[6] The author's commentary follows. 'Who was it that provoked him? Was it not all those whom Moses had rescued from Egypt? Who was it, during all those forty years, that incurred his enmity? . . . those to whom the message first came have been excluded by their unbelief. So he fixes another day, To-day, as he calls it.'[7]

The great value and importance of this interpretation of the Psalm lies in its eschatological indications. There was a first probation of God's chosen people during forty years in the wilderness, and in the end the people were found wanting; the whole generation of those years of wandering was denied entry into the promised land: wherefore the Psalmist

[1] 7: 23, 30. [2] 13: 21. [3] 1: 3. [4] 7: 36. [5] 13: 17–18. [6] 3: 7–11.
[7] 3: 16–17; 4: 6–7.

L.H.–S

foretells another time of trial. The first Exodus was a figure of the eschatological Exodus. What the Epistle to the Hebrews does here is to insist that the moment of the latter Exodus has come: the Psalmist's *hodie* is now, in our own day. Just as Christ on the cross declared to the penitent thief that the paradise of prophecy was already there, 'This day thou shalt be with me in Paradise',[1] so here the long-awaited Exodus is spoken of as actually present: 'Today . . . do not harden your hearts.'

In order to define the mode and meaning of this contemporaneity, we must go back to the Gospel narrative. All interpreters are agreed that the story of the temptation of Christ is framed on the model of temptation of the people of Israel. Both took place in the wilderness, the typical proving-ground, where spiritual warfare reaches its highest intensity. The three temptations of Christ in the Gospel answered to the trials of the people in the desert. The first, to change stones into bread, corresponded to the text of Deuteronomy quoted above: 'he disciplined thee with hunger . . . he would teach thee that man cannot live by bread only, there is life for him in all the words that proceed from the mouth of God.'[2] The second referred to the water which came forth from the rock.[3] The third recalled Mount Sinai, and the Golden Calf.[4]

Another point which is of immediate interest here is the period of the temptation of Christ, which is given as forty days.[5] There is no reason to doubt that this corresponds to a real space of time; but we may wonder why Christ chose that particular period, and particularly why the primitive tradition should have preserved the record of it. When we know that the number forty was, as has been seen, specifically associated with the time of temptation of the Israelites, in all Jewish tradition, and particularly in the later tradi-

[1]Luke 23: 43.   [2]Deut. 8: 4; Matt. 4: 4.
[3]Deut. 6: 16; Ps. 95: 9; Matt. 4: 7.   [4]Deut. 6: 13; Matt. 4: 10.
[5]Matt. 4: 2; Mark 1: 13; Luke 4: 2.

tion, it is inconceivable that the same number should have been preserved in the Gospels without a conscious reference to the time of wanderings; and all the more so in view of the correlation between the temptations themselves. There can, in fact, be no doubt that the Gospel narratives of the temptation of Christ were designed for comparison and contrast with the temptations of the Exodus. Christ's faithfulness stands in opposition to the unbelief of Israel. The Day foretold in the ninety-fourth psalm was the day of Christ.

But this is not the end of the story, for the temptation of Christ is one of the mysteries in which all Christians must participate. The Liturgy consists of this participation of the members of Christ's mystical body in the mysteries which Christ, their Head, originally fulfilled. Consequently, at the beginning of Lent, on the first Sunday, the Gospel in the liturgy is the story of the temptation of Christ, as though to indicate the original meaning of Lent. Historically, this season was first of all the time of preparation for baptism, and therefore a time of temptation. The soul of the catechumen is torn between Satan, who seeks to retain possession, and Christ who is calling him into his own kingdom: 'the serpent is there beside the road', as St Cyril of Jerusalem wrote, 'watching those that pass by. . . . His eye is upon all such as are in the way of salvation, that he may devour them. . . . Look to thy soul, lest he take it.'[1]

There is one difficulty in this sacramental typology: the temptation of Christ came after his baptism, whereas the catechumenate which it prefigured comes before baptism. It is also true that the crossing of the Red Sea, which the Fathers accepted as the chief prefiguration of baptism, itself preceded the forty years of wandering in the wilderness. The difficulty was not enough to invalidate the correspondence between the Temptations and the Catechumenate, but it served to embarrass the chronological presentation of

[1] P.G. 33: 361 A–B.

the case. There is, however, one line of typological interpretation in which even the synchronization is right: if the crossing of Jordan by the chosen people is taken as the type or figure of baptism, then the forty years in the wilderness correspond exactly with the time of preparation for baptism, regarded as the entry to the promised land. This view was presented by Origen.[1]

The forty days of preparation for baptism thus refer back, through the forty days of Christ's temptation, to the reality behind the Biblical associations of this number, the forty years' wandering in the wilderness. But this does not mean that Lent has no other Biblical connexions. A single liturgical symbol often proves to be a focus in which several different lines of tradition meet; the water of baptism, for instance, refers back to the deadly waters of the Flood as well as to the outpouring of the life-giving water and the Spirit foretold in the Prophets. So with the forty days of Lent: and indeed the depth of religious meaning to be found in this liturgical season is a direct consequence of the variety of heterogeneous ideas meeting therein.

One more example of the use of the number forty stems again from Mosaic times. It was for forty days (not, on this occasion, forty years) that Moses remained on Mount Sinai. As before, we find that this figure is a well-established element of the traditional narrative. It comes in Exodus: 'So, for forty days and nights, without food or drink, he remained there with the Lord.'[2] Deuteronomy gives the same figure, adding that the time was spent in supplication for the sins of the people,[3] and that it was at the end of the forty days that the Law was given to Moses.[4] Here, then, this symbolic period of time is associated with the new themes of fasting and prayer, as a preparation for receiving the gifts of divine grace.

Then the figure of Elijah comes to double that of Moses, as he journeys through the wilderness to Horeb, which is

[1]P.G. 12: 843 B.   [2]34: 28.   [3]9: 18.   [4]9: 11.

Sinai. On his way, an angel gave him to eat: and 'strengthened by that food he went on for forty days and forty nights, till he reached God's own mountain, Horeb'.[1] There is an echo here of the wanderings of the people in the wilderness, but clearer still of Moses' sojourn on the mountain. Nor was it a mere chance coincidence. Elijah is shown returning to the very source of the Mosaic revelation. The conception is of a fresh start, a renewal of the spiritual life of God's chosen people: the re-iteration of 'forty days', harking back both to the years in the wilderness and to the days in the mount, was calculated to stress the parallelism.

In the Jewish apocrypha, the notion of forty days continued to be linked with the idea of a preparation by prayer for the enactment of divine events; but it took on a markedly eschatological bearing. In Baruch 2 we read: 'Go up therefore to the top of that mountain, and there shall pass before thee all the regions of that land . . . and the tops of the mountains, and the depths of the valleys . . . that thou mayest see what thou art leaving, and whither thou art going. Now this shall befall after forty days. Go now therefore during these days and instruct the people so far as thou art able.'[2] These forty days in the mountain are obviously derived from the story of Moses. Again, in the apocryphal books of Esdras, he is represented as a new Moses, receiving instructions from God himself for forty days before beginning to instruct the people.[3]

Elias, Baruch, Esdras, none of these was the new, the second Moses that was to come in the last days to give the new and everlasting Law. Christ alone was the fulfilment of this expectation. The Gospels reveal him as the new Moses indeed, the lawgiver of the new Law: as in the mountain of the Transfiguration, where he appeared in company with Moses and Elias. Seen in this light, his forty

[1] 3 Kings 19: 8.
[2] II Bar. 76: 3–4 (Charles, *Apocr. & Pseudep.*)
[3] 4 Esdr. 14: 23, 36, 44–45.

days' withdrawal into the wilderness takes on a new significance. His fasting unmistakably recalls the fasting of
Moses in the mountain, and the fasting of Elias in the
desert of Beersheba, all alike for forty days. This is, in fact,
a commonplace of Biblical exegesis: Eusebius made the
point in his *Demonstratio Evangelica*.[1]

We have already seen, in connexion with the sojourn of
Moses in the holy mountain, how this period of forty days
was devoted to prayer and fasting, in order to turn aside the
punishment due to the sins of the people of Israel: and how
the forty days thus came to be recognized as a time of penance in view of the judgement to come. This particular
aspect of the forty days reappears in the Book of Jonah,
referring now to the whole people, and not to one servant
of God: 'And when he had advanced into it as far as one
day's journey would carry him, he began crying out, In
forty days, Nineve will be overthrown. With that, the
Ninevites shewed faith in God . . . proclaiming a fast
. . . God may yet relent and pardon, forgo his avenging
anger and spare our lives.'[2] The Book of Jonas, as we know,
was a prophecy. The forty days' fast of Moses has become
the action of the peoples. Jonas's preaching was a figure
of the Church, preaching to the world the call to conversion
because of the judgement to come.

This preaching of penance, which was prefigured in the
successive 'forty days' of Sinai and Horeb, of Ninive and
of the Gospel wilderness, is actually fulfilled, as we shall see,
throughout the whole era of the Church's existence. But it
has also its own peculiar formula in the Christian liturgy,
namely the institution of Lent. We have already shown
how the period fixed for this time of fasting in preparation
for Easter was positively determined by the fasts of Moses,
Elias and Jesus. The connexion is made plain in the
Patristic tradition, and notably by St Augustine (who also
gave currency to various extremely questionable essays in

[1] P.G. 22: 172 A–B. [2] 3: 4–5, 9.

symbolism, borrowed from the Pythagorean mystique of numerology). From a number of relevant passages in the Lenten sermons of St Augustine, we may quote *Sermo CCV*, where he begins by recalling that 'forty' is the product of the number of the Gospels by the number of the Commandments, that it is the number of days that elapse before the animation of the human embryo, and that it has many other applications easily discoverable by a quicker wit.[1] He goes on: 'Moses, Elias, and the Lord himself fasted forty days, to teach us by their several examples, that is, by the Law, by the Prophets and by the Gospel, that our whole duty is not to be conformed or attached to this world, . . . but that we must crucify the old man. Such is the rule of our life, . . . and if this is our daily duty as long as we live, how much more must we do it during Lent, which is not only part of our life, but represents the whole of it? At all times you must not let your heart be weighed down with excess of food and drink; but at this time you must go further and practise fasting.'[2] Here is a particularly lucid account of the meaning of Lent: both as the historical fulfilment of the 'types' of fasting, whether by Moses, or Elijah, or Jesus Christ himself; and as a symbol of the whole life of mankind in its penitential aspects.

We must now attend to the bearings of the last few words of the foregoing paragraph. The institution of Lent has this

---

[1]One of these points deserves particular mention, on account of its liturgical consequences. The idea that the foetus was animated forty days after conception is the counterpart of a belief that the corpse is not finally devitalized until forty days after death. This latter opinion, which was widely held in ancient times, explains why the fortieth day after death was celebrated with special funerary rites. Traces of this practice survived into Christianity, where it acquired a certain eschatological reference; for this particular 'forty days' came to represent a time of waiting, and of purgation, before the soul could be thought fit for its heavenly home. So here again the same period of forty days is a kind of preparation: the fact is worth noting, though the whole context in which it occurs lies right outside any consideration of Lent.

[2]*Serm.* CCV. P.L. 38: 1039–40.

in common with all other liturgical enactments, that it is both a memorial and a prophecy. Hitherto we have been concerned only with the former of these two aspects of Lent, that is, with the sources, so far as these appeared relevant. Turning now to the second aspect, it is at once clear that Lent is not an end in itself, but exists for the sake of something else: liturgical symbolism is there to indicate some historical reality. If now we ask what this is, in the case of Lent (bearing in mind that liturgy is essentially a symbolism of time, wherein the seasons of the year stand for realities in the history of salvation), then clearly the answer must be linked in some way with the idea of preparation. This particular concept has appeared already at various points in our present inquiry,[1] but without attracting any prolonged attention, because we have been more concerned with the probationary and penitential aspects of Lent. It is now time to examine the idea of preparation separately by itself.

It is intimately connected with the periods of forty years, or days, already discussed, and with the interpretations we have recorded. Thus the wanderings of the Israelites in the wilderness, besides being for the destruction of the perverse generation, were also the prelude of entry into the promised land. This episode was consequently taken, and quite properly, to be a figure of the catechumenate, which is essentially a preparation. But while the idea of preparation is evident enough in the interpretation of these forty years, it is clearer still when we come to the forty-day fasts of Moses, Elias, and Jesus, which were all times of preparation directly in view of divine favours. Besides this, the forty days of preparation were sometimes related to eschatological conceptions: for Jonas and Baruch, as for Moses, they

[1]One example which we have not investigated, because it had nothing to do with Lent, was the forty days before the Ascension, where this particular period of time was again associated with the idea of preparation (Acts 1: 3).

signify the expectation of punishment to come upon the sinful world. These fasts were not ordinary acts of asceticism, but were demanded by the divine events awaited.

So it followed easily enough from the Biblical associations of the time, that the forty days of Lent should come to represent the whole life of mankind, regarded as preparatory for the next world. The Fathers, and especially St Augustine, loved to show how this particular significance was in accordance with the nature of the number 'forty'. Of course these congruities are entirely secondary; but even so they are not without foundation. St Augustine starts from the basis that 'four' represents the universe; we need not quarrel with that: 'Four is the symbol of temporal things. . . . The year is divided into four seasons. . . . Four winds are mentioned in the Scriptures'.[1] Then 'ten' concludes the series of primary numbers, whence it implies completeness. The product, forty, is thus appropriate, as a symbol for the fullness of time.

A further reason, corroborating this particular symbolism of the forty days of Lent, was derived from the fact that Lent is a preparation for the fifty days of Pentecost; for the latter period symbolized eternity. The reasons for this were exclusively Biblical: fifty days represents that which is beyond the seven sabbaths, the week of weeks, which itself is a figure of the fullness of time. So the liturgical sequence of forty days followed by fifty days was a striking representation of the passage from time into eternity, from preparation to consummation, from penance to reward: while the liturgical content of the two periods was such as to confirm the nature of that contrast. The bold eschatological outline of the primitive Christian year was thus the product of many factors in combination.

It was St Augustine—naturally enough, in view of his preoccupation with the problems and mystery of time— who worked out this symbolism. In the first place, he

[1] *Serm.* CCLII. P.L. 38: 1178.

showed how the forty days of Lent are a figure of life on earth.

> The number, forty, typifies this present time, our life of travail. . . . Moses and Elias fasted forty days, to teach us that we in this life must renounce the love of wordly goods, for that is the meaning of their unbroken fasting for this space of time; and that is also why the Israelites were taken to wander forty years in the wilderness, before they might go in to conquer and rule over the promised land. Such too is our condition all the days of our life here, subject to innumerable cares and fears and fatal temptations; we are taken as it were through the wilderness by the goodness of providence in our time. But if we fulfil the number of forty, that is, if we repay by holiness of living the goodness of God who bestows his gifts upon us in our time, we shall ourselves be rewarded.[1]

Elsewhere St Augustine takes up the same idea again from the basis of numerological symbolism.

> This number, forty, contains a mystery. . . . I take it to be a figure of this world, through which we make our way under the constant attractions and repulsions of the march of time, the instability and mutability of human affairs, the irresistible flow of change. . . . This number represents the time of this world, whether by reference to the four seasons, or to the four cardinal points. . . . Our duty in our journeying through this world is to abstain from wordly lusts: this is the meaning of the forty-days' fast called Lent—*quadragesima*. The word recalls the teaching of the Law, for Moses fasted forty days; and of the Prophets, for Elijah did the same; and of the Gospel, for we are told that the Lord Jesus fasted for the same length of time.[2]

Over against this, the time of fifty days is a figure of the world to come. 'The number, fifty, represents the time of that joy that no man shall take from us. In the present life we are not yet in possession of that joy; nevertheless, after the days devoted to the Lord's Passion, and throughout the

[1] *Serm.* CCLII. P.L. 38: 1177–8.
[2] *Serm.* CCLXX. P.L. 38: 1240.

fifty days which follow upon his Resurrection, we fast no more, and celebrate by anticipation the coming of that time of joy, singing Alleluia in all our praising of God.'[1] So Pentecost represents eternity as Lent represents time: and the distinguishing marks of Eastertide are all in direct contrast to those of Lent—fifty is opposed to forty, the prohibition of fasting to the precept of fasting, the song of Alleluia to the prayer of supplication.

St Augustine was never tired of bringing out the significance of this contrast of the liturgical seasons, as a symbol of all history in the largest sense: 'Just as the season of Lent, coming before Easter, is a figure of the toils and sufferings of this mortal life, so the joyful days that follow Easter symbolize the future life in which we shall reign with the Lord. At present we are passing through the life represented by Lent; we have not yet come into possession of the life represented by the fifty days that followed the Lord's resurrection.'[2] And again: 'I think I have given you enough explanation of this great mystery. You know that our duty is to do good during Lent, if we would praise God during Easter. Therefore we spend the forty days before the sacred Vigil in works, in fasting and abstinence, because those days are a figure of the life that now is; but the fifty days that come after the Resurrection of the Lord are a figure of eternal joys.'[3]

It may be observed that St Augustine embodied his theology of history and his eschatology in two different systems of liturgical symbolism. There is, first, the structure of the week, wherein he was familiar with the distinction between the seven days, symbolizing the natural creation, and the eighth day, symbolizing eternity: in this system it is Sunday that stands for eternal life. Secondly, there is the other system which we have been discussing in the present chapter,

[1] *Serm.* CCX. P.L. 38: 1051–2.
[2] *Serm.* CCXLIII. P.L. 38: 1147.
[3] *Serm.* CCLII. P.L. 38: 1178–9.

where the forty days represent the entire duration of time, and the fifty days represent the world beyond time. This duality of approach is characteristic of the freedom of the patristic use of symbols: but it is also true to say that the two systems emphasize two distinct religious ideas. In the former, the seven days are the time of the first creation—the eighth is the time of the new creation, beginning with the resurrection of Christ, continuing in baptism, fulfilled in glory. In the second system, the forty days are the time of conversion, the emphasis is more on asceticism and less on the natural creation; the fifty days that follow are the time of spiritual bliss.

CHAPTER EIGHT

NOTIONS OF ESCHATOLOGY

THE most distressful and catastrophic periods of history have at all times provided inspiration for apocalyptic writers. The Hebrew prophets regarded the fall of Jerusalem not only as the punishment of the chosen people but also as the first act in a judgement upon the whole world. Again about the year 1000 men thought the world was coming to an end. Lamennais' *Paroles d'un Croyant*, the apocalypse of the nineteenth century, was written in the expectation of a judgement to fall upon the men of his time. And there is a *petite peur* of the twentieth century, lately identified by E. Mounier: a tide of pessimism running through the present generation, flowing from the recognition of imminent danger, whence some people suppose that the end of the world is at hand.

It is a very difficult subject. The prophets of doom are always liable to be suspect: where is their authority? Was it not Christ himself who told the Apostles, 'the day of it and the hour of it are unknown to you'?[1] Besides, these warnings of the last day have so often been belied in the event, that we are inevitably somewhat sceptical of all such predictions. Yet it remains true that the idea of the last judgement is at the very heart of the Christian philosophy, even though curiosity about the date of it is to be deprecated.

Everybody agrees, albeit with some individual qualifications, that the Prophets foretold the last judgement: everybody, even including the rabbis. But how to situate this judgement in history, whether to see the fulfilment of this

[1] Matt. 25: 13.

prophecy in the coming of Jesus Christ—on these questions, opinions greatly differ. A first obvious division is between Jews and Christians, for this is the fundamental issue in all their disputes, 'whether or not Jesus is Messiah?' that is, he that comes to fulfil the judgement, to bring this world to an end, to inaugurate the new world. Now as always, for M. Edmond Fleg just as much as for the Alexandrian rabbi Trypho, who argued with St Justin in the second century, this is the great question.

But the controversy is not only between Jews and Christians. The Christians themselves are far from being united as to the meaning of 'New Testament eschatology', or the relation between the coming of Jesus and the end of the world. Much ink has flowed in the discussion of this matter during the last half-century, particularly in Germany and England. Much, indeed, depends upon the answer: for it determines what we think of Christ, of the Church, of Christianity—in a word, the most important things in life.

One extreme position is that taken up notably by Albert Schweitzer, who had made a name for himself as a Biblical critic before he went to his Central African hospital, which he now never leaves except to give an occasional recital in America. Schweitzer made the discovery that Christ several times appears to have spoken of the end of the world as close at hand. These passages must be taken literally. Hence the judgement, in these passages, can only have meant something that was in the future—and, to be more precise, the near future. This interpretation is technically called 'consequent' or 'immediate' eschatology. As it happens—for good or ill—the end of the world has not come about. The conclusion that Jesus was mistaken was not too much for Schweitzer; but this is rather an important statement to be made on such slight and doubtful grounds. The question arises whether it is not rather Schweitzer who was mistaken in his idea of what Jesus meant.

It seems clear, at least, that the prediction of an early end of the world was not the whole message of Jesus, since another school of thought is able to maintain that the end, in his teaching, was not in the future at all, but was already realized in himself. This interpretation is called 'realized' eschatology: its chief representative is the Anglican C. H. Dodd. There is certainly a good deal of New Testament evidence for it; and there is certainly much truth in it, perhaps most of the truth. Indeed the essence of the Gospel message is to declare the accomplishment of prophecy in Jesus Christ, the new Adam of the new Paradise, and the new Moses of the true Exodus.

But in Dodd's eyes this essential truth fills the whole picture, to such an extent as to leave no room (now that the end has come) for any further useful activity. History since Jesus is a sort of remainder, and theologically insignificant. From this position it is but a step to that of Bultmann, who regards all ideas of a future judgement as nothing but apocalyptic myth: holding that the only judgement is each man's momentaneous relation to God, and the only end, the ineluctable consequence of each decision in this kind. I would call this an 'existential' eschatology.[1] Bultmann's language and thought recall those of his master, Heidegger, and occasionally those of Sartre. It is indeed a kind of existentialism in Biblical exegesis.

Dodd and Bultmann are both perfectly right in insisting, the one upon the fact that the end has already come in the person of Christ, the other upon the immediacy of the crisis of each moment. But they are both wrong in trying to reduce the whole of the Gospel to this one message. Oscar Cullmann, on the other hand, proposes a solution which it is easier to reconcile with the texts as a whole. On his interpretation, Christ's resurrection was the essential historical event belonging to the end of created time; there can never happen anything of comparable importance in future. But

[1]Rather than 'timeless' or 'supra-historical'; these terms, used by Fr Mollat, could be ambiguous.

there is still something to wait for, because this supreme event has yet to fructify in all its consequences. The first Christians were impressed with the nearness of the end precisely because of the overwhelming importance of the event itself: the end was not chronologically near, but 'at hand' because its decisive elements were essentially accomplished. This interpretation may properly be called 'anticipated' eschatology.

Cullmann's point of view enables him to take full account of the New Testament teaching, though he is perhaps too exclusively concerned with the beginning and the end of the 'last days', to the neglect of the interim in which our lives are spent. There is then room for one more interpretation, in close conformity with the whole Christian tradition; it may be called 'initiated' eschatology, in a formula taken from Fr Donatien Mollat, who thus indicates the outlines of the position he adopts: 'With Christ, the time of judgement has really started, the last days really begin. These are days of crisis and decision, which we have to recognize and appreciate. . . . They continue so long as the Son of Man is present in his brethren and in his fellowship. . . . They will be completed by the Second Coming, with the establishment once for all of God's Kingdom.'

Between the inauguration of Judgement at the time of Christ's first coming, and its fulfilment at his coming again, Christian life in its entirety is thus a continual judgement. Fr Mollat puts it admirably: 'The mystical presence of the Son of Man in all men imports an unsuspected eschatological dimension into all human relationships, that is to say into all history at all times. Mankind is now face to face with the Son of Man at every moment of existence: the judgement is *now*.' It will be seen that this conception subsumes and reconciles the historical and the existential interpretations. Judgement does indeed consist now from moment to moment in the relation of man to God; but that is because mankind is historically going through the time of judgement. And this process has only begun; it looks forward to the Last Judgement for the final ratification.

Granted so much, there are still questions unanswered; first of all as to the imminence of the end. Kümmel held that Christ expected a certain lapse of time between the Resurrection and the Second Coming, which, however, he thought would be very short. Guy has rightly pointed out that this was not compatible with the teaching of St Paul, who for his part regarded the Church as the realization of the messianic kingdom: in this connexion he quoted Dodd's observation that 'Paul "has claimed the whole territory of the Church's life as the field of the eschatological miracle"' [1] —a position which is simply meaningless, if the end of all things is immediately at hand. On this basis, then, the texts which proclaim judgement as imminent are not to be taken as referring solely to the last things, but rather to the whole sequence of eschatological events to come. So in St Luke's Gospel, judgement is associated with the fall of Jerusalem in A.D. 70, but this was only one of the earliest acts in the full process. [2]

A second question remains, as to how much of the New Testament eschatology derives from the Jewish apocalyptic literature, and how much should therefore be discarded as ephemeral and obsolete. Rudolf Bultmann's extreme opinions on this point are well known: he would consider the entire historical conception of eschatology as a derivative of extinct literary conventions. Hence the requirement to 'demythologize' the New Testament eschatology, until nothing is left of of it but an existential attitude of disengagement. Kümmel has shown, in an important article, how Bultmann's radical criticism of the formal patterns of expression in Christ's teaching succeeded in evacuating all

[1] *The N. T. doctrine of the last things* (Oxford, 1948), p. 127.

[2] This is in line with the conclusions of M. André Feuillet who has shown that Luke 17: 28 and 18: 8 are not to be distinguished as two successive phases, but that both refer singly to the forthcoming fall of Jerusalem as an element of the judgement to come.

L.H.—T

its historical relevance; and how he was thus forced into the conclusions of his bitterest opponents, the Harnackite liberals, who interpret the Gospel as an ethical sermon rather than an eschatological kerygma.

It is nevertheless true that New Testament eschatology is recorded in part under the influence of apocalyptic inspirations. This accounts for such conventional themes as the clouds wherein the Son of Man shall appear and the sound of the trumpet to announce his coming; or the location of Hades underground, or of the devils in the air. All this belongs to a literary tradition, and does not affect the substance of what is taught, though admittedly it is not always easy to draw the line between convention and content. There is food for thought in what Kümmel has to say about this. Guy makes the useful point that the eschatological passages in Matthew are richer in apocalyptic details than the corresponding passages in Mark; as though this conventional material belonged, not to the substance of the evangelical message, but to its adaptation for a particular cultural milieu.

Here, then, are a number of apparently sound conclusions, leading to an integral view of the manifold and complex teaching of the New Testament on the subject of the Judgement, without minimizing any of its aspects. But this is not all. Certain necessary consequences follow, which have a bearing on our ideas about life. We do not have to elaborate a theory of the eschatological significance of nuclear weapons; all we have to do is to read the New Testament, as interpreted by any normal Professor of biblical exegesis, and then to work out what it means.

First of all, it means that the Last Things have already begun. The resurrection of Christ is presented as the first and decisive act of the last day. The Word of God took humanity to himself in the Incarnation, and cleansed it through his precious blood, and brought it into his Father's house for ever at his ascension. The work of salvation has been substantially done, everything essential has been secured already. This colours the whole Christian view of history. It is incompatible with an evolutionary theory looking forward to any future event of comparable importance, or any future development transcending Christ.

On the other hand, this work of Judgement which Christ has substantially completed has not yet produced its due consequences throughout mankind and throughout creation. For many people this is a principal stumbling-block. Nothing seems to have been changed: before and after Christ, men are equally enslaved; history is still dictated by the will to power and the greed of gold. There is little sign of the arrival of that time when, as Isaias foretold, 'they will melt down their swords into plough shares'.[1] And turning to even more essential matters, mankind is still a prey to suffering and death. 'The whole of nature, as we know, groans in a common travail all the while' until 'nature in its turn will be set free from the tyranny of corruption'.[2] We are still waiting for that Judgement that will destroy the world of corruption and establish a kingdom of saints.

This twofold relationship to something achieved and to something awaited specifies the current phase of time, which is the epoch of the Church. It is the period of grace allowed to mankind for the acceptation of the judgement which Christ has substantially won, and so escape the Judgement to come. The Church's preaching is eschatological in character, consisting in an announcement of the danger that threatens the human race, with notice of the way of salvation, the Ark of the Church, affording the only safe passage through the deep waters of the Judgement. The Church's baptism is eschatological in intent, being a sacramental anticipation of the last day. Every baptized person belongs already to the Church of eternity, the Church beyond the Judgement, and shall escape the judgement to come. 'Baptism,' says Fr Mollat, 'constitutes the messianic

[1]Isa. 2: 4.   [2]Rom. 8: 22, 21.

fellowship of the saved under the shadow of judgement: the Church is born of water and fire.'

The paradox of Christianity is the integration of these two things, fulfilment and expectation. On the one hand it is true that we are already 'risen with Christ';[1] 'we are sons of God even now'.[2] Christianity is thus the possession in advance of good things to come; 'we have already begun to reap our spiritual harvest.'[3] The Christian attitude is not a servile fear, but a filial trust as 'heirs of God',[4] for whom the fullness of possession is of right. But on the other hand it is equally true that this possession is something we can lose: 'what we shall be hereafter, has not been made known as yet'.[5] Christianity is thus an expectancy. Hence, in this situation of suspense, comes the characteristic quality of crisis in the whole period of the Church. However long it may last, it is always nothing but the moment of transition from one world to another, always in the tension of a climax.

What is true of individual lives is here true of communities as well. The fourth gospel emphasizes particularly the personal aspect of the judgement here and now: the Apocalypse shows the same judgement at work in the field of history. Fr Huby accurately described the aim of the latter book as being 'to enable us to appreciate through faith the immediacy of God's judgements in historical events'. Even the disasters of history thus take their place in the conception of a world undergoing judgement, among the events presaging the last day. But it is especially important in this connexion to avoid drawing facile parallels between the visions in the book of Revelation and the circumstances of our own time: and above all to remember that earthly defeat, from the Biblical point of view, is no more necessarily a mark of divine reprobation than temporal successes are a mark of election. It is a most dangerous error for a nation to count its victories for righteousness. Political messianism is poles apart from Christian eschatology.

[1]Col. 3: 1. [2]1 John 3: 2. [3]Rom. 8: 23. [4]ibid. 8: 17. [5]1 John 3: 2.

We have already discussed[1] the masterly dissertation of Herbert Butterfield on this theme. On any theory of temporal rewards for virtue, as he pointed out, we should have to conclude that there is no nation in the world today standing higher in the divine favour than Soviet Russia, which alone derived nothing but gain from two world wars. And indeed this does seem to be the conclusion of those modern Christian writers who misuse such terms as 'the verdict of history' to cover a restatement of the theory of temporal retribution (which was already discredited in the time of Isaiah). It would follow by the same reasoning that Germany must be the object of an altogether special reprobation.

The mere enunciation of these two statements is enough to provoke a doubt of their validity: for all nations have sinned, and the judgement of God is upon them all: but his judgements are unsearchable. It may be that the nations he loves best are most chastised (which would at least conform to the ordinary ways of his working), and that, on the contrary, those nations which enjoy visible prosperity are left in their blindness, serving merely as instruments for God's good purposes towards other nations, and destined afterwards to be broken and cast aside. But a theory of this sort would also go far beyond the evidence. Only one thing is certain, as Butterfield pointed out, namely that any system of interpretation of history which claims to find within the course of history itself a justification of the system, breaks down upon application to reality. The conception of history as the judgement of God upon a sinful world offers the only prospect of resolving its apparent contradictions.[2]

There is a false and superficial notion of eschatology, which consists in an attempt either to determine the time

[1]*Supra*, pp. 96–103.
[2]Fr Mollat for his part also properly lays stress upon the fact that Christians remain liable to sin throughout this life, and cannot be certain of salvation in virtue of their baptism.

of the Last Judgement, or to define its categories. If we seek to find out times and seasons, we are in danger of illuminism, or alternatively of a sort of computers' apocalyptic, owing more to Nostradamus than to St John; dangers of which Christ was the first to give Christians warning. If we seek to forecast the verdict, we are in danger of pharisaism, finding others guilty and justifying ourselves; and pharisaism, whether personal or collective, is directly opposed to the Gospel, whose first principle is that all men are sinners. Mollat and Butterfield speak with one voice on this point: and may serve as examples of another notion of eschatology, utterly removed from all idle speculation, belonging in fact to the deepest realities of human existence. This is the doctrine which reminds us that the days of our life, long or short, are the last days; we are always spiritually on the threshold of the next world. This is the doctrine which reminds us that our time is a time of crisis, in the etymological sense of the word, a time when men and nations are continuously judged in the secret places of the heart. And this is how Christianity provides the solution of both the essential problems of our time and of all times, the problem of history and the problem of existence.

PART III

CHAPTER ONE

COURAGE

THE Christian character is the faithful echo in each
individual soul of the rhythm of the history of salvation. It consists in a practical awareness of the fullness
of time; it is determined by the knowledge that, with
Christ's coming into the world, the decisive event in human
history has already taken place. This world is already
judged. The critical phase of history has begun, the period
of the Church, a time of crisis, wherein nothing is stable or
permanent, everything is provisional: a time when Christ
is always coming, an unfinished Advent. The initial text
of the Lord's preaching defines these conditions: 'Repent.
he said, the kingdom of heaven is at hand'[1]—*Dominus enim
prope est*, 'the Lord is near'.[2] The whole of the Church's
time consists in this proximity of the Second Coming, and in
its constant realization through the coming of Christ into
souls and peoples. In the same way, it is a time of decision,
in which men may exercise their choice, for Christ or
against him. The essence of the Christian calling is this, to
have seen that the moment of choice had come, that it
would no longer do to settle down in a quiet life, that one
had a soul to make, to meet a time of crisis, that one's whole
life and personality must be directed towards the resolution
of this crisis, through the Christian mission to the world.

It follows that a primary characteristic of the Christian is
courage: a readiness, in reliance upon the power of God
(not on his own), to face every kind of difficulty, whether
this arises from the actions of men or of things or of evil

[1]Matt. 4: 17.   [2]Phil. 4: 5.

spirits. 'Such, through Christ, is the confidence in which we make our appeal to God. Not that, left to ourselves, we are able to frame any thought as coming from ourselves; all our ability comes from God.'[1] So this trustful confidence does not mean self-confidence, or self-sufficiency; it comes from God 'since it is he who has enabled us to promulgate his new law to men. It is a spiritual, not a written law; the written law inflicts death, whereas the spiritual law brings life.'[2]

If we are to describe this quality of mind, we must first consider its origin, as indicated by St Paul in the words just quoted, namely God himself. The source of the apostle's courage lies in the recognition that the work in which he is engaged is not his own affair; he is the servant, the agent in a much bigger business. This is a most important point. So long as a man is endeavouring to inculcate his own way, as a philosopher seeks expression for his private intuitions, or a man of action tries to exert a personal influence, he can never elude the question whether he may not be mistaken. Hence there will be a tincture of diffidence and caution in what he says and does—or, if there is none, he will be thought shallow and conceited.

The psychological attitude of the missionary is altogether different. The apostolic type has no bent or special inclination for the work he is called to do—he is, often enough, badly frightened of its dangerous responsibility. He becomes a messenger of the Gospel, not because of some natural predisposition for the active life, but simply because God has picked him for the job. 'It is, then, with the fear of the Lord before our minds that we try to win men over by persuasion . . . No, we are not trying to recommend ourselves to your favour afresh; we are shewing you how to find material for boasting of us, to those who have so much to boast of outwardly, and nothing inwardly . . . When a man becomes a new creature in Christ, his old life has disappeared, everything has become new about him. This,

[1] 2 Cor. 3: 4–5. [2] ibid. 3: 6.

as always, is God's doing; it is he who, through Christ, has reconciled us to himself, and allowed us to minister this reconciliation of his to others. Yes, God was in Christ, reconciling the world to himself.'[1]

The missionary idea is explained in the Pauline formula: 'we are Christ's ambassadors'.[2] At first, the apostle was a private person, living his own life. Now he has a public and official position; it is his duty to tell the world the good news: for the Church is not a private corporation, but an agency of God, the official machinery through which he promulgates the Gospel in the world. The Church's mission, throughout the intervening period before the second advent, is to summon mankind to do penance because of what is to come: 'Repent: the kingdom of heaven is at hand.' This distinctive character of the Church's work is necessarily found in the work of its members.

That, then, is the very basis of the missionary's imperturbable conviction. Once on the mission, the anxieties of doubt and irresolution become unimportant. When a man is in post, the only thing that matters is the job: his personal circumstances do not count; difficulties are all in the day's work. When a liaison officer is sent up the line with a message, he does not have to worry about whether he particularly wants to go just then, or not; the message has to be delivered. Someone has to be informed: he is sent to tell them: they must be told, at all costs, whatever happens to him.

So with the missionary. Men must be told, so as to get ready for the judgement to come. That is what God has sent him for. Danger is largely irrelevant. The missionary life is commonly dangerous, subject to attack from men, from things, from the powers of darkness. Never mind, the job must be done; that is all that matters. Hence his quiet confidence. He has a mission to fulfil, and everything else is put aside: 'his old life has disappeared, everything has

[1]ibid. 5: 11–12; 17–19. [2]ibid. 5: 20.

become new about him.' The newness of life was revealed
to him, with a dazzling brilliance, when once he grasped the
aptness and fullness of time, the world, and God. Till then,
he had been pottering about his daily round, when suddenly
he saw a great light: the outward appearance of things
seemed to be stripped away; he looked down, as into an
abyss, and his eyes were opened to the depths of spiritual
reality, the inwardness of the world's drama. Seeing these
things, he knows there can now be only one course for him,
that is, the discharge of his mission: 'we are ambassadors',
legatione fungimur; I am in post, I have a mission to fulfil, a
duty to perform—not for the sake of any human good cause,
but in the service of the Holy Trinity. The apostle is sent out
by the three divine persons; he is sent out to the heathen; he
is sent out for the purpose of announcing the Second Coming. *Omnium sanctorum minimo* . . . 'On me, least as I
am of all the saints'.[1] *Minimo*—why should it be me
that God picked out? me, 'less than the least'—for St Paul
was a bad speaker: and whether for this reason, or because
of a lack of 'presence', he made no great impression in personal encounters. The Corinthians said of him that he wrote
'powerful' letters from a distance, but when he came himself, there was nothing to him.[2] So he had no special
aptitude for his work—rather the reverse. *Minimo*—
less than the least; he might well wonder why God had
chosen him: but all this was of no consequence; the question did not arise, for he had in fact been chosen, and must
now get on with the work, and keep at it to the bitter end.
Indeed he was all the easier in his mind for the knowledge
that he himself had nothing to do with the arrangement,
that he was not to rely on his own resources, that, humanly
speaking, everything was against him. How was he, a Jew,
to deal with all these Romans and Hellenes? What equipment had he, to dispute with the stoic and epicurean philosophers of the day, at Athens? He had neither health nor

[1]Eph. 3: 8.   [2]2 Cor. 10: 10.

strength, he suffered from an obscure complaint (probably of nervous origin)—how could he stand up to the rigours of constant travel by sea and land, often in terrible conditions? None of these things was of any consequence at all, except as showing the divine power that was at work within him: 'I will not boast about myself, except to tell you of my humiliations'.[1]

Why should he take a pride in his weakness? Because it was just this which proved that the strength that was in him was God's, that his achievements were not the result of human wisdom and argument, but of the power of God within him, which he served. *Servus verbi Dei*—a servant of the word; as such, he serves: nothing else matters. He knows perfectly well that it depends on God alone to make his service effectual. 'We have a treasure, then, in our keeping, but its shell is of perishable earthenware; it must be God, and not anything in ourselves, that gives it its sovereign power.'[2]

How is this confidence to be defined? What is its characteristic expression? It consists in a quiet readiness to face every difficulty. This quietness is a most important feature —there is no violence or tension about it, but a constant peace of mind; unperturbed by contradiction, by danger, by any kind of obstacle; incapable of despair or discouragement, because, once again, there is a duty to fulfil. 'Such, through Christ, is the confidence in which we make our appeal to God. Not that, left to ourselves, we are able to frame any thought as coming from ourselves; all our ability comes from God.'[3] What if life is full of danger? 'We are being hampered everywhere, yet still have room to breathe, are hard put to it, but never at a loss; persecution does not leave us unbefriended, nor crushing blows destroy us; we carry about continually in our bodies the dying state of Jesus, so that the living power of Jesus may be manifested in our bodies too.'[4] The theme is thus developed in a

[1]ibid. 12: 5.　[2]ibid. 4: 7.　[3]ibid. 3: 4–5.　[4]ibid. 4: 8–10.

subsequent passage: 'We take heart, then, continually, since
we recognize that our spirits are exiled from the Lord's
presence so long as they are at home in the body . . . We
take heart, I say, and have a mind rather to be exiled from
the body, and at home with the Lord; to that end, at home
or in exile, our ambition is to win his favour . . . It is,
then, with the fear of the Lord before our minds that we
try to win men over by persuasion.'[1]

'Here is the time of pardon; the day of salvation has come
already.'[2] Once again the same theme of the καιρός, the
due season, the hour that is come: this is the accepted time,
the moment of opportunity, of crisis, of decision. This day
of salvation lasts throughout the whole time of the Church
on earth, through God's mercy who allows this period of
grace for men to make up their minds—and only for that.
The suspension of judgement does not mean that God has
withdrawn his immediate presence; he is always at hand;
only, in his long-suffering kindness, he grants time for all
nations to come to repentance.[3] The days of grace are intended to let the Gentiles take their successive decisions, to
provide for each people in turn to be presented with the
good news, and to make their choice in the light of it.

'Here is the time of pardon; the day of salvation has come
already. We are careful not to give offence to anybody, lest
we should bring discredit on our ministry; as God's ministers, we must do everything to make ourselves acceptable.
We have to shew great patience, in times of affliction, of
need, of difficulty; under the lash, in prison, in the midst of
tumult; when we are tired out, sleepless, and fasting. We
have to be pure-minded, enlightened, forgiving and gracious to others; we have to rely on the Holy Spirit, on
unaffected love, on the truth of our message . . . now
honoured, now slighted . . . They call us deceivers, and
we tell the truth; . . . dying men, and see, we live; punished, yes, but not doomed to die; sad men, that rejoice

[1]2 Cor. 5: 6, 8–9, 11.   [2]ibid. 6: 2.   [3]See 2 Pet. 3: 9.

continually (*Gaudete in Domino, semper* . . .); beggars, that bring riches to many; disinherited, and the world is ours.'[1] The whole passage depicts the missionary's transcendent freedom of spirit; he is free of all human attachment, free in poverty or in plenty, able to follow his calling in all manner of circumstances, because his single concern is to obey that call.

This trustful confidence of the missionary becomes apparent chiefly in regard to three kinds of difficulty that face him: the first being obstacles put in his way by his fellow men. The apostle's duty is to promulgate his message publicly, to the public authorities: for example, the official leaders of thought. So St Paul goes to Athens, and there, on the Areopagus, confronting the best minds of his day, the cream of the epicurean and stoic schools, he announces the Gospel of Jesus Christ and the news of his resurrection. Fully conscious of his technical inadequacy in philosophical argument with these great men, he was in no way deterred from telling them what he had to say. The power of the Gospel does not depend on the persuasive force of human reasoning. The Gospel upsets human arguments and analyses, drives men out of the pattern of earthly discourse. To this extent it must necessarily give offence: but there can be no question of making it less unwelcome by trimming it to the measure of human wisdom. The missionary must put up with contradiction, remembering that his Master suffered the like before him. If his word is to be effective, this will not be because of the way he puts it, but because his Gospel is a power at work in the world, the effective word of the Creator. There is no need for us to make this word tell, but only to speak it. Of course we must do this as well as we can, lest our own carelessness should hinder men's acceptance of it. We must understand the mentality and the traditions of our hearers. But, once again, it is the word, only the word, that works, changing

[1] 2 Cor. 6: 2–10.

men's hearts: the creative word that can 'make a clean heart' in a man. If we had faith enough, the hardest of hearts could be touched, for things which are impossible to man are possible with God.

The apostle has also to face the official authorities of government—a most important aspect of the work of evangelization. In a pagan world, the Gospel wears the appearance of a crime against organized society. It is significant that Christ himself was summoned before a court of justice; it was in court that he found occasion to declare himself and his programme officially, before properly constituted authority. As Peterson has said of the martyrs, this was his statement of the 'claim that the kingdom of God is an authentic form of government'. There is jurisdiction in the kingdom of heaven over the kingdoms of this world; it is accordingly a very significant occasion when the representatives of the former are summoned to appear before the representatives of the latter. In these circumstances, the promulgation of the Christian message takes on its fully official character: the accredited herald of the kingdom of God proclaims his Master's titles to the public authorities of the kingdoms of this world. So it was in the life of Christ, who gave his final testimony before the Sanhedrim, the official court of Jewry, and again before the Roman procurator, Pilate. And his condemnation was in the forms of law. The kingdom of this world had refused to acknowledge the legal validity of the kingship of Christ.

Throughout the Church's history, this public affirmation of rights is constantly made; it is clearest when a Christian has to appear before the officers of government. Thus the early martyrs, brought to the bar of official justice, used this position to preach the Gospel, vindicating Christ's claim to be the true king: and for this they suffered according to law. The same situation has been repeated all over the world, Christians being everywhere liable to arrest in the name of the law for the crime of Gospel. In our own time, the same contrast appears between the claim of the earthly City to be the sole political entity, treating the Church as a private concern, and the claim of the kingdom of heaven to be the official representative on earth of the Blessed Trinity, entitled to make official communications to the constituted authorities. Civil governments have their own valid powers within their proper field of activity, and the Church must recognize the fact: that is of course—and beside the point. But the right of preaching the Gospel is absolute, inalienable; whenever it is challenged by any political system, Christians are obliged to vindicate it, even at the cost of their lives. The issue is perfectly simple: Christian missionaries are on active service, they can tolerate no interference in the execution of their duty. Martyrdom is simply the limiting case of this situation.

A second category of obstacles is the dangers that come from inanimate things. A missionary's life is apt to involve risks. No considerations of physical safety may ever deter him from his evangelistic duty. Freedom of spirit in the midst of mortal perils, the calm trustfulness of total unconcern, is a commonplace of missionary stories. It is not that these men take risks for fun, or as part of a cult of living dangerously; the idea of going out on the mission to indulge a taste for adventure is a fairy-tale: they have, however, a quiet conviction of being in the hands of God, so that nothing whatsoever can befall them but by his permissive will. Thus it was that St Francis Xavier, storm-tossed in the China Sea, while all about him gave way to panic, himself could be more perfectly recollected than ever, utterly resigned to the will of God and enjoying the highest perfection of mystical union.

But the third kind of peril that an apostle has to face is the most formidable of all, for his combat is not only with flesh and blood, but with the powers of darkness and disincarnate forces of evil. His calling, under God, is for warfare, not only against human opponents and material difficulties,

L.H.—U

but even more against spirits. He has to face tangible obstacles, and the hostility of princes; but worse than all is the enmity of him whom the Scripture calls 'the prince of this world'. His field of action is in the spiritual world; his aim is the conversion of souls; he operates in the darkness where his quarry lies captive. He is perfectly aware of the ghastly danger of his enterprise, knowing full well that the Enemy will exert his power to the utmost to hinder and frustrate the spread of the Gospel. The apostle himself expects to be tempted to the limit and subject to every interior trial: he knows that God will allow this, for the sake of the essential victory to be won in the overcoming of temptation. Consequently, he is never afraid, let the powers of darkness do their worst; for he knows he is in God's hands, and that Christ has conquered them all beforehand in his passion and in his rising again.

'The weapons we fight with are not human weapons; they are divinely powerful, ready to pull down strongholds. Yes, we can pull down the conceits of men, every barrier of pride which sets itself up against the true knowledge of God.'[1] It does not matter what manner of men we are, how unsuitable we may find ourselves. That is not what we have to look at. The tools in God's hands may be poor, fragile things, shrinking, cowardly, feeble creatures—he will work wonders with them if only they truly believe in him: it is his pleasure thus to show that their power is of God and not of man. . . . So, and only so, the apostolate is truthful evidence, showing what God can do, and not what mankind does. The greater the missionary's infirmity, the more splendid his testimony, for then no one will be inclined to give him credit for what is achieved, but the glory will be God's alone.

[1] 2 Cor. 10: 4–5.

CHAPTER TWO

POVERTY

W E have seen, among the leading characteristics of
St Paul's missionary life, how the consciousness
of his official duty to give news of God to men
enabled him to overcome every sort of obstacle. He would
not be stayed by the forces of nature, or by the hostility of
opponents, or by interior trials. Yet there was no sense of
strain in this unremitting labour, but peace of mind and
freedom of spirit; because he knew so well that it was not
his doing, but the power of God at work in him. That was
the source of all his strength: he knew he was God's instrument for a particular purpose, which he fulfilled accordingly.

This meant in practice that he was committed to an extraordinary existence, the dramatic qualities of which we may
now consider in more detail. His life was spent in the thick
of the world's tragedy: by this we mean not only the tragedy
of contemporary civilization, but of all time; not the tragic
conflict of economic and political forces, but the interior,
spiritual conflict which is the essential tragedy of mankind.
As we have repeatedly said, the real history of the world
consists in this spiritual warfare that is continually waged
around us for the possession of the souls of men, the
battle between the forces of Christ and the forces of his
enemies.

Now the point about St Paul was that he allowed himself
to be completely absorbed in this conflict: he gave himself
up to it without reserve; his chosen attitude was the absolute
negation of any escape, or flight, or withdrawal from the

storm-wrack of the human struggle into any private quiet-ude.[1] He lived at the very heart and focus of the spiritual tragedy of man, in what Péguy called *'le centre de misère'*: he was embarked once for all in an impossible venture, fraught with every kind of danger and hardship. However appalling the conditions of his existence, this was the life to which he had dedicated himself absolutely; he had resigned his freedom of choice.

It was indeed what we may call missionary poverty, this total destitution which St Paul so conspicuously endured in the single-minded quest of God and of souls: but the first point I should wish to emphasize is that St Paul's poverty was not an artifical self-imposed condition; it was an intrinsic element and immediate result of his self-dedication. Anyone who takes Christ seriously will find himself involved in the same consequential pattern: it is all up with him. But that is how he will find the true life, the life of love . . . 'disinherited, and the world is ours'.

St Paul was a broken man, a man on the run: we can see this in all sorts of ways. To begin with, his reputation was in ruins, as he himself constantly insisted. It was the first thing he gave up. It was simply not possible for him to serve Christ and the world at the same time, to please God and to please men. From the moment of entering Christ's service he was incessantly being required to do things that would shame and degrade him in the world's sight, so that the world, seeing nothing in him to admire or even to like, necessarily despised him and treated him (in his own telling language) as an 'offscouring',[2] a useless waste-product. From the point of view of the world, there was just nothing to be made of him; so he was of no consequence at all, he did not count.

St Paul said so himself, more than once, and particularly in the second Epistle to the Corinthians, where he described

[1]Contrast the popular fallacy that faith is 'a comfortable retreat into security'.   [2]1 Cor. 4: 13.

the trials in which his apostolate involved him: 'And now, to further that work, we entreat you not to offer God's grace an ineffectual welcome. (I have answered thy prayer, he says, in a day of pardon, I have brought thee help in a day of salvation . . .) We are careful not to give offence to anybody . . . as God's ministers, we must do everything to make ourselves acceptable. We have to shew great patience, in times of affliction, of need, of difficulty; under the lash, in prison . . . now honoured, now slighted, now traduced, now flattered. They call us deceivers, and we tell the truth; unknown, and we are fully acknowledged; . . . punished, yes, but not doomed to die; . . . beggars, that bring riches to many.'[1]

By his own account, St Paul was dishonoured in the eyes of the world, had lost his good name; no one knew him, or paid any regard to him. The reference is plain enough if we remember what he had done: he had outlawed himself. Being a Jew, his conversion and still more his apostolate was apostasy: Jewry had literally rejected him, just as a Moslem convert to Christianity is an outcast from Islam. So St Paul consented to be spewed out by his own people.

This first option which St Paul was content to make, of infamy, ostracism, contempt, of being taken for a fool—it is the common lot of those who take Christ seriously. It is the same thing every time, the world calls it madness. Anyone who shows the least inclination really to practise Christ's poverty in his own life will be called a crank. He will be accused of trying to attract attention, and condemned for rebelling against the rules and customs of his station in life. But St Paul would surely never have transformed the world about him if he had not first done that very thing, making a clean break with a whole pattern of customs and prejudices which belonged to his own environment just because the following of Christ required such a final breach. A Christian is bound to give offence, and if he does not, it is a bad sign,

[1] 2 Cor. 6: 1–5, 8–10.

for it shows he cannot be so very Christian—the salt has begun to lose its savour. Among Christian people today it must be admitted that Christianity is very largely inoffensive, politically, intellectually, and every way: but that sort of Christianity will never transform anything.

The next thing St Paul had to put up with was the deprivation of all material well-being: that is, he accepted the risk of living in physical discomfort, and had to learn to care nothing for his own welfare or convenience. So it was for him, always, as he said: 'in times of need, of difficulty; under the lash, in prison, in the midst of tumult; when we are tired out, sleepless, and fasting . . . Dying men, and see, we live; . . . sad men, that rejoice continually; beggars, that bring riches to many; disinherited, and the world is ours'.[1]

Two things are to be noticed here: first, the powerful expression 'disinherited'. Indeed St Paul was one who embraced that primary poverty which is called interior, and consists in a real disposition of readiness to forgo anything whatsoever, an absolute detachment from all material possessions. This is what the young Jesuit meant, at the beginning of the *Soulier de Satin*, when he was tied to the mast of his ship: 'For it is true I am attached to my cross, but my cross is not attached to anything.' In a word, it is the perfect freedom of the bond-servant of love. Tied to his mast in the world's stormy sea, St Paul enjoyed the fullness of liberty; never was man so free, compared with all the slaves of their own sensuality, their money, their belongings, their libraries and collections. Only in absolute poverty is freedom complete.

With St Paul, however, it was not only a matter of interior detachment. His actual life was organized on a purely temporary basis. In the second Epistle to the Corinthians, he speaks of the human body as a tent; so long as we are in tents, 'we are exiled from the Lord',[2] *peregrinamur*, we are

[1] 2 Cor. 6: 4–5, 9–10.   [2] 5: 6.

on a journey, a pilgrimage, far from home: our life in this world is always more or less under canvas. We cannot settle, we are homeless, we have no place of our own in this world;[1] so we pitch our tent wherever we can, taking what comes in the way of food and shelter. That is exactly how St Paul really lived on his incessant journeys. The fantastic conditions of his travelling appear from his own description, later in the same Epistle: 'Are they Christ's servants? These are wild words; I am something more. I have toiled harder, spent longer days in prison, been beaten so cruelly, so often looked death in the face. Five times the Jews scourged me, and spared me but one lash in the forty; three times I was beaten with rods, once I was stoned; I have been ship-wrecked three times, I have spent a night and a day as a castaway at sea [this is not quite clear; $\beta\nu\theta\acute{o}s$, the deep, probably here means the open sea]. What journeys I have undertaken . . . in danger from my own people, in danger from the Gentiles; danger in cities; danger in the wilder-ness, danger in the sea, danger among false brethren! I have met with toil and weariness, so often been sleepless, hungry and thirsty; so often denied myself food, gone cold and naked.'[2]

These were the normal circumstances of his way of life; never safe from actual danger at the hands of human enemies or from implacable nature; always unprotected, never settled. Such a life of real poverty was certainly calculated to fortify the spirit of interior detachment, and to enlarge the soul's freedom for contemplation of the things of God.

The third and last tribulation to be considered is interior trials. We must never forget that St Paul renounced, among other things, also the feeling of spiritual comfort; for this might be the last illusion, the error of the noblest minds, the idea that the interior life consists in a stable

[1] 'Every foreign country is a home to them, but they are foreigners in every man's country'—*v. supra*, p. 61.
[2] 2 Cor. 11: 23–27.

equilibrium, as if the Christian aim were to renounce the world in order to find peace and quietness. Certainly if that was what St Paul was looking for, he never found it: from the first moment of his mission, his life was incessantly beset with troubles, as he said in one of the passages we have quoted: 'in times of need, of difficulty . . . tired out, sleepless, and fasting' and subject to every kind of distraction. St Francis de Sales translated the word 'need' (ἀναγκαί) by *angoisses*, in a beautiful commentary on this passage, showing what is meant by interior trials:

Job, in his . . . spiritual life . . . was oppressed with languors, oppression, convulsions, anguish, darkness, and with all kinds of intolerable interior griefs, as his complaints and lamentations bear witness. The great Apostle proclaims to us a general Indifference; to shew ourselves the true servants of God, 'in much patience, in tribulation, in necessities, in distresses, in stripes, in prisons, in seditions, in labours, in watchings, in fastings . . .' Take notice, I pray you, Theotimus, how the life of the Apostles was filled with afflictions: in the body by wounds, in the heart by anguish, according to the world by infamy and prisons, and in all these,—O God! what Indifference they had! Their sorrow is joyous, their poverty rich, their death life-giving, their dishonour honourable, that is, they are joyful for being sad, content to be poor, strengthened with life amid the dangers of death, and glorious in being made vile, because—such was the will of God.[1]

We must remember that giving oneself to God, even in the contemplative life, is no way to get peace of mind, but rather to get into the thick of the fighting. One of the Desert Fathers said to a young monk who complained of temptations: 'I have been here for sixty years, and never had a day's peace. You will not find peace in the desert, but war.' Of course this is not to deny that the Apostle found another kind of peace in the midst of all his tribulations,

---

[1] *Traité de l'amour de Dieu*, IX: 5. (trs. Mackey).

that peace 'which surpasses all our thinking',[1] and is compatible with all that burden of suffering and anxiety which he was content to bear the full weight of, all the sorrows of the world about him. We must never look to find a separate peace of our own in God's service, if this should cut us off from the world's pain.

The following of Christ must always mean bearing a larger share of men's troubles, because it means loving men more. If people believe, as is sometimes suggested, that the interior life is a kind of sublimated egotism, they are mistaken; they have not understood what the interior life is about. A balanced development of the personality, and psychological self-fulfilment, may be valuable human activities; but they are not what we have to expect from Christ our Lord—he has something quite different to offer us: a life of intimate involvement in the thick of suffering humanity, in a world of troubles. So St Paul's life was, in his own vehement words, 'the loss of everything',[2] of everything the world counts gain; honour, comfort, intellectual satisfactions, even the most refined pleasures: his 'outward part' might indeed be said to 'wear down'.[3] Visibly, he was on the high road to ruin and perdition. But only in outward appearance.

In reality, it was a case of 'plenty in the midst of poverty': for these two things are not only not incompatible, they are effect and cause. St John of the Cross said that the only way to find All was to leave all; there is a direct relationship between the unitive grasp of him who is all in all, and the fact of total destitution. That is just the very mystery that St Paul himself described: 'as God's ministers, we must do everything to make ourselves acceptable. We have to shew great patience, in times of affliction, . . . under the lash, in prison. We have to be pure-minded, enlightened, forgiving and gracious to others; we have to rely on the Holy Spirit, on unaffected love . . . now honoured, now

[1]Phil. 4: 7.   [2]ibid. 3: 8.   [3]2 Cor. 4: 16.

slighted, now traduced, now flattered. They call us deceivers, and we tell the truth; unknown, and we are fully acknowledged; dying men, and see, we live; punished, yes, but not doomed to die; sad men, that rejoice continually; beggars, that bring riches to many; disinherited, and the world is ours.'[1]

This is the charter on which all the great Christian saints throughout the ages have relied for their assertion that utter poverty is the highest riches: as St John of the Cross: 'Mine are the heavens and mine is the earth; mine are the people, the righteous are mine and mine are the sinners; the Angels are mine and the Mother of God, and all things are mine; and God himself is mine and for me, for Christ is mine and all for me. What then dost thou ask for and seek, my soul?'[2] And Tauler, the great fourteenth-century Dominican mystic: 'The man who has so completely renounced himself as to wish for nothing, to seek nothing, to keep nothing of his own, shall come into possession of all that God has and is; everything becomes his, according to his measure, as it is God's. Nay more, all that angels and men possess, all that every creature has of worth and of joy and of bliss, all this belongs to him as it belongs to them.'[3]

In the action of putting off and laying aside the things of this world, there is a mysterious acquisition of the fount and origin of things, God himself. Fr Huby, commenting on the words of St Paul, wrote: 'If we try to keep the good things of this life jealously to ourselves, they will enslave us. If we are detached from creatures, we are the masters; we gain thereby not only our freedom, but also the power of religious insight, to detect in creatures the presence and working of God: so that the least thing affords us such joy as the wealthiest miser can never feel': *disinherited, and the world is ours.*

[1] 2 Cor. 6: 4–6, 8–10.
[2] *Spiritual Sentences and Maxims*, trs. Peers, Vol. III, p. 244.
[3] Second sermon for Easter.

The disinterested, selfless contemplation of things and people can be a source of incomparable delight; but we are constantly cheated of this enjoyment by our own self-centred acquisitiveness. So long as we are concerned to get or keep a person's favour, or his good opinion, instead of caring for the person himself, there is a poison in our liking: and it is the same with inanimate objects; so long as the fact of having them for ourselves means anything to us, there is a poison in the owning. Possession defeats itself. But the more we learn to see everything about us as so many wonderful presents, and freely give God thanks for it all without thought of private gain, so much the greater will be our enjoyment.

This kind of poverty is not a special vocation; it is the universal Christian attitude. Nothing belongs exclusively to us, everything belongs to God. We are to be grateful for the wealth of creatures magnificently bestowed upon us, not to seek possession of them for ourselves. Dispossessing ourselves, 'disinherited', we Christians will 'rejoice continually': and our joy is the very happiness of God himself, that beatitude which the Lord has told us belongs to the poor—*Beati pauperes*, poverty is the condition of bliss. These words are an invitation sounding in the hearts of men, continually calling them hence, *ripae ulterioris amore*, into the world of which poverty makes us free.

Poverty is also the condition of spiritual fruitfulness. It is because he is poor that the apostle not only possesses the world, but 'brings riches to many'. How true that is! and how well we know that it is the poor who enrich us. It is more profitable for us to attend to the needs of the poor than to receive all manner of wealth: the most precious gift any one can give us is an appeal, if we respond to it. So it is often the generosity of the very poor that is the most valuable and effective; for when we give people things, this may be a way to avoid giving ourselves, a substitute for the real best gift, which is not the gift of riches, but of poverty. 'Always we,

alive as we are, are being given up to death for Jesus' sake
so that the living power of Jesus may be manifested in this
mortal nature of ours. So death makes itself felt in us, and
life in you.'[1] By our death you live.

This immense wealth which St Paul found in poverty is
essentially love: for pure love is most perfectly made known
in total self-abandonment and the surrender of all things.
We may say, in the words of the Song of Songs, that the
man who has given all his substance in exchange for love,
reckons it as nothing in comparison with what he receives
in return.[2] Truly if we give all for love, we gain all, because
we gain love, which, in the end, is all we need.

Why is this love then to be found in absolute poverty?
Because love means an effective devotion to God, so that the
only thing we take any pleasure in is his good pleasure. It
is what St Francis de Sales, in the *Traité de l'Amour de
Dieu*, calls 'holy Indifference', not meaning a lack of affection, but on the contrary such an affection for God as leaves
the lover indifferent to all else. Little he cares if things are
attractive or disagreeable to human taste; their sweetness is
the sweetness of God's will. No earthly bitterness can spoil
the lover's enjoyment of whatever may be pleasing to God:
and no sweetness can disguise the bitterness the lover finds
in what is not according to God's pleasure.

This is even a fact of common experience. Our pleasure
in human enjoyments which are against God's will is always
morbid: on the other hand, it so often happens that the performance of some duty at the cost of a natural repugnance
turns out to be enjoyable. This pleasure is a sign of love.
'Those whose soul is altogether detached from creatures, so
that the Sun of righteousness can shine into their depths,
will find the Saviour's yoke [that is, the acceptance of his
will]: and this yoke is unimaginably sweet. And they will
find on the contrary an acute distaste and repugnance for
all that is not God. . . . The power of his attraction con-

[1] 2 Cor. 4: 11–12.   [2] Song, 8: 7 (Septuagint).

sumes as it were the marrow of the bones and the blood in the veins.'[1]

A man like Tauler can use such language because he knows what it means. We may say these things because they sound well, but without experience. Tauler obviously knew what he was talking about. For him, as for St Paul, the difference between lying in gaol and lying in bed, or the difference between corporal punishment and physical comfort, had ceased to matter. His life was not organized to take account of these things at all. Most men contrive to arrange their affairs so as to keep out of trouble as much as they can, and to do the best for themselves: but with him, these considerations have no weight; he does not even notice them. So poverty may be called the epiphany of love; more than all else, it makes love manifest, because in poverty there is nothing else but love: as it was in the poverty of Bethlehem that Christ's love was most simply shown.

Even so, all this is still not enough for St Paul, because, in the last analysis, it is no more than an earnest of something else; it is not yet the full possession of his goal. Over and beyond all this there is a longing in him until the measure of his poverty and destitution, his stripes and all the rest of his trials is finally fulfilled, in the total dissolution of his natural existence. Only then, when the veil is torn away from between him and God, will he have all his heart's desire. 'No, we do not play the coward; though the outward part of our nature is being worn down, our inner life is refreshed from day to day. This light and momentary affliction brings with it a reward multiplied every way, loading us with everlasting glory; if only we will fix our eyes on what is unseen, not on what we can see. What we can see, lasts but for a moment; what is unseen is eternal. Once this earthly tent-dwelling of ours has come to an end', —here is the idea of being under canvas; this life is an

[1] Tauler; Sermon for 4th Sunday after Epiphany.

encampment—'God, we are sure, has a solid building waiting for us, a dwelling not made with hands, that will last eternally in heaven. And indeed, it is for this that we sigh, longing for the shelter of that home which heaven will give us . . . Yes, if we tent-dwellers here go sighing and heavy-hearted, it is not because we would be stripped of something; rather, we would clothe ourselves afresh; our mortal nature must be swallowed up in life. For this, nothing else, God was preparing us, when he gave us the foretaste of his Spirit.'[1]

Here we may recall the words of St Ignatius of Antioch on his way to martyrdom, when he besought the Romans, for pity's sake, not to try to save him from that death whereby, he said 'I shall be a man.' So long as this life lasted he was not yet a man. The sorry limitations of earthly existence and the burden of the flesh were obstacles in the way of his transformation by the life-giving Spirit, inhibiting the desires of his soul longing for divine contemplation, and of his heart longing for eternal bliss, and even of his body longing to be transfigured. Seeing all this, he knew he was not yet a man, and would not be until his time came, that time to which he looked forward as to his 'birthday', his *natalitia*: and indeed that is truly the time of our birth, when the biological phase of our existence, the earthly period, is completed, as it were the maturity of a chrysalis, whence the butterfly may emerge untrammelled for its aerial flights.

So there is not only a connexion in general between poverty and enjoyment, but even between the limiting case of poverty, which is Death, and the supreme joy, which is in the beatific vision of God. The poverty of Christ on the Cross included the deprivation of liberty when his hands were nailed, and the deprivation of property when they took away his clothes: but it was the final deprivation of life itself, which he offered up as a free gift, that opened the way

[1] 2 Cor. 4: 16–18; 5: 1–2, 4–5.

to his resurrection. Our inquiry has thus led us into the heart of the Christian mystery, which is the paradox of life in death.

Everything we have said comes down in the end to that participation in the death and resurrection of Christ which is continually enacted in his mystical body and in each of its members. The coupling of poverty and abundance, death and life, delineates the very foundation of the Christian life, the life that is in Christ, in his death and in his resurrection. We died with him and rose again with him in baptism, and his death and resurrection will be fulfilled in us again when our life on earth is over, and when we come through death to the resurrection from the dead. But in the meanwhile all that space of time between our baptism and death still belongs to Christ's death and resurrection. This is the secret of Christian 'mortification', and also of 'vivification', which latter is so seldom mentioned that people get a wrong idea of Christianity, failing to appreciate that it is really life. Vivification is the essential thing; the point of Christianity is to release the springs of love within us. Of course this can only be done through a process of mortification; as St Augustine said, if the domain of charity is to be enlarged, the domain of the flesh must be restricted: but this mortification is all for the sake of life: 'We have a treasure, then, in our keeping, but its shell is of perishable earthenware; it must be God, and not anything in ourselves, that gives it its sovereign power. For ourselves, we are being hampered everywhere, yet still have room to breathe, are hard put to it, but never at a loss; persecution does not leave us unbefriended, nor crushing blows destroy us; we carry about continually in our bodies the dying state of Jesus, so that the living power of Jesus may be manifested in our bodies too.'[1]

[1] ibid. 4: 7–10.

CHAPTER THREE

SINCERITY

'IT is our boast, made in all good conscience, that *we have behaved* in the world, and towards you especially, *with single-heartedness and sincerity* in God's sight, not using human wisdom, but the light of God's grace. And we mean by our letters nothing else than what you read in them, and understand us to mean. I hope that you will come to understand us better; . . . are we not your chief pride, as you are our chief pride, in the day when our Lord Jesus Christ comes?[1]'

Consideration of these last mysterious words may be deferred until the end of the present chapter. What is immediately evident is the quality of utter sincerity, the complete integrity that belongs essentially to the character of the apostle.

*　　　*　　　*

This particular mental disposition is the contrary of any kind of double dealing, any mixture of motives, any want of candour, such as always and only comes from allowing self-interest to interfere with the single purpose of God's glory and service. It often happens that a man who has embarked upon some undertaking to serve God, finds himself gradually and imperceptibly involved in an uncomfortably false position through attending to what other people may think of him or his work, and trying to please them, or to avoid giving offence. Paul expresses himself most forcibly on the missionary's duty not to care in the least whether

[1] 2 Cor. 1: 12–14.

men think well or ill of him. 'Do you think it is man's
favour, or God's, that I am trying to win now? Shall I be
told, now, that I am courting the good will of men? If . . .
I were still courting the favour of men, I should not be what
I am, the slave of Christ.'[1] Here are two distinct points: in
the first place, if I should *seek* to please men, if my motive
were to gain a certain reputation, I should not be an apostle
at all. But secondly, what is more, it would be a bad sign
if I actually *did* please men, for the chances are I should
not then be truly serving Christ. A real servant of Christ
must necessarily give offence sometimes. Too much tender-
ness on this score means scaling down the demands of
Christ, softening the gospel for fear of shocking human susceptibilities: which is a dereliction of duty.

The Epistle to the Galatians is full of this idea. 'Who are
they, these people who insist on your being circumcised?
They are men, all of them, who are determined to keep up
outward appearances, so that the cross of Christ may not
bring persecution on them.'[2] St Paul was writing to Christians who were being talked over by Jews—'have yourselves
circumcised, and escape persecution'. They were offered a
compromise between God and Mammon, between Christ
and the world; a concession, to save trouble. St Paul de-
nounced the suggestion as mere human respect, prompted
by no concern for their true welfare. 'Why, they do not
even observe the law, although they adopt circumcision;
they are for having you circumcised, so as to make a display
of your outward conformity. God forbid that I should make
a display of anything, except the cross of our Lord Jesus
Christ, through which the world stands crucified to me,
and I to the world.'[3] If I keep faith with Christ, I must
incur the world's reproach, it is impossible for me to be on
good terms with the world.

'The world', for St Paul, does not mean 'creation'. Creation is 'very good'; God's blessing is upon it and the Chris-

[1]Gal. 1: 10.   [2]ibid. 6: 12.   [3]ibid. 6: 13–14.

L.H.–X

tian can have no quarrel with it. 'The world' means the whole collection of those human tendencies that go against the Spirit of Christ, vanity, pride, hardness of heart, concupiscence; of which Christ himself said 'I am not praying for the world'.[1] A Christian cannot agree with the spirit of this world, because there is a direct incompatibility between it and the spirit of Christ. So it is natural for the Christian to be thoroughly disliked; his whole behaviour is a living reproach. He has no love for the world's ideals; this in itself is an intolerable position, because it amounts to a judgement and sentence passed upon the world. Therefore the world hates him.

The disinterested sincerity that marks the true apostle is defined in the First Epistle to the Thessalonians: 'Our appeal to you was not based on any false or degraded notions, was not backed by cajolery. We have passed God's scrutiny, and he has seen fit to entrust us with the work of preaching; when we speak, it is with this in view; we would earn God's good opinion, not man's, since it is God who scrutinizes our hearts.'[2] The essence of perfect sincerity in conduct is to care for nothing but God's judgement of our actions: not to vary our attitude to suit the company we are in, not to hold one opinion when alone and adopt another in conversation, but to speak and act as in the sight of 'God, who scrutinizes our hearts'. There must be an effort to keep our words and deeds true to our real character. Sincerity means trying to make the outward man ever more and more like the inner man—not aggressively, of course; but simply being true to oneself, so that no human respect shall make us false.

Elsewhere, St Paul contrasts this character with that of 'false apostles' who seek the favour of men. 'We do not, like so many others, adulterate the word of God, we preach it in all its purity, as God gave it to us, standing before God's presence.'[3] False teachers adulterate the word of God, like cheating tradesmen, or publicans that water the wine: the

[1]John 17: 9.   [2]1 Thess. 2: 3–4.   [3]2 Cor. 2: 17.

goods they deliver are not the pure wine of the Word, but a mixture, with some of the Word in it, as, after all, there is still a little wine in the tavern liquids, but drowned in extraneous elements. They do not speak the word in its purity. Their wares are not as advertised. Their conduct is not dictated by the single duty of doing God's will.

This special quality of sincerity is chiefly exhibited in two ways, of which the first consists in a pure intention—that is, caring only for the judgement of God upon our behaviour, and nothing for the judgement of men; being more concerned, whatever we do, about his good pleasure and displeasure than about theirs. This is one of the essentials of spiritual life. As a normal rule (if we would not deceive ourselves) we are influenced by consideration of the good or unfavourable opinion of others; we are concerned to keep up a certain character in our neighbours' estimation. And on the other hand we are not especially careful about our condition in God's sight, or we should not so often neglect the things that he alone sees, like private prayer and secret acts of kindness. We pay more attention to those good works, undertaken for God's sake indeed, which nevertheless appear before men, so that our own reputation is involved in them. The utter sincerity of doing things which no one can ever know about just as well as the things other people can see, indicates a high degree of perfection. But it is a fundamental Gospel requirement: 'When you pray, you are not to be like hypocrites, who love to stand praying in synagogues . . . to be a mark for men's eyes . . . But when thou art praying, go into thy inner room and shut the door upon thyself, and so pray to thy Father in secret.'[1] The want of a pure intention subtly and slightly spoils everything we do, so that our life is half a lie; we can never be quite at ease with ourselves.

Now this will not do. 'We ought to be regarded as Christ's servants, and stewards of God's mysteries. And this is what

[1]Matt. 6: 5–6.

we look for in choosing a steward; we must find one who is trustworthy. Yet for myself, I make little account of your scrutiny, or of any human audit-day; I am not even at pains to scrutinize my own conduct. My conscience does not, in fact, reproach me; but that is not where my justification lies; it is the Lord's scrutiny I must undergo.'[1] It does not matter at all what other people think of me—I do not even know what to think of myself: all that matters is the Lord's verdict; the one thing I care for is Christ's judgement of me. 'You do ill, therefore, to pass judgement prematurely, before the Lord's coming; he will bring to light what is hidden in darkness, and reveal the secrets of men's hearts.'[2] Then that which is of real worth will be brought to light, the hidden treasure of charity, humility, prayer; then the good work done in secret simply for God's sake will appear in all its splendour: but then, too, the base metal of our own mixed motives will show up in all its worthlessness and sham. Our whole wealth then will consist in the handful of really genuine things we may have done in our lives, the few acts of real charity or of real prayer, withdrawn from the sight of men, done in the sight of God alone.

This has a special reference to the apostolic life. The missionary must do his duty without heeding the judgements of men, 'now honoured, now slighted, now traduced, now flattered'.[3] This duty is to bear witness to the truth, to declare things as they are. 'Being entrusted, then, by God's mercy, with this ministry, we do not play the coward; we renounce all shame-faced concealment.'[4] Everything we do is done in public, everything is in the sight of men. 'There must be no crooked ways, no falsifying of God's word'—not saying one thing to a man's face and another behind his back—' it is by making the truth publicly known that we recommend ourselves to the honest judgement of mankind, as in God's sight. Our gospel is a mystery, yes, but it is only a mystery to those who are on the road to perdition; those

[1] 1 Cor. 4: 1–4.　[2] ibid. 4: 5.　[3] 2 Cor. 6: 8.　[4] ibid. 4: 1–2.

whose unbelieving minds have been blinded by the god this world worships', the devil, 'so that the glorious gospel of Christ, God's image, cannot reach them with the rays of its illumination. After all, it is not ourselves we proclaim; we proclaim Christ Jesus as Lord, and ourselves as your servants for Jesus' sake. The same God who bade light shine out of darkness has kindled a light in our hearts, whose shining is to make known his glory.'[1]

The mission is the official promulgation of the gospel. The apostle has the Holy Trinity's commission to publish abroad among the heathen that the risen Christ has inaugurated the age of grace and brought salvation to the world of men. He has nothing to do but to proclaim this word of truth—he has no time for plotting and trickery or for diplomatic finesse. He has no use for evasions, 'yes and no': his whole duty is an affirmation, 'yes'. 'As God is faithful, the message we delivered to you is not one which hesitates between Yes and No. It was Jesús Christ, the Son of God, that I . . . preached to you; and that preaching did not hesitate between Yes and No; in him all is affirmed with certainty.'[2] In Christ there was only 'yes', he is wholly witness of truth. 'In him all the promises of God become certain . . . it is through him that we say our Amen.'[3] The divine promises are fulfilled in his person, and himself is witness to their fulfilment.

*   *   *

Besides this interior singleness of view and purpose, there is another manifestation of the virtue of sincerity, this time directed outwards: it is what St Paul describes in a favourite series of expressions as 'unaffected love',[4] or 'sincere love':[5] 'make sure that your charity rings true'.[6] This 'unaffected love' consists simply in the pursuit of others' good. Normally, when we wish others well, we also want them to be

[1]ibid. 4: 2–6. [2]ibid. 1: 18–19. [3]ibid. 1: 20. [4]ibid. 6: 6.
[5]Rom. 12: 9. [6]2 Cor. 8: 8.

grateful for our kindness; we should like them to be pleased
with us; it is nice to be appreciated. Our benevolence
suffers the admixture of a number of other feelings. But a
really disinterested charity means that we are happy when
others are really better, when they love God, even if they
have forgotten all about us.

St Paul states the difference in terms of an actual experience of his own. It is clear that he had been accused of self-
seeking and ambition: for he defends himself by showing
that he had not sought any personal gain from his apostolic
labours—'Be generous with us; it is not as if any of you
could say that we had wronged him, or done him harm, or
taken undue advantage of him. I am not finding fault with
you when I say this; I have told you before now, we hold
you so close in our hearts that nothing in life or in death can
part us from you. With what confidence I speak to you.'[1]
Again, still more explicitly: 'I impoverished other churches,
taking pay from them so as to be at your service. I was
penniless when I visited you, but I would not cripple any of
you with expenses; . . . I would not, and I will not, put
any burden on you.'[2]

Then, in the First Epistle to the Thessalonians, he insists
upon the point that he has not claimed even the marks of
respect to which he was properly entitled. 'We have never
asked for human praise, yours or another's, although, as
apostles of Christ, we might have claimed importance
among you. No, you found us gentle as babes in your
company; no nursing mother ever cherished her children
more; in our great longing for you, we desired nothing
better than to offer you our own lives, as well as God's
gospel, so greatly had we learned to love you. Brethren, you
can remember how we toiled and laboured, all the time we
were preaching God's gospel to you, working day and night
so as not to burden you with expense. Both you and God
can witness how upright and honest and faultless was our

[1] 2 Cor. 7: 2–4. · [2] ibid. 11: 8–9.

conduct towards you believers; it is within your knowledge
that we treated every one of you as a father treats his children, encouraging you, comforting you, imploring you to
lead a life worthy of God.'[1]

Is there to be no seeking after glory? is every object of
ambition to be rejected? Our Lord himself would not look
to his own reputation;[2] 'when a man seeks to win credit for
one who sent him, he tells the truth, there is no dishonesty
in him'.[3] St Paul was occasionally obliged, as he put it, to
'boast' in self-defence. 'I might boast of the powers I have,
powers which the Lord has given me so as to build up your
faith, . . . and I should not be put in the wrong.'[4] 'Once
more I appeal to you, let none of you think me vain; or, if it
must be so, give me a hearing in spite of my vanity, and let
me boast a little in my turn . . . If so many others boast
of their natural advantages, I must be allowed to boast too.
You find it easy to be patient with the vanity of others, you
who are so full of good sense.'[5] He had to defend himself,
because the accusations and attacks directed against him
involved also the message entrusted to him; he could not
bear the kind of hostile criticism that might hinder the
Word of God. Thus he was induced in the interests of truth
to vindicate himself from certain unjust charges: for otherwise the very Word of God would suffer, the gospel would
fall into some measure of disrepute.

It was only because the Corinthians were so much influenced by these personal considerations that St Paul had
to condescend to any kind of self-defence. For his own part,
the whole question was quite unimportant. To be a Hebrew,
of the seed of Abraham, and so forth, meant nothing to him.
But he found himself confronted with people to whom
these things meant a great deal: he had to accommodate
himself to their little world; so, although he really cared
nothing for the subject of discussion, he was drawn into

[1]Thess. 2: 6–12. [2]John 8: 50. [3]ibid 7: 18.
[4]2 Cor. 10: 8. [5]ibid. 11: 16, 18–19.

bestowing some pains upon it. Here we meet the perennial question of the place of mundane activities on the Mission. Undoubtedly, it is by the power of God alone that his kingdom will come: so why should missionaries start by building universities and teaching mathematics, or by devoting their charitable activities to the care of men's bodies? Is that the way to establish the kingdom of Heaven? Clearly not; the only way is to preach the Word: but human preparations will help the message to tell. It will not make the good news any better—the gospel remains gospel: but if it is wrongly presented, the Word of God will not be rightly valued.

All the same, St Paul makes his apologia with a great deal of irony. He will not take himself seriously, he keeps a sense of proportion. Forced as a he is to make good his human pretensions, he will not value these things above their true worth. None of them really matters. It is only the grace of God that turns the hearts of men. Knowing this, he is free to make use of human means just as far as they will serve, and equally free to discard them. Here is the key to the authentic missionary attitude. The human approach is there to be used; it would be ridiculous to omit it: but everything must be kept in proportion. The Word of God is not bound by any rules of method. It works in the power of preaching and of prayer, and supernaturally.

There is a proper place for everything. St Paul says, first, 'If so many others boast of their natural advantages, I must be allowed to boast, too.'[1] Next, he says 'If I must needs boast, I will boast of the things which humiliate me'.[2] In the end, my real glory is not in such human gifts as I may have, but in the power of God at work within me: a glory that is not mine at all, but belongs entirely to God. My real achievements, when all is said, have nothing to do with the puny human efforts I may have made to serve the gospel; my great work is what God's word has brought about in me and through me, and I cannot boast of this because

[1] 2 Cor. 11: 18.   [2] ibid. 11: 30.

the praise of it all belongs to God. Honour where honour is due. 'I will not boast about myself, except to tell you of my humiliations. It would not be vanity, if I had a mind to boast . . . More than ever, then, I delight to boast of the weaknesses that humiliate me, so that the strength of Christ may enshrine itself in me. I am well content with these humiliations of mine, with the insults . . . when I am weakest, then I am strongest of all.'[1]

[1]ibid. 12: 5–6; 9–10.

CHAPTER FOUR

ZEAL

'IF you would only bear with my vanity for a little! Pray be patient with me; after all, my jealousy on your behalf is the jealousy of God himself; I have betrothed you to Christ, so that no other but he should claim you, his bride without spot.'[1] St Paul is thinking of the Churches he has won for Christ, betrothed to the Lord. His affection for them is anxious, exacting. He cannot bear any suspicion of infidelity in their engagement; the very thought of them falling short of their promises to Christ is intolerable to him. As he says, he is 'jealous' of them; but this quality of mind requires some further elucidation, for the idea of 'jealousy' has unpleasant associations. Elsewhere in the New Testament, jealousy sometimes stands for the feeling of resentment against any perfection in others that we ourselves lack; this is certainly one of the vilest deformities of which human nature is patient. Yet the Scriptures also use the word in quite another meaning, to denote something of great religious worth, belonging in particular and primarily to God himself.

It is actually stated in the Bible that 'the very name of the Lord bespeaks jealous love'.[2] Like 'the wrath of God', this terminology is somewhat disconcerting; but it is simply the vivid presentation of one attribute of the living God, namely his absolute refusal to tolerate any rival in the affections of men. It is important to be accurate here: it is only the worship due to God alone that he will in no case consent to share; there is no question of forbidding the indulgence of

[1] 2 Cor. 11: 1–2. [2] Exod. 34: 14.

ordinary human affections in their proper place. But nothing and no one may trespass upon the exclusive right of God, his primacy, his unique claim of worship. No creature may ever be treated as God.

It is important to recognize this background, if the idea of 'zeal' is to have, from the first, its due status and worth. It is often the case that New Testament words have suffered a certain degradation in contemporary language. Among other examples, the most striking degeneration has affected the words 'charity' and 'edification': but also the word 'zeal', when divorced from its theological connotation. We have to sweep aside all modern imagery and associations of ideas if we are to restore the primitive dominant idea of zeal as belonging to the divine jealousy, God's intolerance of competition for the true love of God. Zeal, in men, is simply the characteristic attitude of those who take God's side, and consequently will not accept, any more than he does, any shortcomings in giving him his due of worship, any failure to love him as he should be loved: zeal means suffering and indignation because men do not keep faith with God. Zeal, so understood, is essentially and directly connected with love itself: it represents the ardour of love, the demanding, insatiable aspects of love.

This scriptural use of language derives, of course, from customary usage in respect of something that is lawful and valuable in human life, and is seen at its best in the jealous regard that husbands and wives have for each other, inasmuch as they will have no intrusion of third parties, or reconcile themselves to any idea that love once given can ever be withdrawn or transferred. Essentially, that is a noble attitude of mind, and simply gives expression to the quality of singleness in human love. Scripture transposes the same attitude of mind into the context of divine love, because the whole Bible is there to show that the bond between Jehovah and the Israelites, and between Christ and the soul, is also a single, exclusive and irrevocable union. The whole range of imagery and emotion associated with human love is similarly transposed, to show the various aspects and requirements of the love of God.

The first mention of God's jealousy in the Bible is in Exodus, where idolatry is forbidden. 'Thou shalt not carve images, or fashion the likeness of anything in heaven above, or on earth beneath . . . to bow down and worship it. I, thy God, the Lord Almighty, am jealous in my love.'[1] The text is as clear as can be. God's jealousy means that he does not tolerate idolatry: we are to bow down only before him; he will not have us make an idol of any creature. In this respect he is jealous of his name and of the glory that belongs to him alone. There is one whole category of human dispositions that God reserves strictly for himself, so that we are not in any circumstances entitled to transfer them to any created object.

The same injunction is constantly to be found in the prophetic books, where the strictness of God's demands upon his people in this respect is much emphasized. It is simply and finally inadmissible that God's people, with whom he has made an exclusive covenant, and whose God he is, should go astray after foreign idols. This kind of unfaithfulness is exactly what is often called in the Bible the 'adultery' of the chosen people; or as Ezekiel has it, their brothel-keeping—in a famous passage, perhaps the finest in all the literature of the covenant. It begins with Jehovah reminding Israel of its origins, like a foundling baby; 'on the bare ground thou wert cast away . . . that day of thy birth'; and how Jehovah took up the poor child, and gave her life, and bestowed his own beauty upon her. 'All the world heard the fame of thy loveliness; I had made thee so fair, says the Lord God, utterly fair! Fatal beauty, fatal renown, which emboldened thee to play the harlot, lavish thy favours on every passer-by, and be his! That thou shouldst use those garments of thine to make curtains for

[1] 20: 4–5, Cf. 34: 14; Deut. 32: 16; Jos. 24: 19; Ps. 77: 58.

thy hill-shrines . . . Salve is none, says the Lord God, for
such a heart as thine, set on following a harlot's ways . . .
Such punishment thou shalt have as unfaithful wives have;
to my jealous anger thy life must make amends.'[1]

The whole passage is inspired with the terrible strength
of God's love, and all the violence that the Bible predicates
of God, to the scandal of rationalizing pharisees, who call it
anthropomorphic, themselves preferring a properly abstract God, who will stay in his sky and give them no
trouble. The God of the Bible is quite different; he is a God
in love: and when one is in love it is unbearable that the
beloved should be false. So here we see his love in action,
fiercely intolerant of any betrayal by the souls he loves; he
will not put up with sin. We find it so easy to overlook our
offences against God, but he does not get used to them at
all—he cannot bear us to commit sin. According to a profound idea developed by Guardini, this corresponds in a
mysterious way to an actual suffering in God himself. For
while it is true that God is impassible, yet there is indeed in
him something analogous to what we recognize as 'suffering':
it is this irreducible intolerance of unfaithfulness, the
impossibility of coming to terms with it. God's holiness
and purity are utterly incompatible with all sin, but the
most abhorrent are the sins of souls that he has chosen
and reserved to himself, bestowing all his best gifts upon
them.

The violence of the divine jealousy is seen first in the
punishment which God inflicts upon the faithless one, as
we saw in the sixteenth chapter of Ezekiel, and as appears
again in Hosea. 'See if I do not hedge her way about with
thorns, fence in her prospect, till way she can find none!
Then, it may be, when her gallants she courts in vain, she
will have other thoughts: Back go I to the husband that was
mine once; things were better with me in days gone by. Yet
I it was, did she but know it, that bread and wine and oil

[1] Ezech. 16: 14–16, 30, 38.

gave her, gave her all the silver and gold she squandered on Baal.'[1]

But when God chastises his people, that is not the end of the matter, for it is essentially not the satisfaction of retribution that he is seeking to obtain: to him, vengeance is not sweet. All he wants is to win men's hearts, and that they should be converted. So his punishments are always only intended to bring the faithless one to some consciousness of her guilt, whether through the pangs of remorse, or through the ensuing tribulations. As we saw in the last quotation, the thought came to the adulteress to say 'Back go I to the husband that was mine once; things were better with me in days gone by.' The essence of chastisement is thus to bring home to the sinner the bitterness of sin, so that she may want to come back. It is one of the lover's stratagems whereby God, who is always on the watch for every human soul, endeavours both by trials and by consolations to win possession.

Among the strangest of these mysterious ways is God's provocation of jealousy in the faithless beloved; he pretends to have forgotten her, to be caring for another, so as to make her jealous. Thus we find in Deuteronomy that when the Lord saw the wrongdoing of his people, he 'was roused to anger when he saw it, saw his own sons and daughters defying him. I will turn away from them, he said, and see what comes of it; here is a rebellious race, a thankless brood. They have deserted me for a god that was no god, phantoms have been my rivals; now I will desert them in my turn, for a people that is no people of mine; their rivals shall be men as impious as themselves.'[2] So that when he turned his face away from them, and appeared at that time to be forsaking them, this was to make them feel sorry not to be his beloved people any more.

St Paul developed the same idea in the Epistle to the Romans, which is a key text for the understanding of the

[1]Os. 2: 6–8. [2]Deut. 32: 19–21.

mystery of Judaism. 'Tell me, then, have they stumbled so
as to fall altogether? [that is, are we to suppose the Jews'
apostasy will be for all time?] God forbid; the result of their
false step has been to bring the Gentiles salvation, and the
result of that must be to arouse the Jews to emulate them.
Why then, if their false step has enriched the world, if the
Gentiles have been enriched by their default, what must we
expect, when it is made good? (I am speaking now to you
Gentiles.) As long as my apostolate is to the Gentiles, I mean
to make much of my office, in the hope of stirring up my
own flesh and blood to emulation . . .'—here is St Paul
playing God's own game: he too is trying to make the Jews
jealous by paying attention to the heathen, so that one day
they shall be angry at being neglected for a rival, and begin
to want a little attention themselves. 'If the losing of them
has meant a world reconciled to God, what can the winning
of them mean, but life risen from the dead?'[1]

Zeal, then, or jealousy, is primarily our jealous God's own
zeal, the refusal to share divine honours with another: it is
also the passion that God's friends feel for him; knowing
him as they do, they cannot bear to see him slighted. To be
zealous for God means not being able to put up with any
disobedience to his will, or anything contrary to the hallow-
ing of his name. Among various Old Testament characters
who showed this kind of zeal, the most ancient was Phinees, who figured in a scene of brutal violence and blood-
shed: such scenes are not uncommon in the Old Testament,
but in this one the inspiration evidently comes from a pas-
sionate love of God. Phinees saw one of the children of
Israel bring a Madianite woman, a heathen, into the camp.
It was absolutely forbidden under the Jewish law for a Jew
to marry a heathen; the man's action was literally sacrilegious, which is the key to a true understanding of the story:
it was a case of defilement affecting the whole people

[1]Rom. 11: 11–15.

through complicity in the worship of false gods. It was done 'in full sight of . . . the whole multitude that stood weeping at the tabernacle door. Whereupon Phinees, son of Eleazar, son of the high priest Aaron, left his place among the multitude weapon in hand, and followed this Israelite into the place of shame; man and woman both he pierced through . . . With that, the Israelites were rid of the plague that had befallen them.'[1] Jehovah sets great store by the purity of his people: Phinees knew it, and therefore he gave concrete and violent expression to the vengeance of that God who will not have his spouse defiled. Jehovah praised him for the exercise of what he called '*my* indignation': 'Phinees . . . has averted my vengeance from the sons of Israel; a man roused to such indignation in my cause, that my own indignation has spared them.'[2] The very enormity of this episode conveys some idea of the rigour of God's claim.

Another character who powerfully represented the divine jealousy was the prophet Elias, the great witness to the holiness of God.[3] In the Third Book of Kings, it is recorded that when he was a fugitive from persecution, he went into a cave to spend the night; 'and all at once the Lord's word came to him, Elias, what dost thou here? Why, he answered, I am all jealousy for the honour of the Lord God of hosts; see how the sons of Israel have forsaken thy covenant, thrown down thy altars, and put thy prophets to the sword! Of these, I only am left, and now my life, too, is forfeit. Then word came to him to go out and stand there in the Lord's presence; the Lord God himself would pass by. A wind there was, rude and boisterous, that shook the mountains and broke the rocks in pieces before the Lord, but the Lord was not in the wind. And after the wind, an earthquake, but the Lord was not in the earthquake. And after

---

[1] Num. 25: 6–8. [2] ibid. 25: 11.
[3] The parallel between Phineas and Elijah is brought out in 1 Macch. 2: 54, 58.

the earthquake a fire, but the Lord was not in the fire. And
after the fire, the whisper of a gentle breeze. Elias, when he
heard it, wrapped his face in his mantle, and went out to
stand at the cave door. There a voice came to him, Elias,
what dost thou here? I am all jealousy, said he, for the
honour of the Lord God of hosts; see how the sons of Israel
have forsaken thy covenant, thrown down thy altars, and
put thy prophets to the sword! Of these, I only am left, and
now my life, too, is forfeit.'[1] It is to the man who is jealous
of God's honour that Jehovah reveals himself in the still,
small voice that stands for the simplicity of his spiritual
being. St Paul quoted this episode, and Elijah's words—'I
am the only one left . . .'—with reference to the handful
of Jews among his own contemporaries who were believers
in Christ. Though the children of Israel had forsaken the
new covenant, these few were left, these only, a faithful
remnant of Israel to stand up for God and keep his new law:
'So it is in our time; a remnant has remained true; grace
has chosen it'.[2]

Another example of jealousy, or zeal, in the Old Testament, and one which is especially significant for us, occurs
in one verse of a Psalm: 'Was it not jealousy for the honour
of thy house that consumed me; was it not uttered against
thee, the reproach I bore?'[3] The magnificent expression in
the second line, where the Psalmist feels as his own all the
ignominy and contempt in which men hold God, was applied
by St Paul to the person of the Saviour:[4] but Christ himself
re-enacted the first line, when he purged the Temple.
'The paschal feast which the Jews keep was drawing near,
so Jesus went up to Jerusalem. And in the temple there he
found the merchants selling oxen and sheep and pigeons,
and the money-changers sitting at their trade. So he made a
kind of whip out of cords, and drove them all, with their
sheep and oxen, out of the temple, spilling the bankers'
coins and overthrowing their tables; and he said to the

[1] 3 Kings 19: 9–14. [2] Rom. 11: 2–5. [3] Ps. 68: 10. [4] Rom. 15: 3.
L.H.–Y

pigeon-sellers, Take these away, do not turn my Father's house into a place of barter. And his disciples remembered how it is written, I am consumed with jealousy for the honour of thy house.'[1] We ought not to allow God's house, the holy temple, to be turned into a trading establishment: that is, the Church of God is not to be a commercial enterprise of any sort, there must be no corruption of its sanctity by human interests. Christ would not have his Father's house profaned; and we know that the temple, in the holy scriptures, always stands for the Church—the temple in question here is not so much, or not only, the stone temple of Jerusalem, but the spiritual house built of 'stones that live and breathe',[2] the temple of the Catholic Church. Christ will have no profanation of this temple, and the scourge of the Gospel story is always in his hand to drive out the salesmen. We are not always ready to appreciate this side of our religion, the fierce intransigence of God's claim upon us: we are much too easily reconciled to the defilement of God's Church, and the shoddiness of average Christianity; we are used to it; but a zealous soul will never make the best of any bad job, as Péguy said in his original *Jeanne d'Arc*: '*c'est quelqu'un qui n'a jamais pris son parti rien.*' There is no making the best of sin and of the unfaithfulness of Christians. The Church is betrothed to Christ, 'his bride without spot'.[3] To see this chaste bride corrupted by seducers, whoever these may be—to see a soul alienated from the faith by the preaching of false prophets, this is enough to break the heart of a real Christian: he is not going to put up with that, he cannot bear it, he will not have it. That was St Paul's feeling all through the Second Epistle to the Corinthians. He loved his Corinthian converts with all a father's love for his children, because he had given them to Christ: and now false teachers had been to Corinth, and led their souls astray by fine speaking, so that St Paul would hardly know them again. The family tie was broken: a sha-

[1]John 2: 13–17.   [2]1 Pet. 2: 5.   [3]2 Cor. 11: 2.

dow had fallen between him and them, because there was a shadow between them and Christ. That was too much for St Paul; it maddened him—there are passages in his letter where he is absolutely consumed with passion, as though the violence of God's own jealousy possessed his heart.[1]

Of course this fiery jealousy is united in the divine being to the deepest mercy, 'demanding all things and forgiving all things' as Jacques Rivière well expressed it: but the intransigence conditions the indulgence; they go together. Indeed we must forgive seventy times seven times. God is always ready to forgive the worst sinners, but that does not mean he can ever tolerate sin. It was noticed that Christ went about with sinners and whores; but there never was in him the least suspicion of connivance in the sin of any man or any woman. A fellow-feeling for sin is by no means a good way to win over the sinner. Not but what there may still be a measureless love of sinners, an inexhaustible capacity to forgive, an infinite mercy; only all this mercy must be grounded on something unshakeable if it is to be any good. If we are really going to help those we love, they must find something solid in us at bottom; we shall do them no good unless they like us the better for not giving way to them. In this case, but only in this case, we are different from them, we represent something other than the self which so often disgusts them. What they want of us is to be able to go on admiring us, even when their very admiration is a constant reproach to themselves; it is a reproach they want to be able to feel, and it is something they expect of us.

At this point we may return to the consideration of that eleventh chapter of St Paul's Second Epistle to the Corinthians, from which we began this inquiry, and see how the notion of zeal or jealousy is enriched with all its Old Testament associations. 'If you would only bear with my vanity for a little'—he is not going to be reasonable any more, but like one madly in love. 'Pray be patient with me; after all,

[1]See Origen, *Hom. Ex.* VIII: 5.

my jealousy on your behalf is the jealousy of God himself; I have betrothed you to Christ, so that no other but he should claim you, his bride without spot, and now I am anxious about you. The serpent beguiled Eve with his cunning; what if your minds should be corrupted, and lose that innocence which is yours in Christ? Some newcomer preaches to you a different Christ, not the one we preached to you; he brings you a spirit other than the spirit you had from us, a gospel other than the gospel you received; you would . . . be patient with him.' But this cannot be the case: 'I claim to have done no less than the very greatest of the apostles', mine is only the one Gospel. Next then, St Paul accuses himself; it was his fault that his Corinthians have been unfaithful, because he could have no sufficient ascendency over their minds; they knew him so well that his faults were an obstacle to their conversion. Or 'perhaps you think I did wrong to honour you by abasing myself, since I preached God's gospel to you at no charge to yourselves? Why, I impoverished other churches, taking pay from them so as to be at your service. . . . As the truth of Christ lives in me, no one . . . shall silence this boast of mine.' He is tortured with anxiety lest the fault should be his. But after all, since the Corinthians have allowed the false teachers to take great liberties with them, he, St Paul, may as well speak out, too, and let them hear what he has to say. 'You let other people tyrannize over you, prey upon you, take advantage of you, vaunt their power over you, browbeat you! I say this without taking credit to myself'— the more fool I; if I had known you would let yourselves be carried away by false prophets, I need not have been so gentle with you myself; I would have told you more of my mind, and asked more of you to begin with. 'As if we had no power to play such a part'—I ought to have been bolder, more exacting: if that was what you found so charming in your seducers. . . . But St Paul cannot keep it up. 'I have given way to vanity; it was you that drove me to it; you ought to have given me credentials, instead of asking for them. No, I have done no less than the very greatest of the apostles, worthless as I am . . . I will gladly spend and be spent on your souls' behalf, though you should love me too little for loving you too well. Ah, you say, that may be; I did not lay any charge on you myself, but I preyed upon you by roundabout means, like the knave I am.'[1]

The special importance of this passage for our purpose, in analysing the quality of apostolic zeal, is the way in which St Paul identifies his own cause completely with God's; this scene between him and the Corinthians is essentially a scene between them and God. He cannot be on a proper footing with them unless they are at peace with God and keep the faith. So much plainly appears at the beginning of the epistle, where St Paul opens his heart, quite simply, and tells them of the misunderstanding that has arisen between them and him. 'On this I was resolved in my own mind, that I would not pay you a second visit on a sad errand. Was I to make you sorry? It meant bringing sorrow on those who are my own best source of comfort. And those were the very terms in which I wrote to you: I would not come, if it meant finding fresh cause for sorrow where I might have expected to find cause for happiness. I felt confidence in you all, I knew that what made me happy would make you happy too. When I wrote to you, I wrote in great anguish and distress of mind, with many tears. I did not wish to bring sorrow on you, only to assure you of the love I bear you, so abundantly.'[2] This sounds like lovers' jargon—and so, indeed, it is: but the affair is God's affair, and wholly supernatural. St Paul really wanted the Corinthians to make him happy when he came to see them; but as they had been unfaithful, he had to make them sorry first: he had to sadden them by telling them what was on his mind; but all the while he wanted them to realize that the sorrow he was obliged to make them feel was for their

[1] 2 Cor. 11: 1–5, 7–8, 10, 20–21; 12: 11, 15–16.   [2] ibid. 2: 1–4.

own good, to bring them back into a right mind. So, when he hurt them, it was not for lack of love, but on the contrary it was just because he loved them, and wished above all things to do them good; and he was hurt himself because the Corinthians did not realize this, and nursed a grievance against him.

The great lesson which emerges from this passage is the truth that a sincere love must give us the strength and courage even to offend the beloved when this is for the beloved's own good. That is the crux of the matter. St Paul had to hurt the Corinthians because he had to make them ashamed of themselves, and bring them back to good behaviour. He was writing 'not to bring sorrow on you, only to assure you of the love I bear you'; and 'even if I caused you pain by my letter, I am not sorry for it. Perhaps I was tempted to feel sorry. . . .'[1] He had been afraid he might have gone too far, but now he knew everything was all right again; there was no more need to worry. 'I saw how my letter had caused you . . . momentary pain, but now I am glad; not glad of the pain, but glad of the repentance the pain brought with it. Yours was a supernatural remorse . . . Supernatural remorse leads to an abiding and salutary change of heart.'[2] The pattern of St Paul's feelings is plain enough to see: for all the complexity of his expression, it is essentially a simple story. The Corinthians had been unfaithful; St Paul, in a transport of grief, had rebuked them; they had taken offence, and he had felt anxious lest he might have said too much. But after all the Corinthians had realized that his reproaches were only meant to bring them to repentance, and they did repent. So now St Paul had got them back again, and all his peace of mind and happiness along with them.

The first thing to notice about St Paul's share in this episode is his utter lack of self-interest. 'I have betrothed you to Christ.' We may recall what was said in St John's

[1] 2 Cor. 7: 8. [2] ibid. 7: 8–10.

Gospel about the Baptist: 'the bridegroom's friend . . . rejoices at hearing the bridegroom's voice.'[1] So here: the Apostle wanted nothing on his own account; his jealousy was nothing but zeal for God's sake. The only thing he cared about was that souls should love God. If it should happen that he found a bad influence at work, he must combat it for the sake of souls to be saved; and in this case a personal element crept in: but St Paul was visibly uncomfortable about it. All he really wanted was for Christ to possess the souls of men: so long as the Churches were faithful, he was perfectly happy, he asked no more than this; this was his reward, and nothing else mattered. He was thus entirely free from the least tendency towards empire-building, and from any possessiveness in regard to particular souls and particular churches. In this way, St Paul's feeling was poles apart from clerical despotism, which is indeed a caricature of real apostolic zeal; for the latter requires us to love souls only for Christ's sake, and never for our own: it means that we may never do anything with the idea of keeping people to ourselves, because it consists in such a great love of souls as to make us happy in their welfare even when it is none of our doing. That is the essence and the specific character of disinterested love: we must be glad whenever any good influence is at work; there must be no monopolizing of a soul. The importance of this rule is capital, for the alternative is self-seeking, a hidden corruption to destroy the purity of apostolic zeal. But this is not by any means to say that a harmful influence should not be vigorously attacked: in this situation, the case is altered, for we have no right to acquiesce in the subjection of a soul which is under our care, or connected with us in any way, to bad influences. If it is our duty to be unselfishly glad of every good influence, it is just as much our duty to fight to save souls from what we know is bad for them. Christ's spouse must not turn adulteress: we ought to have that intuitive quickness of

[1]John 3: 29.

perception, that penetrating insight which will enable us to detect, almost to feel, an infidelity. For we know that the seducer is none other than Satan, who was once an angel of light, and who can use the outward appearance of goodness for his purpose of enticing a soul away from whatever is really good for it. Sometimes he will turn a soul back from the true course of its own perfection by the attraction of something else that is good in itself, but less perfect, and represents for that particular soul a real infidelity. We must be able to defend souls against themselves: it is all part of apostolic zeal.

Such zeal springs originally from the love of God, but it comes from the love of men too; for we know that the real happiness and full perfection of men consists in fidelity to their calling and to the love of God. We have to help others to be true to themselves, help them not to make a botch of their lives, help them to persevere in their own main task and to obey God's call to each one of them. So doing, we shall further at one and the same time both the rightful claims of God upon each soul, and the best interests of the souls of men. If this is our aim, with a purely spiritual and holy motive, and also with some degree of supernatural intensity of purpose (for the love of God is a devouring fire), then we have spiritual zeal, which is apostolic and godly. We must work to help others to find their own way to God, even if it means offending them, or hurting them, or on occasions opposing their wishes and good pleasure: we must be able to show that we disagree—it is often the best service we can render them. They must have someone around who can say 'no' to them, when everyone else is saying 'yes' for fear of giving offence. They must be taught that there is someone who suffers when they are unfaithful or slack. Then, when they come to themselves, like the unfaithful wife in Hosea, they will say: 'Back go I to the husband that was mine once; things were better with me in days gone by.' That is the conversion of a soul, when the interior call is heard, to go back to the true home, the Father's house, where the soul always knew that real happiness was to be found, even when leaving it for the sake of adventure and out of curiosity. But for this to happen, there must be someone who is truer to that soul than it is to itself, a witness to the contrast between the real personality and what seems to have become of the person. Apostolic zeal, properly so called, is the kind of love that expects the most of the beloved: it is real love. Doing good does not always mean being nice, as we must constantly be reminded; on the contrary, being nice to people is often the reverse of doing them good. Charity is not to be confused with the sort of facile condonation that often does duty for it.

Finally, zeal means being active. Just as the divine jealousy is no mere passive attribute, but a living force, perpetually at work—just as the jealous God manifests his own zeal by breaking in upon the lives of men, disturbing them in their perverse amusements in order to awaken a nostalgia for something else and stimulating their better selves: so the true apostolic zeal is a busy and consuming activity. Yet true zeal is not tactless; it is essentially courteous, but constantly watchful: instinctively preserved from the indiscretion that marks the self-seeking busybody, who is after proselytes and conquests, like a sportsman after game for his table. The zeal of Christ is not like that at all. It is no business of ours to gain a reputation for our influence in a particular direction, or to claim the credit for a particular success. As soon as our zeal begins to be tinctured with any fondness for power and responsibility, or with any concern for our own influence over others, then at once we are in danger of being indiscreet, and missing the mark altogether. Real zeal comes from pure love, and has all love's instinctive tact.

CHAPTER FIVE

GNOSIS

THE existence of gnosis, that is, a higher or extra-ordinary kind of knowledge, belonging to the sphere of religious activity, has presented Christianity from the beginning with a serious and difficult problem. Already in St Paul we find a repudiation of 'the wisdom . . . of this world's rulers',[1] and pre-eminence given to charity as the only genuine mark of a true ministry of the word: while he also tells how he was 'carried up into Paradise, and heard mysteries which man is not allowed to utter'.[2] Such contrasts still occur in the world about us today. On every hand, bogus mystics, materialists and spiritualists alike, claim to possess the ultimate truth of reality. Even within Christianity, the evaluation of supranormal knowledge is a controversial matter; the Church recognizes this phenomenon as a bright jewel in her crown and as a distinguishing mark of her intrinsic holiness; but at the same time she constantly insists that any anxious or inquisitive pursuit of these extraordinary ways is a dangerous illusion; and constantly reiterates that charity is better. We shall do well, therefore, to begin by briefly indicating the nature of Christian gnosis, as contrasted with false gnosticisms, and with spurious derivatives of the true original.

Prophets and prophetism have become fashionable topics again in our own day; and no wonder, since prophecy is essentially an intuitive interpretation of the historical process. A revival of the prophetic spirit follows immediately upon a rediscovery of the historical conception of reality.

[1] 1 Cor. 2: 6.　[2] 2 Cor. 12: 4.

But the contemporary revival of prophecy is open to the same criticism as contemporary notions of history. The word 'prophetic' is often used to describe such historical concepts as the class-war, or technological progress: in this context the term is misapplied, for it conveys an impression of absolute validity, whereas the subject-matter is here wholly relative. Such misuse of language is characteristic of the false prophets of 'the wisdom of this world's rulers, being indeed inspired by him who is called the Prince of this world. It has ever been the single aim of true prophecy to denounce these misconceptions, whereby men interpret history as they would like to have it, conformably with their will to power and their selfish lusts: the true prophet teaches a contrary view of history as God makes it, confounding worldly projects and ambitions. Our present concern is with this sort of prophecy, which alone affords a right understanding of the historical process and enables us to play our effective part in it.

Real prophetism is the business of such as are allowed into the secrets of history by its maker, the Holy Ghost, who thus makes use of them to fulfil the purpose of history. In that Spirit who alone 'can find out the depth in God's nature'[1] they look beyond all earthly and outward seeming, and enter into the knowledge of the ways of God, which pass all understanding. Therein is all their greatness, for they are entrusted with the secret of God's designs; their natural endowments are relatively unimportant—it is well if they are men of talent, but that is not essential. Jeremiah was handicapped by a stammer, but he was nevertheless the Lord's man. The quality required of a witness is truthfulness. What God requires of his witnesses is that they should not testify of themselves, but of him that sent them.

If a missionary is to testify before men concerning the mind of God, he must first enter into that mind himself, he must be led by the Holy Ghost into 'the depth in God's

[1] 1 Cor. 2: 10.

nature, he must contemplate with awe the scale and bold-
ness of the divine plan. The soul of the Blessed Virgin was
enlightened at the time of her Visitation by such a spiritual
vision of the ways of providence, so that she cried out, in the
Magnificat, 'My soul magnifies the Lord . . . because he
who is mighty . . . has wrought . . . wonders.'[1] 'Mag-
nify' means to recognize the greatness of God's work, to
stand amazed at the magnificence of his operations.
Generally, men fail to see these things, being blinded by the
spectacle of earthly grandeur, and unaware of the glory of
God. They are readily moved to admiration of temporal
achievements: the power of the great nations opposing one
another in our time, or the dynamic influence of the human
mind evinced by such as Nietzsche, or Marx, fill them with
astonishment, even while they forget the immeasurable
might of God's activity.

What the Holy Ghost does for the apostolic man is to raise
up his understanding from the plane of human activity to
the level of the divine working. For, indeed, as the Lord
said to Isaiah, he does not 'think as you think, deal as you
deal'.[2] Men have their own ideas, but these are not God's;
men would like to organize the world in a certain fashion,
but this is not God's fashioning; men pursue a goal which
is not God. There is some relationship between these two
distinct worlds, but it is not one of identity. The Apostle is a
man whom the Holy Ghost has taken up into the ways of
God, and whom he will help to co-operate in them, making
him instrumental in their fulfilment; as we may see in the
case of the Prophets throughout the ages of Old Testament
history.

Today the Holy Ghost still affords us the same religious
understanding of the historical process, the same spiritual
insight into the realities of our own time. Thus when we
look at contemporary events we may see further than the
children of this world, who perceive only the outward husk

[1] Luke 1: 46, 49.　　[2] Isa. 55: 8.

of things; we need not explain everything in terms of the conflicting material interests of classes and nations. Behind the scenes, another conflict is engaged, between Christ and the powers of evil, for the possession of nations and of souls. It is only the Spirit of God that enables us to transcend the limitations of human insight, and to read the unanswerable riddle of our times.

Gnosis comprises this intuition of the religious meaning of history, but also the knowledge of history's last end, which determines its entire course. It has been justly observed that gnosis, in St Paul's thought, the supernatural knowledge which is the fulfilment of faith, essentially consists in an anticipated experience of beatitude. This is a fundamental contrast between Christian mysticism and every other. Gnosis is not simply a deeper knowledge of the intelligible reality beyond the life of the senses. It is no mere transparency of the veils of sense, such as allows the Hindu mystics (like the ancient neo-Platonists) a certain experience of the life of the spirit. It is on the contrary something absolutely beyond the scope of human intelligence, something that cannot be known except by the man whom God brings to such knowledge: it is the unfathomable recesses of God's mind. 'How deep is the mine of God's wisdom, of his knowledge.'[1] as St Paul wrote in the Epistle to the Romans. God had allowed him a sight of what is 'prepared for those who love him',[2] a glimpse of the hidden realities of the world to come, the City of God: he had given him a foretaste of that blessed union with the Holy Trinity which the soul may enjoy for ever hereafter, but which here we know in part, as in a glass, darkly. St Paul had to bear this witness to the Blessed Trinity in the midst of the pagan world; to give him courage for such a work, God deigned to let him into the secret of these things by anticipation, so that he could speak of them with the unmistakable accent of conviction, defying contradiction by

[1] Rom. 11: 33. [2] 1 Cor. 2: 9.

the obvious authenticity of his experience: 'There is, to be
sure, a wisdom which we made known among those who
are fully grounded; but it is not the wisdom of this world,
or of this world's rulers, whose power is to be abrogated.
What we make known is the wisdom of God, his secret, kept
hidden till now; so, before the ages, God had decreed,
reserving glory for us. (None of the rulers of this world
could read his secret, or they would not have crucified him
to whom all glory belongs.) So we read of, Things no eye has
seen, no ear has heard, no human heart conceived, the
welcome God has prepared for those who love him. To us,
then, God has made a revelation of it through his Spirit;
there is no depth in God's nature so deep that the Spirit
cannot find it out. Who else can know a man's thoughts,
except the man's own spirit that is within him? So no
one else can know God's thoughts, but the Spirit of
God.'[1]

God may allow us, as he alone can, some acquaintance
and foretaste of these things, to help us through our time
of preparation in this world, lest the taste of earthly satisfactions should grow upon us, and atrophy our impulses of
expectation and longing. So he maintains during this life
a certain eschatological tension, the tension of waiting, making us creatures of hope and men of tomorrow: whence it
comes that we show ourselves in this world as not belonging to the world, because this world is not all the world
to us.

We were born to be sons of God and to live in his glory.
We were invited by God to share in the heavenly banquet
and the companionship of the blessed Trinity. We were
made to live with our Lady and the Saints and to be at home
in the City of God, the New Jerusalem. Therefore we have
no right to involve ourselves in the life of the world or in the
pursuit of its ambitions and pleasures; 'it is for the heathen'
and worldlings 'to busy themselves over such things';[2] but

[1] 1 Cor. 2: 6–11.   [2] Matt. 6: 32.

for our part 'we find our true home in heaven'.[1] We should live through this world as though we were lost in it, as though we did not belong here.

In any case, only the self-deception of blind optimism can mask the truth that this world really is a 'vale of tears'. It is a world of physical distress and economic slavery. Think how many are sick in hospitals, how many are fast imprisoned in the industrial machine, how many languish in concentration camps, how much suffering there is everywhere. We have no right to look the other way when so many people are in such a plight. Our first duty is to do everything in our power to alleviate this distress and to set the people free. Yet we should know what we are about, recognizing that these evils all come from sin, and will last as long as sin lasts, that is, throughout history. Human progress only makes the tragedy grimmer, as we may see on every hand in the horrifying spectacle of sin let loose: mankind hideously divided against itself, men spurred on by the lust of gold and the will to power until they fight, and kill each other with all the latest artifices of contemporary science. With such things before our eyes, we may well say we live in a sinful world. And in fact gnosis means the knowledge of present misery as well as of future bliss.

This is what St Paul meant when he said: 'We find our true home in heaven: it is to heaven that we look expectantly for the coming of our Lord Jesus Christ to save us.'[2] We are prisoners, we are sick, we are wounded, we need deliverance: but for that very reason the first thing is to be aware of it. Of all evils, the worst is not to realize that anything is wrong. A sick man's gravest danger is supposing himself to be in health; a prisoner's worst state is to be so used to the darkness of his cell as to have forgotten the light of day. Most men are so accustomed to the blackness of captivity that they have lost the feeling of any better light—so familiar with the symptoms of their sickness as to have no

[1] Phil. 3: 20.   [2] ibid.

notion of real health. Our 'humbled body', of which St Paul speaks, is so much with them that they have lost all idea of that 'glorified body', in whose likeness Christ would mould them.[1] And the deepest of all these heavy sleepers are perhaps those who have no sufferings of their own to make them sit up and listen; well-fed, satisfied people, who have everything they want, with always enough to eat and enough to drink and enough to keep them happy; people whose lives are so perfectly smooth and even as to afford no opening at all. These can exhibit already in this world a sort of living damnation, impervious to God, impervious to others, closed up in their self-sufficiency, completely lost to all sense of what they are really for.

The Christian gnosis, then, consists in a religious understanding of the course of this world, and an anticipated awareness of the world to come. We have now to inquire what is the place of this higher knowledge in the scale of Christian values. A re-examination of the Second Epistle to the Corinthians will provide the material for an answer. Let us first recall the context of this work: the Corinthians had been carried away by the preaching of certain visitors who boasted of certain divine revelations. These claims made a great impression at Corinth, where visions and apparitions and extraordinary phenomena generally were highly prized —which, incidentally, is not always a very wholesome condition. St Paul had no desire to reinforce his own authority, in contrast to these rival teachers, by reference to his own comparable experiences, though, as we shall see, he might well have done so. The only evidence he would recognize as a guarantee of the worth of his ministry was the faithful constancy of his care for the souls entrusted to him. The genuine apostle was to be known by his charity and sincerity, proving him to be no seeker of his own glory; for it is possible to seek one's own glory even in reference to spiritual gifts, if one aims to attract attention thereby.

[1]Phil. 3: 21.

There is such a thing as vanity, even here; so that the possession of such gifts is not by itself an infallible proof that a
man is doing the work of the living God.

It is to be observed further, that the Church will have
nothing to do with extraordinary graces except in so far as
these are associated with effective dispositions of charity:
this is always the ultimate test. The writings of all the great
mystics are highly instructive on the point. How often
they reveal an attitude of mistrust in regard to private
revelations, or visions, or voices! If such things come to
the soul from God, they are evidence of his wonderful
generosity and worthy of all gratitude, but they are not
to be sought after. The only thing that counts, as St John of
the Cross said, with brutal frankness, is the denial of one's
own will. That alone is substantial: everything else without
exception, even visions and revelations, may be illusory.

For all that, St Paul was too well balanced in his judgements to think of despising spiritual gifts. They are not by
themselves an adequate guarantee of apostolic authority,
but they are real gifts, great gifts, to be greatly esteemed.
It was in order to show how much importance, short of
supreme importance, he attached to the fact of religious
experiences, that he once took the extraordinary step of
writing about his own. Normally, the interior life of the
soul is a secret between that soul and God himself, who is
not pleased to share it with others; but in this particular
case he allowed St Paul to lift the veil for a moment, to
show the wonderful things wrought in him by the Blessed
Trinity: *If we are to boast (although boasting is out of place),
I will go on to the visions and revelations the Lord has
granted me. There is a man I know who was carried out of
himself in Christ, fourteen years since; was his spirit in his
body? I cannot tell. Was it apart from his body? I cannot tell;
God knows. This man, at least, was carried up into the third
heaven. I can only tell you that this man . . . was carried
up into Paradise, and heard mysteries which man is not*

allowed to utter.'[1] This is what gives the testimony of St
Paul, touching the question of extraordinary spiritual gifts,
its special worth. If people who have not received mystical
graces should disparage them, that is not of much consequence for a real judgement. The case is the same as when
people who are not themselves learned speak slightingly of
science; but when Pascal says that 'all the science in the
world is not worth as much as a single act of charity', he is
a competent witness: and so with St Paul, when he tells us
that mystical graces are not the one thing necessary, and
that charity is what matters—he is entitled to be heard; his
opinion carries weight. His account of the matter rings true.
It is comprehensive and fair. Nothing is unduly depreciated:
the splendour of the mystical ways is fully recognized, as
one of the loveliest jewels in the crown of Christian holiness; but yet above all there is charity, rightly understood,
meaning that we do not our own will but the will of him
we love. 'The greatest of them all is charity.'[2]

It is of course true that in real life charity and gnosis do
not conflict. The love of God must always move us to love
our neighbour, and the love of men must always bring us
back to the love of God. Love of God and love of our neighbour are like the ebb and flow of one tide, or the very pulse
of life in one love, just as the life of God himself is at once a
unifying and an expanding, recollection and gift. St Paul
shows this clearly when he says that the personal knowledge
of God is something to be spread abroad: 'I give thanks to
God, that he is always exhibiting us as the captives in the
triumph of Christ Jesus, and through us spreading abroad
everywhere, like a perfume, the knowledge of himself. We
are Christ's incense offered to God, making manifest both
those who are achieving salvation and those who are on the
road to ruin.'[3] Yet this link between charity and gnosis is
still a tension. That is another aspect of the drama, the
tragic intensity, of the apostolic life at all times.

[1] 2 Cor. 12: 1–4.   [2] 1 Cor. 13: 13.   [3] 2 Cor. 2: 14–15.

As missionaries, we find ourselves engaged in two lives at once, and they can even seem to be incompatible. On the one hand we know that our calling is to a life of worship, to take our part in the angelic liturgy, representing before the blessed Trinity in the eternal Trisagion the cry of those who know not God. And at the same time we know we have to serve our heathen brethren, to live among them, to be at their disposal, to answer their incessant calls upon us. So our life is constantly divided between these two opposite requirements. We may feel homesick for the quiet of contemplation while we devote ourselves to the needs of the heathen, but as we pray it is the call of that duty that we hear.

What we have to learn is that this is not something wrong, or avoidable: it is just what being a missionary means. Others may be called to live in the heart of the Christian community, which is the temple of God. The missionary's job is to live in the heart of the heathen world, which is away from God: and his personal vocation is to suffer the pain of that separation. If he feels himself torn in two directions, that is not the fault of particular circumstances, but simply his own free vital response to the scandal and disgrace of mankind's estrangement from God: it is his participation in the mystery of Christ, the Father's missionary, who left the angelic hosts, the ninety and nine peoples of heaven standing round about the throne of God, and went out to look for the lost sheep, and took it on his shoulders, sharing so thoroughly in the nature of sinful man as to be willing, at the climax of his Passion, even to feel himself—somehow—forsaken by his Father.

The cross of Christ is the only means of communication between the heathen world and the blessed Trinity: so we cannot be surprised to find that when we deliberately establish ourselves in the midst of these two, and try to bring them together, this is not possible without the Cross. We must be conformed to that Cross, and carry it, 'carry about

continually in our bodies the dying state of Jesus',[1] as St
Paul said of the true missionary: for this dichotomy we suffer, this strain in our hearts between the love of the most
holy Trinity and the love of a world that is alien to the most
holy Trinity, is nothing but our share which the only-
begotten Son invites us to take in his Passion. He bore in
himself that duality of opposition and conflict, and brought
it to an end in himself, but he only ended it because he had
first borne it. He reaches from one extreme to the other.
Remaining eternally in the Triune Godhead, he yet
descends to the uttermost bourne of human want, and fills
up all the intervening distance. This boundless range of
Christ's action, symbolized in the four cardinal points of the
cross, is itself the hidden meaning and the formal principle
of the missionary's fragmentation.

It is then the very vocation of the apostle to unite, however paradoxically, the love of the Trinity and the love of
the heathen, to belong to both, and to feel the separation
between them. The whole spiritual life of a real missionary
wears this double aspect: every feature of it is marked with
the missionary character. His prayer is apostolic, for he takes
up in it the peoples whom he has spiritually made his own,
offering explicitly to the Father through the Son everything about them that is capable of consecration. His
poverty is apostolic, for it consists in accepting the deprivation of all that he has—his time, his affections, his substance
—by and for the sake of his brethren. He is made over to
them, he is their prey: 'henceforward, we do not think of
anybody in a merely human fashion'.[2] We are destitute of
human wealth; but we hold our single treasure in the
inaccessible secret heart of hearts, the tabernacle where
dwells the blessed Trinity.

[1] 2 Cor. 4: 10.　　[2] 2 Cor. 5: 16.

CHAPTER SIX

HOPE

OF all the psychological attitudes described in the Bible, none is more intimately characteristic of the Christian's active role in sacred history than the quality of hope, which may indeed be called the specific virtue of life in the time-process. On the foundation of the past, hope looks forward to the future in the experience of the present moment: these are the constitutive aspects of its definition. Its whole basis is in elapsed events, the actual promises of God and the beginnings of their fulfilment. Its movement is wholly towards futurity, in the expectation of the kingdom of God, whose establishment is to be the culmination of history. Here and now it is nothing but a faithful patience undismayed by trouble and difficulty, the very character of a spiritual man.

Hope does not mean optimism. Optimism is easy: it consists in supposing that everything is sure to work out in the end, automatically. In a more analytical form, its conception of evil is of a certain transitional dislocation or disturbance, which will rectify itself, as it were a growing-pain. By this elimination of all that is tragic from the problem of evil, optimism would destroy the very nature of hope. To delude men into thinking that the remedy for human ills is in their own hands is actually to put them out of the way of salvation. One example of this fallacious optimism is the Marxist dogma that a change in the economic conditions of life suffices to transform mankind. But even apart from materialism, the same dangerous illusion recurs in other systems, for instance when the mere act of withdrawal from

the world of the senses is proposed as the way for mankind
to find itself and attain to the Absolute.

Pessimistic doctrines, by comparison, seem far more sensible, for at least they take some account of the tragic
element in the life of mankind: and this is something that
can hardly be denied in the contemporary world, with all
its injustice and cruelty, and with the observable incidence
of suffering and death. The merest intellectual probity demands that we should face these facts, even though (or because) it takes more courage to do so than to indulge in
illusory fantasies. Besides, it is of the essence of pessimism
to recognize the fact of man's inability to improve his own
lot; in this respect, those who have seen furthest into
human nature are all pessimists, like Angustine, Pascal, and
Kierkegaard; and Péguy graduated from an optimistic socialism towards the despairing position represented by the
second *Jeanne d'Arc*. The attitude of despair is a precondition of hope; for the first act of hope is a cry for help, which
springs from the awareness of a desperate situation.

Pessimism itself, by definition, stops short of this decisive
act. Consequently the various philosophies of despair, although they offer a means of access to the virtue of hope,
themselves do not attain it. Some of these preach resignation as the only becoming attitude for a wise man, on the
theory that if we cannot ourselves change our lot, we can
only put up with it. Hence the wisdom of the Stoics in
former times, and now the appearance of serenity in the
resignation of such as André Gide. For others, as for Albert
Camus, the monstrous absurdity of a world at odds with
mankind leaves us with no real option apart from the attitude of revolt—the dignity of mankind requires at least that
we should say 'No' to a world we cannot change and may
not tolerate.

Christianity, too, starts from the awareness of a desperate
situation, a helpless servitude, a want of all possible remedy.
To this extent Christianity shares the pessimistic outlook,

and the Christian hope derives all its character from this
starting-point. That is why the doctrine of original sin is so
important, for it is nothing but the theological formulation
of the desperate condition of our affairs. It is indeed for
exactly the same reason that the optimists execrate this
doctrine. But the distinctive quality of our hope is that we
are not resigned to our servitude: we have given up all expectation of winning our own freedom, but we then appeal
(against all the evidence) to Another. Wherever this appeal
is made, wherever a man looks out from this miserable
estate for help whence it may be forthcoming, in a word
wherever a prayer is uttered, there is hope—maybe not the
theological virtue of hope, but real hope nevertheless. It is
a movement towards Almighty God, and as such it is a grace
bestowed. This turning to God for help is rare among us,
simply because it presupposes a really difficult renounce-
ment of self. Mankind has a passion for autonomy: we love
to have only ourselves to thank, to be self-sufficient. We
prefer a modest competence of our own getting to greater
riches in another man's gift. The average man of our time
considers it a mark of weakness to seek God's help: it seems
to him a bigger thing to rely on oneself. Marxism is a symptom of this state of mind, being an effort of mankind to
make man, to take over the Creator's work in relation to the
future of the race.

There is of course one way in which a man can give up,
which is a kind of quietism: in this case, reliance on God is
no more than a convenient excuse for not trying; but that is
a vile caricature of genuine hope. Hope is the attitude of a
free will which has already reached the limits of its own
activity; we may adapt a Pascalian formula and say that
there is nothing more voluntary than this abdication of the
will. The fact is that grace and glory are beyond our reach,
and it is only by an act of hope in God, who alone can bestow his gifts upon us, that we can anticipate possession
of the unattainable. It is a monstrous abuse of Christ's

atonement to make of it no more than a labour-saving
device. Christ came among us to break the bounds of our
natural human existence, and to afford us a way of access
into the boundless life of God himself.

Hope is thus compounded of humility and trust. It takes
us out of ourselves, so that we may rest in God; but only by
an act of heroic renunciation: it requires of us an absolute
dispossession of self, keeping nothing back. That is why we
find it hard. There is a substratum of doubt and fear in us
that almost always persists in some degree, a fundamental
insecurity that is not wholly overcome; perhaps we would
not even have it otherwise, because it is really a disguised
reluctance to give ourselves utterly away. But the life of
the spirit is ours from the moment when we rest in God
unreservedly, with our whole weight.

                    *   *   *

Thus far we have spoken of the human approach, on the
level of natural religion. The essence of the Christian revelation is that God has answered the appeal of mankind: so
that our hope is now grounded in God's fidelity to his own
word. According to the Epistle to the Hebrews, Abraham
relied on the promises of God when he left his home for a
land which he was to inherit, 'without knowing where his
journey would take him.'[1] But if Abraham's hope was based
exclusively upon a promise, we are better off now; for the
promise made to Abraham has been largely fulfilled since
then, and that which has been granted already is a guarantee of all the rest to come. Thus we have seen how the Old
Testament Jews could build their hope of ultimate salvation
upon the mighty works which the Lord had done at the
time of their Exodus from Egypt. But for the Christian believers there is far more than this. The resurrection of
Christ is the fulfilment in fact of all the substance of the
promise. Henceforth our hope is immovably established on

[1] Heb. 11: 8.

the foundation of the entire previous course of sacred history in all its solid reality. In Christ, the Word of God united himself with the nature of mankind; and that for ever, irrevocably. Christ has taken possession of futurity. 'It is his own blood . . . that has enabled him to enter, once for all, into the sanctuary; the ransom he has won lasts for ever.'[1]

It must not be forgotten, either, that the course of sacred history, which is the ground of our hope, was not concluded in the visible presence of Christ on earth, but is continued in the life of the mystical body, the Church. The mighty works of God accomplished during two millennia of the Church's existence give us further justification for hoping that they will go on. This is the special significance of the witness of the Saints, wherein the author of the Epistle to the Hebrews rightly saw one of the chief grounds of the Christian hope; 'since we are watched from above by such a cloud of witnesses, let us . . . run, with all endurance, the race for which we are entered.'[2] The Saints are not indeed the ultimate support upon which we found our hope, but they are surely an obvious and immediate support. What God has done in them affords us a reasonable case for hoping that he will do the same in us. They have shown us the way in which they would persuade us to follow them. They have gone before us in Christ's footsteps, entering into the world of heaven, whither the great cloud of them irresistibly attracts us who come after.

The whole past history of the Church is exhibited in the persons of all these her principal witnesses and champions, for our contemplation, and to encourage our hope for the future. Since we know that the Holy Ghost through the power of grace raised up such as St Martin and St Boniface, St Catherine of Siena and St Bridget of Sweden, in the midst of the heathen, and among the divisions of Christianity, and from the collapse of social order, we know that

[1]ibid. 9: 12.   [2]ibid. 12: 1.

God can raise up saints also in the world of our own time, heathen as it is, and divided, and ruinous. The 'great multitude' described in the liturgy of All Saints is always growing; and there may seem to be a special applicability to our own time in the particular addition that this multitude is 'taken from all nations and tribes and peoples and languages'.[1] Please God we too may be caught up in this crowd and carried along with it 'before the throne in the Lamb's presence'.

All we are waiting for is that the fruits of a victory which is already won should be distributed to all the predestined peoples—that these should enter into the full glory of God, the Holy Trinity, where Christ and his Virgin Mother, as we know, have entered already. The Assumption of our Lady reveals a further depth in the mystery of hope: an ordinary woman, a human creature who was nothing more, lives now in the glory of the Trinity, to give us the plainest guarantee. Everything that has been accomplished is a pledge of what remains to be accomplished. Our hope now is fortified by the fulfilment of past hopes to look forward towards fulfilments to come. This can be observed also in each individual life. We may be unfaithful, but God is always faithful, and never takes back his word. Whenever we turn back to him, his promise never fails us. Our baptism is a divine promise, an engagement whereby God has bound himself; we can deny ourselves the grace of baptism, but we cannot be unbaptized. The eternal covenant is love in bonds—whether in baptism or in any other of the sacraments, and throughout the ministry of the Church. The Eucharist is the sacrament of the Covenant, recalling the essential event and assuring the very foundations of our hope.

In these conditions, hope implies a perfect confidence in God, and absolute frankness with him. Our relationship to him is no longer servile, but filial. Between friends, there

[1] Apoc. 7: 9.

can be a community of goods: between us and God there is the same community. As sons, we are entitled to our divine patrimony: this was the purpose of Christ's mission, as he said, 'that every request you make of the Father in my name may be granted you'.[1] In Jesus Christ we may 'come boldly before the throne of grace'.[2] Our approach should be that of sons who know the Father's love: this is the specific quality of Christian prayer—a filial colloquy with the Father, for Christ's sake and in his name. The prayer of Abraham set us an example of this freedom: 'I have taken it upon me to speak to my Lord'[3]; that is the liberty of the Saints at prayer.

The Christian hope is thus unshakeably assured upon the foundation of something that has already been won for the human race and for each human soul. But there is more to come, beyond what has been achieved; hope belongs, by definition, only to such as are in this half-way state. It is a trustful, patient expectation, free from all anxiety because the outcome is assured in Christ. St Paul compares the position of the Christian believer to that of the heir apparent, whose title is sure, but he has not come into his inheritance. You are already, so he wrote to the Colossians, 'risen with Christ. . . . Christ is your life, and when he is made manifest, you too will be made manifest in glory with him.'[4] St John wrote to the same effect: 'We are sons of God even now, and what we shall be hereafter, has not been made known as yet.'[5]

The primary object of our hope, according to St Paul, is resurrection; because this is essentially what we have not already received. There is a death of the body, and a death of the soul: of these two, the latter has already been destroyed in holy baptism. But we have not yet been set free from the *miseria*, the burden of mortality, the corruptibility of our flesh which issues in sickness, in pain, and at last in death. Our aspiration is towards the completion of what

[1]John 15: 16.   [2]Heb. 4: 16.   [3]Gen. 18: 27.   [4]Col. 3: 1, 4.
[5]1 John 3: 2.

has been begun, the total conquest of life over death; the
burden of the flesh is grievous to be borne; not that we would
be rid of the body, but that the body should be freed of its
servile estate. 'We ourselves . . . groan in our hearts,
waiting for . . . the ransoming of our bodies'[1] and here we
come to the second Epistle to the Corinthians: 'if we tent-
dwellers here go sighing and heavy-hearted, it is not because we would be stripped of something; rather, we would
clothe ourselves afresh; our mortal nature must be swallowed up in life'.[2] So the Christian hope looks forward to
the development in the visible universe of all the consequences of that new creation which has already taken place
in the unseen spiritual world. 'Your life is hidden away now
with Christ in God. Christ is your life, and when he is made
manifest, you too will be made manifest in glory with him.'[3]
So St John spoke of the future 'making known' of the sons
of God. And it is not only we ourselves that await this
development: 'creation is . . . waiting for the sons of God
to be made known. Created nature has been condemned to
frustration . . . with a hope to look forward to; namely,
that nature in its turn will be set free from the tyranny of
corruption.'[4]

It is worthy of attention that our hope is not restricted to
salvation alone, but to the redemption of all creation. There
is no suggestion of liberating spirit from matter, for matter
itself is a part of the work of God's hands. The Word of God,
by whom all things were made, came to deliver all things
from corruption. Christians are too often regarded as spiritualists, enemies of the body, indifferent to the visible
world: whereas they are no more spiritualists, in that sense,
than they are materialists. Matter is something precious,
being God's creature, and for that very reason we long for
its deliverance from the bondage to which it is subjected.

Yet though the whole destiny of creation is embraced
within the objective of our hope, our chief concern is

[1]Rom. 8: 23.   [2]2 Cor. 5: 4.   [3]Col. 3: 3–4.   [4]Rom. 8: 19–21.

obviously with the destiny of mankind, and especially with the salvation of the peoples of the earth, which is one distinct element in our expectation. While we await the end of time, to bring about the universal consummation of the redemptive work which is already accomplished but is still unseen, we look first for the extension to all mankind of the salvation Christ has won for us. This is something we expect to come before the end, while there is still time: this is the most immediate object of hope. It would not be too much to say, therefore, that the virtue of hope directly envisages the work of the Mission.

The Bible explicitly teaches us that the promises of salvation are for all nations. From the time of the promise given to Abraham, God gave him this assurance: 'in thee all the races of the world shall find a blessing.'[1] When the chosen people alone enjoyed the blessings of the Covenant, this was a temporary arrangement, which the prophets foretold would be extended to all men; 'Thy gates shall stand open continually . . . make way for the wealth of the nations that shall flow into thee'.[2] This promise was fulfilled in Christ; the wall of separation was broken down, and all the old heathen nations had access to the sanctuary. But now that the Covenant is open to their participation, they still have to come in: that which has been freely granted in principle has yet to become effective in practice.

Before all the great nations can dwell under its shadow, the tree, which is the Church, must grow: and that takes time. We know how, in the case of each individual soul, the process of being transformed into the likeness of Jesus Christ is a gradual business: we know how we are always too impatient about it. We would like Christ to come into our lives all at once. We should wish, and we are right to wish it, that the love of Jesus should take such a hold of us as could never be loosened, so that he should reign in our hearts, and we ourselves no longer be as now, constantly unfaithful

[1]Gen. 12: 3. [2]Isa. 60: 11.

to him, for ever turning away from the living God, turning back to our idols. That is what we want, and we do well to want it: but the Lord in his wisdom will not have it so. For he is wise, and knows how the imperishable stuff of true spiritual love is to be made up in our hearts, by continuous piecemeal faithfulness in our lowly works of prayer and un-ambitious acts of charity, rather than by the fervour of an instant, blazing and vanishing like a fire of straw.

It is the same with nations. The Word came 'to spread fire over the earth'[1] when he was made man; this fire must spread to the ends of the earth till every human society has been kindled in urnt—but this takes time, as we know. We of the first cultures to be evangelized, the Western civiliza-tion, needed to have patience, the patience of missionaries, to support us as we await the coming of the latter days, when all the others shall have entered in. Such a patience, having its roots in the love we bear towards those who have not yet received the Gospel, such a conviction of the Chris-tian mission in the world, is the only way to make any functional sense of the present situation of Western Christendom, and consequently the only preservative against the danger of decay which threatens our society.

This same patience leads also to a deeper understanding of events. In connexion with the growth of the soul, we have just seen how the love of God gradually deepens down from the plane of feeling into the foundations of the spiri-tual life, and how this is effected through the long night when the soul lives by faith. So nations, too, have their dark nights. At the present day, there are peoples in the spring-time of their conversion, rejoicing in their first experience of Christianity, newly-betrothed to Christ in the spirit: while other peoples are in the throes of a mystical trans-mutation. Holy Russia is going through such trials as St John of the Cross described, and all the while her Chris-tianity is being purged of its dross, until in after ages she

[1] Luke 12: 49.

may come back to us with the gift of a new and purer faith. And those Western countries that are torn with schism and heresies suffer in another dark night of crucifixion, bearing the bitter cross of separation and division. So that the deferment of Christ's second coming is no neglect, no absenting of himself, but is all part of the mysterious design of his eternal love.

Through the night of pain and sorrow, while 'the whole of nature groans in a common travail', under 'the tyranny of corruption', 'waiting for the sons of God to be made known',[1] have we no better answer to offer than a patient expectation? It is at least one answer, for we know that the time of waiting is an effect of God's love: 'The Lord is not being dilatory over his promise . . . he is only giving you more time, because his will is that all of you should attain repentance, not that some should be lost'.[2] We are also to be long-suffering, for if our agony is protracted, this, we know, gives more time for repentance, and allows more souls to be saved. Missionary charity is the one all-sufficient explanation of judgement deferred.

Is there no more we can do? Of course we can and should labour for the deliverance of mankind from present bondage in temporal things, but we know that no such deliverance can touch the root of the trouble; we cannot thus do away with sin and death. Accordingly, the Scripture goes further than that. There is another passage in the Second Epistle of St Peter that I had not particularly noticed until a Chinese protestant pointed it out to me one day: 'All so transitory; and what men you ought to be! How unworldly in your life, how reverent towards God, as you wait for, and *hasten* [σπεύδοντας] the day of the Lord'.[3] So the Bible tells us that we can do something to hasten the Lord's coming and the transfiguration of a world set free. What kind of collaboration is this that is open to us?

[1]Rom. 8: 22, 21, 19. [2]2 Pet. 3: 9. [3]ibid. 3: 11–12 (Vulgate: *properantes*. Knox has 'wait eagerly').

Christ said that 'this gospel of the kingdom must first be preached all over the world, so that all nations may hear the truth; only after that will the end come'[1]: and St Peter wrote that the Lord delays his coming 'because his will is that all of you should attain repentance, not that some should be lost'.[2] When, therefore, we are also told that we are not only to 'wait for' but to 'hasten' 'the coming of the day of the Lord', this clearly can only mean one thing: we are to labour for the evangelization of the world, on the Mission. So an active zeal for the Second Coming is nothing but missionary charity: with all patience, we are to be doing—not as though the aim were to hasten the end regardless of the souls that perish, but hastening the conversion of souls in order that the end may come.

That is the consummation for which we wait, while trying to speed it. We are part of the process of achievement, which is itself the Christian mission. The grace of Christ would envelop all that is left of the heathen world, clothing all that part of wounded humanity that is still unfulfilled—not that it should be 'stripped', but 'clothed afresh': whatever is of real worth is not to be destroyed, but purged and transfigured. All taint of corruption and mortality is to be done away, but that which is life is to be clothed with the vesture of grace.

For it is an essential element in the Christian virtue of hope, and one too often mistaken when we think of hope as belonging exclusively to our own individual salvation, that it bears always upon the wonderful works of God in his creation. It looks for the Lord's coming again, to bring all history to its ultimate goal; its object is nothing less than the destiny of all mankind. Our 'earnest longing'[3] is the redemption of the whole world. It is important to keep this in mind, because otherwise the virtue of hope might seem to be in some way selfish, as Fénelon uneasily felt it was, because he misunderstood it. Hope is really concerned with

[1]Matt. 24: 14. [2]2 Pet. 3: 9. [3]Phil. 1: 20.

the salvation of all mankind, and with our own salvation only inasmuch as we belong to the human race.

It is a matter of obligation to hope to be saved; and it is not always easy. Some people who find no difficulty in believing that Christ is the Saviour, may yet be grievously tempted to doubt whether this can really apply to them: and indeed the sight of our sins brings us to a just conviction that we do not deserve it. But it is just the distinguishing characteristic of Christian salvation that it is offered to sinners. What Christ asks of us is to believe in his forgiveness; we are too chary of this act of faith, which needs, it is true, a great deal of love.

Our hope, the hope of mankind, then, is for 'ourselves', its object is 'us': St Thomas poses the question whether it is possible to hope for 'others',[1] and concludes that 'it is possible to hope for someone else when one is united to him by love'. True hope lives on charity, and the tragedy that belongs to hope lies in anxiety for another's salvation. The missionary is a man who feels this tragedy, a man with a positive awareness of souls that perish, a man whose love for these souls leads him to feel hope for them, and in that hope to labour at works of love that may perhaps be for their salvation.

Thus in conclusion we may see the special connexion between hope and history. The object of hope is the final destiny of the world and of the whole human race. At various times throughout the Christian centuries there has been what we may call an excessive tendency to focus attention upon the destiny of the individual human soul. In this way, the 'particular judgement' has somewhat overshadowed the 'general judgement' of the last day. A truer sense of the scale and proportions of Christianity will not narrow it down to this exclusive concern for individual salvation, but will see in it a call to work for the salvation of the world, that is, to take part in history.

[1] *Summa Theologica* II–II: 17, 3.

L.H.–AA

INDEX

Aaron, 205, 212, 217
Abraham: covenant with, 1, 3, 17, 28, 80, 142, 187, 188, 344, 349; choosing of, 19, 80, 111, 139; position of, 48, 49, 118, 137, 145; and guests, 67, 70; in Islam, 111; and Christ, 189; prayer of, 347
Absolute: faith in the, 89; attainment of the, 342
Absolute being: idea of, 155, 156
Absolutism, 15
Abydenos, 50
Academic history, 96
Acts of the Apostles, 18, 57n., 111, 149n., 224, 256–7, 264n.
Adam: as type, 140; and Christ, 189, 190, 271; sin of, 246, 247
Adoptionist solution, 189
Advent (Daniélou), 19n.
Advent of Christ, 199, *see also* Nativity
Aegean civilization, 38
Aeons: two contrasting, 253
Affinities, in symbols, 134
Africa, 35, 38, 40, 44, 58, 171, 181, 270
Agape; love, 42
Akkadian civilization, 38
ἀκολουθία: law of successiveness, 241–51
Alchemy, 122, 123
Alexandria: Hebrew bible translated into Greek, 37; Jews of, 154, 270; theologians of, 189, 232
All Saints liturgy, 346
Allegorism, 141, 144
Alpha and Omega: Christ, 82, 195
alter Christus, 215
Ambition: apostolic, 310–13
Ambrose, St, 228, 231, 232, 234, 235n., 254

Amem-em-ope, 120
America, 34, 93, 133, 270
Angels: fallen, 15, 31, 32, 47, 49, 54, 328; of God, 31; of nations, 46–56; and Abraham, 70; lore of, 120; of Satan, 209, 211
Anger: defined, 154, 155; God's, 255
Anglo-Saxons: as missionaries, 63
Annunciation, the, 6, 332
Anthony, St, 77
Anthropomorphic: of God, 154, 155, 317
Anticipated eschatology, 272
Anti-historicism, 184
Antioch: theologians, 189
Apocalypse, the: *see* John: of Isaiah, 216n.
Apocalypse of History (Lampert), 30n.
Apocalyptic books, 188, 217, 218, 219, 220
— writers, 120, 269, 273, 274
Apocrypha, the Jewish, 51, 261
Apollinaris, 192
Apologetics, 140, 161
Apostolic life: *see* missionary
— teaching, 141
— type, 282–3, 332
Aquinas: *see* Thomas Aquinas, St
Arab world: in ferment, 34; contribution of, 58; exiles of, 59; and hospitality, 67
Aramaic language, 36, 40
Aravinda, the, 112
Archetypes, 13, 94, 109, 127, 134–5, 139, 206
Arikah: sage, 120
Aristotle, 27, 42, 241
Arithmetic: and symbolism, 124, 255
Armenia, 59

355

Religion: function of, 100
Religions: non-Christian compared with Christianity, 107–21
Renaissance, the, 25, 97
Renunciation, 343, 344
Repentance, 157, 162, 197, 198,
281, 283, 286, 326, 351
Repetition, endless, 1, 2
Resentment, 314
Resignation, 342
Ressentiment, 155
Resurrection, the: historical, 1,
111, 139, 142; of Christ, 3,
12, 32, 129, 178, 186, 194, 195,
201, 206, 207, 209, 212, 249,
257, 268, 271, 273, 274, 287,
302–3, 344; decisive event, 3,
7, 10; as type, 6, 141, 142;
position of Barth, 10; of the
body, 11, 29; and Passover, 19,
142; central point, 29; new in
Christianity, 108; and symbols,
131, 145; in God's design, 149,
act of creation, 150; general;
195, 250n., 303, 347
Retribution, 161
Revelation: unchanging, 12; and
heathen religions, 19, 110; of
God in history, 111, 142, 145;
and metaphysics, 128; and
myths, 136, 145; of divine
through creation, 137
Revolt: attitude of, 162, 163, 342
Revolutions, 83, 91
Riesenfeld, H., 221n.
Righteousness of God, 150–1, 159
Rilke, 144
Rivière, Jacques, 323
Rock: symbol, 150, 153, 208
Roi du monde (Guénon), 123, 127
Roman civilization, 35, 39, 40, 56
— rites: *see* Catholicism
Romans, Epistle to the (Paul), 18,
83n., 111, 115n., 137, 140n.,
197, 201n., 249n., 275, 276,
309n., 319, 321, 333, 348, 351
Romantic civilization, 15
Rome: fall of, 11; Petrine, 41
rouah (Hebrew), 117
Rousseau, Dom Olivier, 42
Russia, 59, 81, 93, 277, 350
Rust, E. C., 14

Sabbath, the, 4, 221n.
Sabbaths, seven, 265
Saccidananda, 117
Sacraments, the: as types, 8, 225,
238, 254; continuing God's
work, 10, 12, 141; and contemporary problems, 78; importance of, 83; and pagan
rites, 117; and symbols, 130;
and creative acts, 139; of the
Church, 201; in history of
salvation, 203–4; and mystical
life, 232, 234; and love, 346.
See Eucharist and Baptism
Sacramentum Futuri (Daniélou),
52n., 187n., 195n., 215n.
Sacred history: and beginnings, 3;
defined, 4; continues, 9–10;
import of current history, 10–11,
12; and secular history, 14, 16,
24, 27, 80–1, 83, 94, 106;
reality of, 88; and *historia*, 103–
4, 105; and events, 139, 140;
subject matter, 149; as one
process, 241 et seq, 345; eschatology of, 253
Sacrifice: in primitive ritual, 109;
of Christ, 193
Sages, 112, 115, 119, 120
Saints, 63, 94, 95, 102, 115, 173,
181, 210, 275, 298, 334, 345–
6, 347
Salvation: irreversibility of, 2;
through Resurrection, 10;
through man, 90; through
Jesus, 112, 113; through faith,
113, 353; plan of, 163; in
Christ, 165–6, 182; of humanity, 201, 348–9, 352, 353;
present reality, 207, 274–5,
286, 309. *See also* History of
salvation
Salvation Army: work of, 69
Sanctification, 10, 204
Sanctity. *See* Holiness
Sanhedrim, the, 288
Sapiential books, 120–1, 218
Sarah, 6
Sartre, 91, 92, 271
Satan, 209, 210, 328
Saul: reign of, 257
Saul (St Paul), 114